elizabeth falkner's
DEMOLITION
DESSERTS

RECIPES FROM

CITIZEN CAKE

elizabeth falkner's
DEMOLITION
DESSERTS

Elizabeth Falkner

with Ann Krueger Spivack

Photography by Frankie Frankeny

Illustrations by Ryan Falkner

TEN SPEED PRESS
Berkeley | Toronto

To my mom and dad, Sherry and Avery Falkner, who taught me how to be a loving rebel with many causes.

Copyright © 2007 by Elizabeth Falkner
Photography © 2007 by Frankie Frankeny
Illustrations © 2007 by Ryan Falkner

Ten Speed Press
PO Box 7123
Berkeley, California 94707
www.tenspeed.com

Distributed in Australia by Simon and Schuster Australia, in Canada by Ten Speed Press Canada, in New Zealand by Southern Publishers Group, in South Africa by Real Books, and in the United Kingdom and Europe by Publishers Group UK.

Cover and text design by Betsy Stromberg

Library of Congress Cataloging-in-Publication Data

Falkner, Elizabeth.
  Elizabeth falkner's demolition desserts : recipes from citizen cake / Elizabeth Falkner ; With Ann Krueger Spivack ; Photography by Frankie Frankeny ; Illustrations by Ryan Falkner.
    p. cm.
  Includes index.
  ISBN-13: 978-1-58008-781-0
  ISBN-10: 1-58008-781-7
  1. Desserts. I. Spivack, Ann Krueger. II. Title.
  TX773.F285 2007
  641.8'6—dc22
                        2007020384

Printed in China

2 3 4 5 6 7 8 9 10 — 11 10 09 08 07

CONTENTS

1 | A STUDY IN CHOCOLATE CHIP COOKIES

2 | THE CHOCOLATE CRAWL

3 | FRUITSCAPES

8 | CORE RECIPES

ACKNOWLEDGMENTS

A cookbook requires a ton of patience, time, and work, and a number of people gave me vital support along the way. Thanks to Aaron Wehner, my editor, and Ten Speed Press, for encouraging me to do this book for years and letting me make it my own. To Betsy Stromberg, for getting my punk rock sensibility and coming up with a kickin' design. To Ann Krueger Spivack, for taking this on with me and devoting herself to all things Elizabethan. To Amy Vogler, our amazing recipe tester, for coming up with the questions before Caremi did. And to my fantastic brother Ryan Falkner, for taking my simple direction for Caremi and bringing her to life. Thanks to copyeditor Sharon Silva for being exacting as well as gracious, and to proofreader Jasmine Star, for the last, careful read. Yo, to Frankie Frankeny, for the perfect, delicious photography and the fun time we had shooting it. And thanks to Liv Blumer, my literary agent, for being persistent.

Thanks Sara Ko and John Mark, for living Citizen Cake since the beginning and staying with it as it continues to grow. Thanks to Jill Hinchman, for listening to me rant. Thank you Angie Heeney, Jenny Robinson, Sean Forsha, William Pilz, Yuko Fujii, and Luis Villavelazquez and everyone at Citizen Cake and Citizen Cupcake, for giving me the space I needed to work on this project. And thanks to all my chefs, cooks, and bakers, who push themselves to invent things I would never imagine and have dedicated their lives to the most gratifying medium and craft to work in. To all of the investors at Citizen Cake and Citizen Cupcake, and Orson, thank you, thank you!! And to all of our customers, especially our regular customers, we love you!

Thank you to all the farmers and producers we adore in Northern and central California—you make my job a pleasure and an adventure. A special thank you to Greg, Holly, Robert, and Stephen at the Culinary Institute of America, Greystone, for the annual pasty chef retreat, which inspires the nation's top pastry professionals to create their best work. Thanks to Sherry Yard, for making Spago a superfun place to work from when in So Cal.

To my family, for always being proud of me, and for encouraging my ongoing pursuit of my passion. To my amazing partner, Sabrina Riddle, who endured months of waking up to the sound of the ice cream machine running—thanks for your insight, wisdom, passion, desire for change, impeccable fashion sense, and love.

This book would not have happened without the works and inspirations from Avery Falkner, Jason Falkner, Elvis Costello, Talking Heads, the Cure, Pierre Hermé, David Lynch, Martha Stewart, Madonna, Richard Serra, Jean-Paul Gaultier, David Bowie, Quentin Tarantino, Frank Gehry, Marie-Antoine Carême, Jane Campion, Sofia Coppola, Christine Manfield, Mark Rothko, Frank Stella, Franz Kline, Masaharu Morimoto, Dif Juz, Cocteau Twins, the Adrià brothers at El Bulli, Yoshitomo Nara, Comme des Garçons, Chrome Hearts, and Orson Welles.

INTRODUCTION

Dessert for me is an art form. My usual approach is to take a classic—apple pie, carrot cake, tiramisu—and rethink it. The initial image that comes to mind is wonderful and comforting, but then I always ask myself the same question: How can I turn this dessert upside down and come up with a new way to look at it and eat it? Other times, I will create a dessert that is entirely new, sometimes building it around one extraordinary ingredient or an unfamiliar flavor combination. I am inspired by all kinds of things, from exotic sugars to architecture to song lyrics, and I think of desserts as whimsical, fun, wild, stunning, exciting, and, of course, delicious.

In the pages that follow, you will learn how to make many of my favorite desserts. My hope is that they will inspire you to think creatively and begin building your own dazzling desserts.

❖　❖　❖　❖　❖

I come from a creative family. My father is a painter, my mother has always been a creative multitasker and a great cook, one brother is a musician and composer, and my other brother, whose illustrations grace this book, is an

1

illustrator, actor, and performer. My dad exposed me to the works of the modernists, such as Rothko, Stella, Still, Klein, Lichtenstein, Calder, and Diebenkorn, at an early age. And then there was Julia Child. My mother and I would watch her shows together, and I especially loved how Julia took her cooking seriously but kept her sense of humor. If you combine the works of the modernists with Julia Child and the influences of every American kid growing up in the seventies—the Beatles, the Moody Blues, Pink Floyd, Snickers bars, and the television show *ZOOM*—you get an idea of how the creative part of my brain works.

Growing up in Southern California, I imagined myself directing movies some day. When I began to focus on experimental filmmaking, I moved to the Bay Area to attend the San Francisco Art Institute. I produced installations and films built around audience participation, including *Black Espresso, Black*

Sorbet, a film scene–dessert experience that I created for the audience.

While still in school, I worked part-time at the original Williams-Sonoma store on Sutter Street in San Francisco. My coworkers and I would skim through all the new cookbooks when they came in. Julia Child, Marion Cunningham, and James McNair all came into our store. It was a totally different celebrity scene than I was used to, but I was into it. I was dining in some of the hottest restaurants of the time—Stars, Chez Panisse, Zuni, Monsoon, Rosalie's, and Eddie Jacks—and before long I was leaning toward cooking as a profession.

After graduating in 1989, I worked in a small film production company during the day, and at night washed dishes and plated *croques-monsieur* and Caesar salads at Café Claude, a French bistro in downtown San Francisco. The café bought many of its desserts wholesale, and when I offered to make the apple tart, cheesecake,

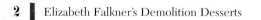

and bread pudding, as well as the chocolate mousse and crème caramel, my offer was quickly accepted. The response was great. A month or so later, when chef Julia McClaskey left, I was given her position, and I ran with it for a year.

During that same time, I worked as a *stagiaire* at Masa's, the famed four-star French restaurant headed at the time by chef Julian Serrano. My friend Daniel from Masa's, who had his coffee at Café Claude every morning before heading to work, mentioned one day that there was an opening in pastry. I immediately ran up the hill and asked Julian for the job. I worked for one year— an amazing year—at Masa's alongside pastry chef Alicia Toyooka, who had been hired by founding chef Masa Kobayashi.

The early 1990s was an exciting time to work in restaurants in the Bay Area. While California cuisine was taking hold in the rest of the country, chefs in San Francisco were looking abroad for inspiration, incorporating ingredients and techniques from foreign cuisines into their cooking. Elka, a restaurant opened by Elka Gilmore and Traci Des Jardins in the Miyako Hotel in Japantown, was one of the first restaurants to serve Pacific Rim cuisine, a then-new term for food rooted in a California-Mediterranean style but influenced by Asian kitchens. After dining at Elka, I decided I had to find a way to work there. At that point, I had been one of Alicia's assistants for a year, and I was anxious to learn more and move up. But there was no place for me to go at Masa's. So I called Traci, introduced myself, and told her how amazing I thought her food was. I then showed up with sketches of my desserts, a sample menu, and some desserts for Traci to taste, and I got the job. At Elka, I was able to experiment with many Japanese ingredients and aesthetic concepts, which I am still drawn to in my work today.

When Traci opened Rubicon in San Francisco's Financial District, the first California venture for New York–based restaurateur Drew Nieporent, I went with her. During my three years there, I learned a great deal from Traci about balance and restraint. I was also able to *stagiaire* with François Payard at Daniel in New York and spend every free moment working stints with Mary Cech, a pastry chef who made a huge impression on me when she was at San Francisco's Cypress Club. Mary introduced the architecture that had begun to appear in East Coast desserts to West Coast restaurant kitchens.

At Rubicon, I honed my skills and pushed myself and my team to create inventive desserts. My recipes started to reflect my interest in different cultures and abstract ideas. Titles began playing an important role on our menus, too. They were a way to sell the desserts through intrigue and suggestion, rather than just by listing what was in them. Names like A Chocolate Tart Named Desire and Baked Hawaii gave diners familiar frames of reference while making it clear that they should expect something different and original.

Customers began asking me to make cakes for their birthdays and weddings. Soon, I was making so many cakes outside of the restaurant that I thought someone needed to open a bakery, a great bakery, in San Francisco.

In 1997, I opened the original Citizen Cake along with my pastry chef, Sara (Cameron) Ko, who I had begun working with at Rubicon. The original Citizen Cake location was on an obscure corner in San Francisco's South of Market neighborhood. Not surprisingly, the bakery proved a drastic shift, moving from plating desserts to making cakes, breakfast pastries, and breads that needed to hold up in a display case. Plus, Sara and I had to become early-morning bakers, rather than late-night dessert makers.

Two years into it, I was feeling that our location was too small and too remote, so we moved to Grove Street in

Hayes Valley, near City Hall, where we are today. In the process, we grew to be a full restaurant and pâtisserie serving breakfast pastries; cakes, cupcakes, and cookies to go; ice cream; brunch, lunch, and dinner; and—traveling full circle—my plated desserts. I love thinking about the architecture of cakes and the simplicity of shortbread cookies, but plated desserts are my favorite expression of pastry, because they give me the freedom to juxtapose components with different textures and temperatures.

In the ten years I have owned Citizen Cake, I have constantly shaped and reshaped my style of cuisine. Often a regular customer who has tried lots of our desserts will say, "Elizabeth, I miss Pokemon's Purse. Any chance you'll bring that back?" Pokemon's Purse was a dessert I created after my first trip to Japan. It is a rich chocolate cake neatly wrapped in a thin layer of vibrant yellow mochi to look like a purse, with Spanish peanuts

on top. When you cut through the ever-so-slightly-crisp mochi, you get a hit of warm chocolate cake and a kind of Snickers bar effect from the peanuts. I liked it too, but Pokemon's Purse in its original form had its moment (as did Pretty in Peach, with its peaches, cardamom froth, and peach sorbet; or Blueberry Hill, which was a very cool combination of sautéed blueberries and corn with corn crumbles and bacon ice cream).

Although my staff and I look back on past creations fondly, we also want to keep moving forward. If Pokemon's Purse ever reappears on our menu, chances are it will take a different form, because every day in the kitchen we learn more, discover more flavors to play with, come up with new ideas we want to try. I think of the Elvis Costello album *This Year's Model*, and that same notion applies. I believe that our desserts get even better as they evolve, and the constant process of discovery is the best part of my work.

This book is a compilation of my past creations (in some cases updated to suit my taste today), as well as some of the most recent desserts from Citizen Cake. I purposely start with a chapter devoted to chocolate chip cookies to demonstrate how even something so basic and iconic can be taken in many directions. The progression from classic chocolate chip cookie recipe to the book's first plated dessert, Chocolate Chip Mania, is a snapshot of my creative process.

If you have some basic cooking or baking experience, try making the major desserts as they are written and photographed, with all of the components. If you aren't as comfortable in the kitchen, you can start with the "minimalist version" that accompanies most of the recipes. I have written the recipes so that you can prepare the desserts the same day you will be serving them.

But some advance planning can take the pressure off, particularly when making the multicomponent desserts, so I have provided a make-ahead timeline when appropriate. For every dessert in this book, think balance and restraint: a five-component dessert works only if you use a light touch with each component.

The Core Recipes chapter at the end of the book provides the raw materials for you to assemble your own pastry creations. I hope you will forge your own dessert-making path, putting together the components exactly the way you like and drawing from the rest of the book, other sources, and your own inspiration. Consider any mistakes part of the process of discovery. In fact, sometimes mistakes turn out to be better than what you set out to create. The cook who made the first fallen chocolate soufflé cake didn't start out thinking that the cake would fall, but what came out of the oven was fabulous.

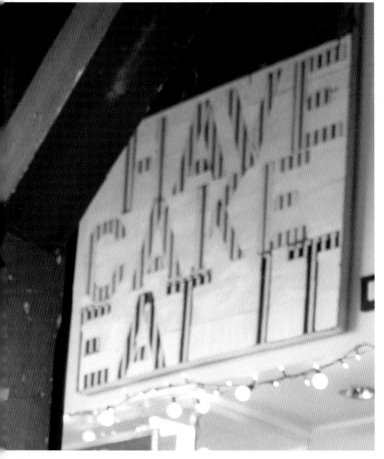

Since we are on the topic of being bold, I want to introduce an ambitious little baker, Caremi Keiki, who is going to appear on some of these pages. Caremi Keiki has big ideas. She wants everyone to know that dessert is necessary in our lives. "People smile when they see dessert coming, and that's important," she says.

Caremi likes to make larger-than-life sculptures from dessert ingredients. Sometimes she gets carried away, literally, and while she is quite clever and a bit of a show-off, I'm fully behind her point: always have as much fun making dessert as eating it.

CAREMI KEIKI

INGREDIENTS,
POWER
AND OTHER
EQUIPMENT

TOOLS,

ou don't always need to use the most expensive ingredients when you cook, but every ingredient you use will influence whatever you are making. And the fewer ingredients in a dish, the bigger the role each one plays. Creating a new dessert often begins with just one or two perfect ingredients. These might be flawless raspberries from a farmers' market or the candy cap mushrooms I use to make ice cream. But the inspiration can also be butter, brown sugar, chocolate, or another staple in my pantry. Don't undervalue the contributions these everyday ingredients make to your desserts.

Tasting is key. Taste constantly before you begin cooking and throughout the process. I recommend keeping a notebook handy to jot down how the flavor and appearance of a dessert changes when you switch to a different butter or sugar. If you're not into notebooks, just notice how trading out one ingredient for another changes the final result.

I use organic produce almost exclusively and organic dairy products whenever I can. Chocolate is the one area where "organic" on the label doesn't guarantee a better-tasting product, as you will discover in the entry on chocolate that follows.

Whenever you cook, there is a fine balance between enhancing the flavor of an ingredient and letting that ingredient speak for itself. The more you cook and the more you taste your ingredients before you start cooking, the better you will become at letting your ingredients have their full say.

Dairy: Butter, Buttermilk, Cream, Milk, Yogurt

I use unsalted butter because I like to control the amount of salt in my recipes. The recipes in this book were tested with brands of butter found in most supermarkets, such as Land O'Lakes and Challenge. But as more and different types of butter appear in the market, it is worth trying them. Taste different farm-style butters and see how some can seem grassier, while others might have a floral note. By all means experiment with higher butterfat butters (often called European-style), but don't worry if all you have in the fridge is standard American grocery store butter.

Freshness is the most important quality in butter. Butter picks up odors easily, so wrap it well before refrigerating or freezing it. Taste and smell your butter before you begin cooking. If you detect any odor or off flavor, get some fresh butter.

I like to cook with both yogurt and buttermilk, and I have used many different brands. Just as artisanal butters can have subtle differences, so too can yogurt and buttermilk. My locally available Straus low-fat yogurt is tangy and more liquid, while Greek-style yogurts are always wonderfully creamy, whether they are full fat, low fat, or no fat. Try the various brands in your area to see which ones you like.

I try always to use organic dairy products, because of all the ingredients I consume every day, I want dairy, and milk and cream in particular, to be free of hormones and antibiotics. I also want the animals to enjoy a healthy diet, have access to pasture, and live in a generally stress-free environment. I believe that taking part in a chain of kindness to other creatures is ultimately better for our own bodies. You can do research on the products available in your area to find out which ones meet the criteria that are important to you.

Chocolate

Organic is not as great a concern with chocolate as it is with dairy products. Makers of the best chocolate often buy beans from small farms that practice organic methods, even if they are not certified organic. Also, today many growers in the cacao industry are moving toward the fair trade, sustainable, and organic practices that have been taken up by an expanding segment of the coffee industry.

Although there isn't a major brand of premium chocolate that I don't like, at Citizen Cake we do use specific brands for different purposes. For recipes that call for dark or bittersweet chocolate, we like Scharffen Berger, Valrhona, and El Rey; for milk chocolate, we use El Rey for its dark-chocolate qualities; and for white chocolate,

we typically use El Rey as well (if you are not a fan of white chocolate, this one will change your mind). I also like to use both Guittard and Ghirardelli for dark, milk, and white chocolate, because they are made in the Bay Area and are widely available.

I've only recently started using natural cocoa powder from Scharffen Berger. Dutch-processed cocoa powder will work for the recipes in this book, but natural cocoa powder tastes more like chocolate (see Resources).

Eggs

All the recipes were tested with large eggs. I use organic eggs whenever possible. I love buying eggs at the farmers' market in San Francisco, because they are so fresh. It is amazing what a difference a really fresh egg can make to a recipe.

Spices

I love the unexpected savory note a spice can add to a cocktail or a dessert, such as a sprinkle of cayenne on top of a Watermelon Margarita (page 188) or an Upside-Down Pineapple Parfait (page 80). But before you sprinkle anything from that dusty jar that has sat at the back of your cupboard for a year, take a whiff. If the scent is faint or the spice looks gray, discard it. Time is the enemy of all spices, and you want to use only bright, colorful powders with a fragrance that kicks you awake. If your spice doesn't give you a little hit of aromatherapy, it won't do much for your food.

When you take the time to grind a whole spice, you will be amazed at how much more flavor you will taste. For example, take cardamom straight from its pod, barely crush it in a mortar and pestle, and then stir the black flecks into the whipped cream for Lovelova (page 89). The same whipped cream with a little powdered cardamom stirred in won't have the same poetry or depth.

Sometimes using a fresh spice is easy: whole nutmegs and cinnamon sticks are readily available in most grocery stores. To extract the best aromas in desserts that call for infusions, such as ice creams and syrups, use whole spices, or spices that you have barely broken apart in a mortar. Roasting whole spices, such as fennel seeds, before you steep them will bring out more flavor, though you can skip this step if you are baking the spices in a dough or batter.

If all you can find are ground spices, by all mean use them, but seek out fresh ground spices to experience what a difference they can make in your cooking. If your regular market doesn't have enough turnover to ensure freshness, try small ethnic markets, your local farmers' market, or the Internet (see Resources).

White Sugar, Brown Sugar, and Molasses

I use cane sugar, rather than beet sugar. As with butter, all the recipes in this book were tested with sugars easily found in most well-stocked supermarkets, though you may need to hunt a little harder for less refined sugars, such as muscovado or turbinado.

When it comes to brown sugar, I am a fanatic and enjoy the rich flavor of dark brown sugar almost as much as I enjoy chocolate. High-end grocery stores such as Whole Foods are carrying more types of sugar each year. Try enticingly dark, fragrant sugars, many of which are made in small batches and often have their own unique characteristics. Sometimes, if all I can find when I begin cooking is light brown sugar, I add a touch of molasses to give it the bitter intensity I like. Unsulfured molasses is best, and blackstrap molasses, which has the most intense flavor, is the type I buy most often. (For more information on sugars and molasses, see page 29.)

Vanilla Beans and Extracts

I like to cook with vanilla beans whenever I can, especially when making ice creams and custards. These days, you will find many different types of both beans and extracts in high-end markets and cookware stores, such as Williams-Sonoma and Sur La Table. Vanilla is grown in lots of different places, from Madagascar to Tahiti to Mexico, so I like to try the various products, whether in bean or extract form, to compare their flavor. I tend to use Madagascar Bourbon beans, but I like Tahitian beans, too, especially for tropical desserts. If using extract, check the label to be sure it is free of additives. The label should read water, alcohol, sugar, and vanilla. If it contains any scientific-sounding ingredients, choose another bottle.

One final word about vanilla extract or such flavorings as Cointreau or Grand Marnier. They are all volatile, meaning they contain alcohol, which evaporates into the air. Because stirring releases some of the fragrance and flavor prematurely (you want to keep every bit of flavor you can), the less you stir these volatile ingredients the better. That is why they are added as late in the game as possible.

GENIUS CAREMI, IS THIS A DESSERT "HAPPENING"?

YES, KIND OF YOKO ONO, DON'T YOU THINK?

AH—I SEE YOU ARE INFLUENCED BY THE CONCEPTUAL ART MOVEMENT.

I obviously have many tools in my restaurant kitchens and bakery that you don't have at home. But I tested all of these recipes in my home kitchen, where I don't have many "professional" tools. In fact, until I started working on this book, I was using a small hand-cranked ice cream maker, and I was excited to try out my new "pro-style" machine at home for testing the sorbet and ice cream recipes.

Before you go out and buy any power tool, keep this in mind: these tools are all based on the movements and dynamics of the human body; for small-scale baking, our hands sometimes do the job better than the best machine. We make very good chocolate chip cookies at Citizen Cake, but they can't compare to the cookies I make at home. Cookies mixed with a spoon in small batches taste better. Plus, it seems like less work to mix ingredients with a whisk than to drag out the big stand mixer and then have to clean it afterward. But because some of you are unwilling to set aside your stand mixer, many of the recipes include instructions for mixing by hand, with a handheld mixer, or with a stand mixer. For just a few recipes, a stand mixer is a necessity. But for most of them, the only power you need is your own muscles.

Here is what I use at home and what you will find handy for making the recipes in this book.

Baking Sheets

At home, I like to bake cookies, sheet cakes, tartlets, and other items on 13 by 19-inch heavy-grade aluminum baking sheets, also known as half sheet pans, or 9½ by 13-inch baking sheets, or quarter sheet pans. I always use parchment paper to line the pans, so I don't bother with nonstick baking sheets, although they will work, too.

Blenders: Immersion and Stand

Nothing beats a handheld immersion blender for puree-ing, blending, or emulsifying sauces while they are still in the pan. A stand blender is a necessity for herb oils and for some types of pureeing or blending. For both types, choose a brand that will last, but don't spend extra for a bunch of unnecessary attachments.

Cocktail Shaker

A classic bartender's shaker is essential for cocktails. Style counts for this tool. Buy one that is good-looking, and be sure to buy a strainer if the shaker doesn't include one.

Cutting Boards

I most often use a large board made from synthetic material because it cleans well and doesn't dull my knives. For small jobs, I like the book-sized boards made from sustainable bamboo.

Electric Mixer

As much as I like to whip cream, beat egg whites, or stir up a batch of cookies by hand, I have to admit that a reliable electric mixer can be a sound investment for home bakers. For marshmallows in particular, a stand mixer is necessary. You would have to work too hard without one. If you don't have a stand mixer, don't go out and buy one—unless you plan to make marshmallows often. Handheld mixers will work for any of these jobs except for marshmallow making.

Graters

I use a Microplane grater for grating citrus zests, cinnamon sticks, whole nutmegs, and chocolate, and I consider it an indispensable tool. A box grater works well if you need a large amount of grated cheese or vegetables. Microplane makes different-sized graters, but my favorite medium-sized one grates everything from cheese to citrus zest to chocolate to horseradish root.

If you like fresh ginger, a ginger grater is a cool thing to have. They are made of ceramic or porcelain and have little teeth that grate the ginger without losing any juice. Find inexpensive models in urban Chinatown or Japantown markets, or try Sur La Table or Williams-Sonoma.

Ice Cream Maker

I only recently bought an electric ice cream maker for home and I love it. It wasn't an exorbitant investment, and now I can easily make lots of different ice creams at home. You can get an expensive model, but I prefer mid-range-priced machines from a manufacturer that I know and trust. Look for a model with a canister that fits into the freezing chamber, a timer, and easy-to-clean parts.

Juicer

I am a fan of inexpensive, easy-to-clean Mexican-made juicers: basically two plastic handles that end in a hinged press. When you put a lemon or lime half in the press and squeeze, you get lots of juice easily, which is why you see bartenders using these for margaritas. A wooden reamer works well, too.

Knives

Pastry chefs are not known for having the sharpest knives, maybe because we use our knives to cut things like plastic for tuile cookie stencils and to chop nougatine shards, hardened slabs of caramel, or chunks

of chocolate. Despite this constant abuse, I keep my knives sharp for safety reasons: it's worse to cut your finger with a dull knife. Also, cutting fruits and vegetables with a sharp knife is much more efficient, and you will have better results from clean cuts rather than shaggy ones. Get your knives professionally sharpened—these days many grocery stores offer knife-sharpening services—and use a steel to maintain the edge. Avoid mechanical sharpeners, which can saw away the knife's metal.

In my home kitchen, I use a serrated knife to chop chocolate and slice bread and cake, a good paring knife to peel and slice fruit or make a *brunoise* of strawberries, a comfortable-in-your-hand chef's knife to chop herbs, and a sashimi knife to create paper-thin slices of anything (in this book, pineapple or fennel).

Mandoline

A mandoline makes quick work of slicing anything, from fennel to pears to strawberries. You don't need to buy a top-of-the-line mandoline. I use the small plastic types imported from Japan, and they do a terrific job.

Mortar and Pestle

An old-world mortar and pestle is inexpensive and a beautiful piece of equipment. Mine stays out on my counter, and I use it almost every day to grind spices, crush nuts, and make pastes. If you don't own a mortar and pestle, a mini food processor or a spice grinder (or a coffee grinder reserved for noncoffee use) also works.

Parchment Paper and Nonstick Baking Mats

I line my baking pans with parchment paper. I use non-stick baking mats made of silicone for mixtures that don't have much fat, such as the pecan pralines on page 58 or the blueberry paper on page 115. Silicone mats are also ideal for sugar work, and I feel for any pastry chef who specialized in sugar work before these mats were invented. Look for them in any cookware store.

Pastry Bags and Tips

Both reusable (washable) and disposable pastry bags are available widely and can help with the detailed work of pastry making. I keep a few different tips in my home kitchen: plain tips in different sizes for injecting fillings into cupcakes, and star tips or spaghetti-type tips for creative frosting applications.

Rolling Pin

I am drawn to rolling pins without handles. I just like the feel of a straight, smooth, even club for rolling out dough. If I am baking in a kitchen without a rolling pin, I wipe down a wine bottle, either full or empty, and use that. But you should use whatever type of pin feels comfortable in your hands.

Sifters

I like my drum sieve, which is a wide, tambourine-shaped sieve also known as a tami, for sifting. Most American drum sieves are stainless steel with steel mesh, but models from Asia are sometimes wood with cheesecloth. You can buy a drum sieve in nearly any cookware store, or you can use a mesh strainer or a standard sifter, if that is what you own.

Spatulas: Offset, Icing, and Silicone

Sara Ko, Citizen Cake's pastry chef, makes everyone in our pastry kitchen carry a baby offset spatula in his or her pocket so it's handy for lifting a small cube of cake or a brownie out of a pan, smoothing a meringue, or frosting a cupcake.

An icing spatula is the best tool for frosting a cake. You don't get the same straight sides and smooth top without one.

I use heatproof silicone spatulas in varying sizes for melting chocolate, for cooking and stirring, and for scraping out bowls. Of course, when heat is not involved, an old-fashioned rubber spatula will work, too.

Strainers

I have strainers with fine and medium mesh for straining at home. They also come in handy for draining tapioca and washing fruit, and for sifting if you don't own a standard sifter or a drum sieve.

Torch

If you want to torch meringue without overheating it, you need a butane torch. A torch is also the best tool for giving anything a brûlée finish or for welding together slabs of sugar (if you are serious about your confectionary architecture). If you buy a torch at a hardware store rather than a culinary store, it will cost less and last longer.

A STUDY IN

CHOCOLATE

CHIP

COOKIES

Since junior high school, I have made chocolate chip cookies at least once a week, always tinkering with the ingredients to see how the cookies would change. During my student council days, I would go home during the lunch break, bake a batch, and then carry back warm cookies to the meetings.

I grew up in the eighties, when cookie shops were springing up all over—Mrs. Field's, Famous Amos, and David's cookies were all popular. Every time I took a bite out of one of those boutique chocolate chip cookies, I would think, "I can do better than this," and I'd go home and make another batch of cookies to see how I could improve them. My youngest brother, Ryan (who did the illustrations for this book), called me Libba. When I began making ice cream sandwiches from the chocolate chip cookies I baked, my other brother, Jason, christened them "Libwiches." These days when I visit my brothers, all they ask for is my cookies.

A cookie might seem tame compared to some of the other desserts in this book, but a well-made chocolate chip cookie is a work of art. While the recipe for this American icon has only a few ingredients, their quality and how they are combined can change the taste and texture of the cookie. In the following recipes, you will see how I start with a single concept and take it in a few different directions, before finally deconstructing it and transforming the idea into the more-is-more plated dessert appropriately named Chocolate Chip Mania (page 35).

Here are a few tips to keep in mind as you make cookies:

- Start with unsalted butter that has been allowed to soften at room temperature but is still cool to the touch. If the butter is too warm, the cookies may bake up thin and have a slightly greasy appearance.

- Once the dough is made, chill it in the refrigerator for 30 minutes. Cookie dough (and pie dough) benefits from chilling because it relaxes the gluten that developed as you made the dough, resulting in a better texture once it is baked. If you want to chill it longer—say overnight—you can, but 30 minutes is fine.

- Try to handle the chilled dough as little as possible when shaping the cookies. At our bakery, we use a 1-inch scoop to plop cookie dough onto the baking sheets. It gives us cookies with a consistent shape and it is super-fast (we made 142,000 drop cookies in 2006, so speed is essential). At home, I usually spoon the dough onto the baking sheet. If you like to shape each cookie by rolling it into a ball between your palms, you can, but keep it quick, because cookie dough is easily overworked.

- The cookie doughs in this chapter will keep in the freezer for a couple of months. To freeze, divide the dough in half, roll each half into a log about 1 inch in diameter, and wrap well in plastic or parchment. You don't have to thaw the dough before baking, though it is easier to slice if you let it sit at room temperature for 20 to 30 minutes. Slice the log into chunks 1 1/2 to 2 inches wide, place on parchment-lined baking pans, and bake for 2 to 3 minutes longer than specified in the recipe.

- I like bittersweet chocolate, but it is not easy to find in chip form, so I chop chocolate bars into chip-sized chunks. But you can use standard chocolate chips in any of these recipes.

- Every cookie in this chapter makes a great ice cream sandwich. See steps for making ice cream sandwiches in the Real McCoy Ice Cream Sandwich (page 50).

CHOCOLATE CHIP COOKIES STRAIGHT UP OR WITH NUTS

makes about 3 dozen cookies

After decades of cookie baking, this is the chocolate chip cookie I like best. (For now. My favorites generally last for about six months before I find a new one.) Sometimes I make these cookies with walnuts, and sometimes I leave them out, depending on my mood.

In a large bowl, using a wooden spoon, cream together the butter and brown and granulated sugars until smooth but not overmixed. (I do this by hand, but if you use a stand mixer fitted with the paddle attachment or a handheld mixer, beat on medium speed for 1 to 2 minutes, and then scrape down the sides of the bowl before continuing.) Add the egg, vanilla, and salt and stir just until combined. Sift in the flour, baking soda, and baking powder and stir gently just until combined. Add the chocolate and nuts and stir just until evenly distributed throughout the dough. Cover and refrigerate for 30 minutes.

Position the racks in the upper third and lower third of the oven and preheat the oven to 350°F. Line 2 baking sheets with parchment paper.

Scoop up 1-inch balls of the dough with a spoon or mini scoop and set them 2 inches apart on the prepared pans.

Bake the cookies, rotating the pans after 7 to 9 minutes, for 13 to 17 minutes, or until the cookies are golden brown. If you like a very soft cookie, bake them for 13 minutes. If you like a crisp cookie, bake them for 17 minutes. Transfer to racks and let cool.

I think these cookies are best the day they are baked, but they will keep in an airtight cookie jar for up to 4 days—if they last that long.

8 tablespoons (4 ounces) butter, softened but still cool

3/4 cup (61/4 ounces) firmly packed dark brown sugar

1/2 cup plus 1 tablespoon (4 ounces) granulated sugar

1 (11/2 ounces by weight) large egg

1 teaspoon pure vanilla extract

1 teaspoon kosher salt

11/4 cups plus 3 tablespoons (7 ounces) all-purpose flour

1/2 teaspoon baking soda

1/4 teaspoon baking powder

8 ounces bittersweet chocolate, chopped the size of chocolate chips, or bittersweet chocolate chips (about 11/2 cups)

3/4 cup (3 ounces) chopped walnuts (optional)

CHOCOLATE² CHIP ESPRESSO COOKIES

makes about 4 dozen standard cookies or 8 dozen mini cookies

Because I'm both a coffee person and a chocolate person, it made sense to me to combine them in a cookie. Espresso brings out the bitterness of the chocolate, which means these cookies are good with ice cream because they balance its sweetness.

If you find good white chocolate chips—El Rey, Valrhona, Ghirardelli, and Guittard are four good brands—they are fantastic in this cookie. You can make regular-sized cookies, or you can make mini versions for Chocolate Chip Mania (page 35).

1¹/2 cups (7¹/2 ounces) all-purpose flour

3/4 cup (2¹/4 ounces) unsweetened cocoa powder, preferably natural

1/2 teaspoon baking soda

1/2 teaspoon baking powder

2 teaspoons finely ground espresso-roast coffee beans

1 cup (8 ounces) unsalted butter, softened but still cool

3/4 cup plus 2 tablespoons (7¹/4 ounces) firmly packed dark brown sugar

1/2 cup plus 1 tablespoon (4 ounces) granulated sugar

1 (1¹/2 ounces by weight) large egg

1 teaspoon pure vanilla extract

1/2 teaspoon kosher salt

1¹/3 cups (8 ounces) semisweet, milk, or white chocolate chips, or a combination

In a medium bowl, sift together the flour, cocoa powder, baking soda, baking powder, and ground coffee. In a large bowl, using a wooden spoon, cream together the butter and brown and granulated sugars until smooth but not overmixed. (I do this by hand, but if you use a stand mixer fitted with the paddle attachment or a handheld mixer, beat on medium speed for 1 to 2 minutes, and then scrape down the sides of the bowl before continuing.) Add the egg, vanilla, and salt and stir just until combined. Add the sifted ingredients to the butter mixture in two additions, stirring gently after each addition just until combined. Add the chocolate chips and stir just until evenly distributed throughout the dough. Cover and refrigerate for 30 minutes.

Position the racks in the upper third and lower third of the oven and preheat the oven to 350°F. Line 2 baking sheets with parchment paper.

Scoop up 1-inch balls of dough for full-sized cookies or ¹/2-inch balls for mini cookies with a spoon or mini scoop. Set the large scoops 2 inches apart or the small scoops 1 inch apart on the prepared pans.

Bake the mini cookies for about 5 minutes and the full-sized cookies for about 8 minutes, and then rotate the pans and bake both sizes for another 3 minutes, or until they are puffed and still look a little wet in the center. Transfer to racks and let cool. (Okay, you can sneak a couple of warm cookies, but let most of the batch cool.)

These cookies will keep for 2 to 3 days in an airtight container, but they will be at their most tender the day you bake them.

CHOCOLATE CHIP COOKIES VERSION XS

makes about *4* dozen cookies

The **XS** stands for extreme sugars. This recipe calls for two types, Demerara and muscovado, and you will experience the distinctive texture and flavor of both sugars when you bite into this cookie. Cookies are a good way to experiment with different types of sugar because it is easy to make batches and compare. Plus, cookies are familiar, so you notice when their flavor changes with a change in sugar. Turn to page 29 for more about the many types of sugar available.

Adding toasted ground rolled oats to the dough gives the cookies a toasty flavor and makes the different textures of the sugars even more noticeable. Use old-fashioned rolled oats or experiment by substituting rye, barley, flaxseed, or another type of cereal grain.

In a food processor, pulse the oats for 15 to 20 seconds to refine the texture. Most of the oats will look like coarse sawdust, but you should still have some recognizable flakes when you are done.

In a sauté pan, melt 4 tablespoons (2 ounces) of the butter over medium heat and allow it to cook for about 3 minutes, or until it browns slightly. Add the oats and cook, stirring constantly, for about 2 minutes, or until you can smell a toasty fragrance. Don't overdo it. You want to take the pan off the heat as soon as you detect a hint of toast. Spoon the oats onto a baking sheet or sheet of parchment paper, spread them out with the spoon, and set aside to cool.

In a large bowl, using a wooden spoon, cream together the remaining 12 tablespoons (6 ounces) butter and the muscovado sugar until smooth but not overmixed. (I do this by hand, but if you use a stand mixer fitted with the paddle attachment or a handheld mixer, beat on medium speed for about 1 minute, and then scrape down the sides of the bowl before continuing.) Add the Demerara sugar and vanilla and stir briefly, just to mix. Add the egg and stir just until combined.

Transfer the cooled oats to a medium bowl. Sift together the flour and baking soda onto the oats. Add the salt and stir to combine. Add the dry ingredients to the butter mixture and stir just until combined. (If you are using a mixer, pulse on low speed for 15 to 30 seconds, as the flour will fly up.) Add the chocolate and stir just until evenly distributed throughout the dough. Cover and refrigerate for 30 minutes.

Position the racks in the upper third and lower third of the oven and preheat the oven to 350°F. Line 2 baking sheets with parchment paper.

1¼ cups (4 ounces) old-fashioned rolled oats

16 tablespoons (8 ounces) unsalted butter, softened but still cool

1 cup (about 8½ ounces) firmly packed dark muscovado sugar

1 cup plus 2 tablespoons (8 ounces) Demerara sugar

1 teaspoon pure vanilla extract

1 (1½ ounces by weight) large egg

1½ cups plus 2 tablespoons (8 ounces) all-purpose flour

1 teaspoon baking soda

1 teaspoon kosher salt

8 ounces bittersweet chocolate, chopped the size of chocolate chips, or bittersweet chocolate chips (about 1½ cups)

Scoop up 1-inch balls of dough with a spoon or mini scoop and set them 2 inches apart on the prepared pans.

Bake the cookies, rotating the pans after 4 minutes, for 7 to 9 minutes, or until they are puffed up but still soft, or until done to your liking (see below). Transfer to racks and let cool.

These cookies will keep for 2 to 3 days in an airtight container, but they won't have as much flavor as the day they were baked.

I like a medium-crisp cookie, so I bake my dough for 10 minutes, but experiment until you find the optimal baking time to suit your own tastes.

At **7 minutes**, the cookies are still rounded and so soft they are hard to lift with a spatula.

At **9 minutes**, the cookies are still slightly rounded and are soft when cooled.

At **10 minutes**, the cooled cookies are flatter but still chewy.

At **12 minutes**, the cooled cookies are flatter and crisp.

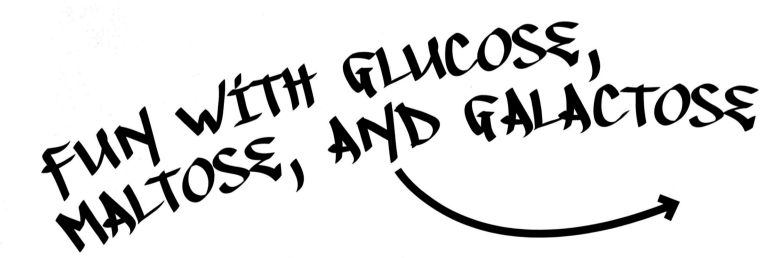

FUN WITH GLUCOSE, MALTOSE, AND GALACTOSE

Sugar

or most of the recipes in this book, the standard sugars found in the baking aisle of your grocery store will work just fine. But there is room to experiment with the artisanal sugars that are now becoming more widely available to home bakers.

My view of sugar changed in the mid-1990s, when I joined a group of pastry chefs and writers invited by El Rey chocolate manufacturers to tour Venezuela and learn more about chocolate. When Flo Braker, Mary Cech, and I visited a Caracas marketplace, we found sugars as exotic as the fruits. The vendors sold their sugar packed into cones called a *papelón*, and the sugar was so unrefined you could see small twigs, flowers, and even bees inside. We stood there trying to figure out how we could pack the cones into our suitcases and bring them home. That experience made me wonder why most of us in the United States have been limited to everyday white and brown sugars. It also inspired the granita in CocoShok (page 53).

Trying a new variety of sugar is a sensory experience. You can open a bag and inhale the aroma of a spicy brown sugar made from sugarcane grown in Mauritius, off the coast of Africa, or of a dark, rich sugar from India or South America. When I have packages of these dark sugars in my pantry, I feel ready to create something new or to make something interesting from a favorite old recipe. A cookie is a good place to experiment, because you won't ruin it by swapping sugars, as long as your total sugar weight stays the same. You can also taste these sugars by adding them to your tea of coffee or sprinkling them over your morning oatmeal.

Most of the sugars described here are available at Whole Foods, Williams-Sonoma, or Sur La Table stores or online through other sources (see Resources).

A Short History of Sugar

Sugar is found naturally in lots of fruits and vegetables, but most processed sugar is made from either beets or sugarcane. The first sugarcane processing was in India, and the Persians, who discovered it when they invaded the subcontinent, kept sugarcane a secret until the Arabs and Berbers carried it to western Europe in the eighth century.

In 1493, Columbus took the sugarcane clippings he had been given on La Gomera, in the Canary Islands, to the New World, and sugar production followed. Caribbean rum, which appeared in the early 1600s, owes its flavor to those same clippings.

Sugar manufacturing boomed in the eighteenth century to meet the growing demand for confectionary, chocolates, and beverages. Plantation owners grew more sugarcane, prices fell, and what was once a luxury for the elite became an everyday staple for the masses.

In the early nineteenth century, during the Napoleonic Wars, the British prevented Napoleon from importing sugarcane from the Caribbean. His response was to ban all sugar imports and push the cultivation of sugar beets. The fact that today most European bakers use beet sugar instead of cane sugar can be traced back to Napoleon and the amount of power he had.

While I have cooked with both cane and beet sugars, I prefer cane sugar and especially like to experiment with less refined versions. The following are some of the sugars you will find in my restaurant kitchen and in my home pantry.

White Sugar

Highly refined, white sugar is the most widely used sugar, by both industry and home cooks. The particles, or granules, come in a range of sizes, but the two most common are medium, or granulated sugar, and fine, or superfine sugar, also known as caster sugar.

Brown Sugar

Refined brown sugar gets its color from molasses, a by-product of sugar processing. Brown sugar can be made from sugar beets or sugarcane, but the brown sugar most commonly sold in the United States is refined white sugar crystals to which sugarcane molasses has been added for flavor and color. (You can easily make your own brown sugar by mixing molasses into granulated white sugar. Add about 1 tablespoon molasses to each cup of sugar for dark brown sugar, and 1 1/2 teaspoons molasses to each cup for light brown sugar.)

Refining sugar until it is white and then reintroducing the molasses to make it brown results in sugar that is consistent in color and taste. But if this is the only brown sugar you use, you are missing out on wonderful flavor variations found in less refined brown sugars. Some of the following

brown sugars are my favorites to experiment with, particularly in the chocolate chip cookie recipes.

DARK AND LIGHT MUSCOVADO SUGAR

Also known as Barbados sugar or moist sugar, muscovado sugar is a natural, unrefined sugar made from the juice of sugarcane. It has a high molasses content and more minerals than most other sugars. Open a bag of dark muscovado sugar and you will feel almost intoxicated by the aroma. This rich, spicy sugar, which is the color of cloves and almost winelike in its intensity, adds incredible flavor to cookies, ice cream, scones, simple syrup (page 215), and the granita for CocoShok (page 54). Light muscovado is also rich and almost creamy. Both sugars have unique flavors and work in all the cookie recipes in this chapter.

DEMERARA SUGAR

Demerara sugar is a tan, coarse-textured, partially refined sugar that varies slightly in flavor from one producer to another. Originally named for the old colony of Demerara in the South American country of Guyana, it is now primarily produced in Mauritius.

TURBINADO SUGAR

Turbinado is a partially refined cane sugar that is processed with steam, which gives it an attractive blond color. It is more fine-textured than Demerara sugar and has a pleasant vegetal flavor.

PANELA, RAPADURA, PAPELÓN, PILONCILLO, AND JAGGERY

All of these names refer to sugars that are basically dried sugarcane juice, unrefined and usually molded into cones or bricks for easy transport. You will find *panela* in Colombia and surrounding countries, *rapadura* is made in Brazil, *papelón* is used in Venezuela and the Caribbean, *piloncillo* is found in Mexico, and jaggery is from India. All of them have been around for centuries and are still widely available, prized, and often preferred over refined sugar in the countries where they are found.

Powdered Sugar

Also known as confectioners' sugar and icing sugar, powdered sugar is granulated white sugar ground to a fine powder and mixed with an anticaking agent, usually cornstarch. Some powdered sugars are labeled with an X designation, which refers to the fineness of the grind. It can range from 4X, which is relatively coarse, to 14X, which is superfine. Most markets carry 10X powdered sugar.

Molasses

When sugarcane is mashed to extract its juice and the juice is then boiled to yield sugar crystals, one of the by-products is molasses. This first boiling produces a particularly sweet molasses. The juice is then boiled a second time to extract more crystallized sugar, and this molasses has a slightly bitter taste. The third boiling, after which most of the crystallized sugar has been extracted, results in a molasses called blackstrap, which is bitter and full of vitamins and minerals, such as iron, calcium, and magnesium. Blackstrap molasses is my favorite type, and I choose the unsulfured brands (no sulfur dioxide has been added to the molasses as a preservative).

CRISP CHOCOLATE CHIP FLORENTINE COOKIES

makes about **3** dozen cookies

These lacy tuile-like cookies, with the added bonus of dark chocolate, are wonderful served on their own or with ice cream. Three things give them their inimitable crunch: a candy thermometer (to tell you when the butter-sugar mixture is the right temperature), nuts crushed—but not too finely—in a food processor, and cacao nibs. Nibs are the edible part of cacao beans, what remains after the beans have been roasted and shelled. They taste like dark chocolate and are incredibly crunchy. Look for them in the baking aisle or bulk-food section of high-end grocery stores, or order them from Scharffen Berger (see Resources).

4 tablespoons (2 ounces) unsalted butter, cut into chunks

1/2 cup (31/2 ounces) granulated sugar

1 tablespoon firmly packed dark brown sugar

1/4 cup heavy cream

1 tablespoon all-purpose flour

1/4 cup (1 ounce) cacao nibs

1/2 cup (2 ounces) crushed hazelnuts, almonds, or walnuts

1/2 teaspoon kosher salt

1 ounce bittersweet chocolate, coarsely chopped

In a saucepan, stir together the butter and granulated and brown sugars over medium heat for about 5 minutes, or until the butter has melted and the mixture begins to bubble. Add the cream and flour, stirring to break up any lumps. Clip a candy thermometer to the side of the pan and bring the mixture to a boil, stirring constantly. Cook, stirring, for about 5 minutes, or until the thermometer registers 225°F. Remove the pan from the heat and stir in the cacao nibs, nuts, and salt.

Pour the mixture into a heatproof bowl and let cool for about 15 minutes. Cover with parchment paper or plastic wrap, pressing it directly onto the surface, and refrigerate for at least 1 hour or up to overnight.

Position the racks in the upper third and middle of the oven and preheat the oven to 350°F. Line 2 baking sheets with parchment paper.

Cut or pinch off pieces of dough the size of large marbles, 1/2 to 3/4 inch in diameter, and place 3 inches apart on the prepared pans. Place 1 or 2 small chunks of chocolate on top each mound of cookie dough.

Bake the cookies, rotating the pans after about 6 minutes, for 12 to 13 minutes. These cookies caramelize and darken quickly, and they will continue to darken slightly even after you take them out of the oven, so remove them when they are still a little lighter than you would like. If any cookies have run together, cut them apart with a butter knife. Transfer to racks and let cool.

These cookies are best the day they are made. Store them in an airtight container at room temperature.

UP TO 1 WEEK BEFORE

➼ make the sauces

UP TO 3 DAYS BEFORE

➼ make the ice cream

THE DAY BEFORE

➼ make the cookies

A FEW HOURS BEFORE

➼ make the blondies

➼ make the chipped cream

JUST BEFORE SERVING

➼ rewarm the chocolate sauces

➼ plate the dessert

MINIMALIST VERSION

Serve a blondie with the ice cream and one or both of the chocolate sauces.

CHOCOLATE CHIP MANIA

blondies, brown sugar–chocolate chunk ice cream, chocolate² chip espresso cookies, chipped cream, dark and white chocolate sauces

serves 6

When my friend Gail Deferrari owned Universal Café, a popular San Francisco restaurant, she served a blondie with caramel sauce and vanilla ice cream that was so good—almost overly sweet the way pecan pie à la mode can be.

Gail's blondie inspired this dessert, the next step in my ongoing affair with chocolate chip cookies: a blondie; brown sugar ice cream with just the right amount of vanilla and salt; mini Chocolate² Chip Espresso Cookies; and chipped cream and dark and white chocolate sauces for an over-the-top finish.

If you are like me and consider baking cookies a kind of therapy, you will want to make every component of this recipe yourself. Otherwise, this can be a dinner-party dessert. Hand out the recipe for each component to a different chocolate chip–crazed friend, make the sauces yourself (they're fast and easy), and then put everything together when you are ready to dive in.

To Make the BROWN SUGAR–CHOCOLATE CHUNK ICE CREAM

Set up an ice bath by half filling a large bowl with ice and water. Have ready a heatproof storage container or bowl that fits in the ice bath and a fine-mesh strainer or chinois.

In a medium saucepan, combine the cream and milk and place over medium heat. In a medium bowl, combine the granulated and brown sugars, egg yolks, and molasses and whisk until smooth.

After about 5 minutes, when the milk mixture just begins to boil (small bubbles will appear around the edges of the pan), remove the pan from the heat. Whisk a few tablespoons of the hot liquid into the egg mixture. Then, while whisking steadily, slowly add the rest of the hot liquid to the egg mixture. Return the mixture to the saucepan and place over medium-low heat. Cook, stirring constantly but gently with a wooden spoon or heatproof spatula, for 3 to 4 minutes, or until the custard begins to thicken. The custard is done when the light lacy foam on the surface vanishes or when you run your finger across the back of the spoon and the line holds.

Pour the custard through the strainer into the heatproof container. Stir in the salt and vanilla. Nest the container in the ice bath. When the

Brown Sugar–Chocolate Chunk Ice Cream

1 cup heavy cream

1 cup whole milk

2 tablespoons (1 ounce) granulated sugar

1/4 cup plus 3 tablespoons (3 ounces) firmly packed dark brown sugar

6 (3 ounces by weight) large egg yolks

1 tablespoon unsulfured dark molasses

1/8 teaspoon kosher salt

1/2 teaspoon pure vanilla extract

5 ounces bittersweet chocolate, chopped the size of chocolate chips (about 1 cup), or bittersweet chocolate chips

custard is completely cool, cover and refrigerate for at least 1 hour or up to overnight.

Briefly stir the chilled custard, and then pour into an ice cream maker and freeze according to the manufacturer's directions. Fold the chocolate into the finished ice cream, and then store in a covered container in the freezer for 1 to 2 hours before you plate the dessert. It will keep for 1 week but will taste best if served within 3 days. You should have about 3 cups. (Keep in mind that this ice cream, with or without the chunks of chocolate, also makes great ice cream sandwiches.)

To Make the BLONDIES

Position a rack in the center of the oven and preheat the oven to 350°F. Lightly butter the bottom and sides of an 8-inch square baking pan or dish and then line the pan with parchment paper (the butter will help hold the parchment in place), allowing the edges of the paper to extend beyond the rim of the pan. The overhang comes in handy when it is time to remove the blondies from the pan: all you have to do is grasp the opposite ends of the paper and lift.

In a medium bowl, stir together the flour, salt, and baking powder. In a large bowl, using a wooden spoon, cream together the butter and granulated and brown sugars until smooth but not overmixed. (I do this by hand, but if you use a stand mixer fitted with the paddle attachment or a handheld mixer, beat on medium speed for about 2 minutes, and then scrape down the sides of the bowl before continuing.) Add the vanilla and eggs and stir until combined. Add the dry ingredients and stir just until combined. Do not overmix.

Pour the batter into the prepared pan.

Bake the blondies for 25 to 30 minutes, or until the center is still slightly soft to the touch but a skewer inserted into it comes out clean. The edges will be golden but darker than the center. Let cool completely in the pan, on a rack if you like. As the blondies cool, they will set in the center but still be fudgy, like a pan of brownies.

Using the parchment paper, lift the blondies out of the pan and peel off the paper. Using a large, sharp knife, trim the edges even, and then cut the square into 6 equal squares or rectangles.

To Make the CHIPPED CREAM

In a bowl, using a whisk, whip the cream until very soft peaks form. (Or, use a stand mixer fitted with the whip attachment or a handheld mixer on medium speed.) Split the vanilla bean lengthwise and, with the tip of the knife, scrape the seeds into the cream. If using vanilla extract, pour it now. Add the chocolate and whisk until soft peaks form.

Blondies

1¼ cups plus 3 tablespoons (7 ounces) all-purpose flour

¾ teaspoon kosher salt

¼ teaspoon baking powder

8 tablespoons (4 ounces) unsalted butter, softened but still cool

¼ cup plus 3 tablespoons (3 ounces) granulated sugar

¾ cup plus 2 tablespoons (7¼ ounces) firmly packed dark brown sugar

2 teaspoons pure vanilla extract

2 (3 ounces by weight) large eggs

Chipped Cream

½ cup heavy cream

½ vanilla bean or ¼ teaspoon pure vanilla extract or vanilla powder

1 ounce bittersweet chocolate, grated or finely chopped

To Plate the Dessert

Make large polka dots on each plate with the dark and white chocolate sauces. Place a blondie in the center of each plate. Put a quenelle (see below) or a scoop of the ice cream on top of the blondie. Put a quenelle or a spoonful of the chipped cream next to the ice cream. Finish by placing 1 or 2 mini cookies between the ice cream and the chipped cream and leaning another cookie against one side of the blondie.

1/3 cup Dark Chocolate Sauce (page 207)

1/3 cup White Chocolate Sauce (page 208)

12 to 18 mini Chocolate² Chip Espresso Cookies (page 24)

making a quenelle

quenelle (pronounced ke-NELLE) is a presentation technique, a way to shape ice cream, sorbet, mousse, ganache, or whipped cream before plating it. Adding a well-formed quenelle, rather than plopping down a scoop (unless, of course, a scoop is in tune with your creation), makes the entire dessert look more polished. Quenelles are usually made from ingredients or mixtures that melt or otherwise lose their shape quickly, so forming one and putting it in place is generally one of the last steps in plating.

Sculpting a quenelle requires a little deftness, but success is mostly about patience and practice. In the savory kitchen, chefs traditionally use two spoons to form quenelles from soft foods like caviar or chicken liver pâté, but in the pastry kitchen, only one spoon is typically used. It doesn't need to be fancy. Start with a regular serving spoon or soupspoon, but make sure it is oval and not round. Warm the bowl of the spoon over the gas flame of your stove top, in hot water from your tap, or in a bowl of boiling water. Don't let the spoon get red-hot; you want only to warm it.

Next, pull the edge of the spoon over the surface of the ice cream, ganache, or mousse. (If you are working with ice cream or sorbet rock hard from the freezer, let it sit out at room temperature for about 20 minutes.) Don't dig the spoon in; instead, skim it along the surface in a single motion, so it forms a small, smooth oval. Place the quenelle on the plate, and clean and rewarm the spoon before starting the next one.

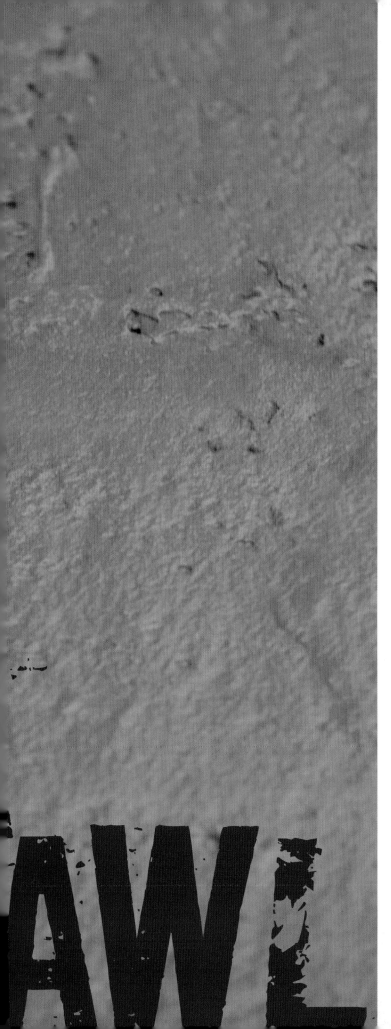

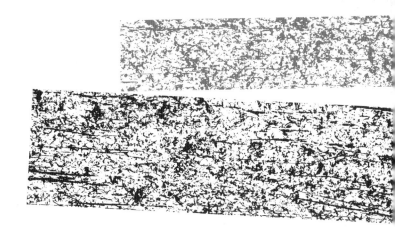

o understand my complicated relationship with chocolate, you have to know that I was born allergic to it, as well as to milk and citrus. I got over the milk and citrus allergies pretty quickly, but the chocolate allergy hung on. When my brother Jason was given a chocolate bar as a treat, I was handed a Planters Peanut Bar or stuck with something made of carob—always a letdown (although I do still like both peanuts and carob today).

Around the age of six, I got into trouble for climbing on top of the refrigerator, breaking into the Ovaltine, and eating it straight from the jar. A half hour after the incident, I remember my mother asking, "Elizabeth, did you eat chocolate?" I looked her straight in the eye and said no. But the hives welting up all over my face and the empty Ovaltine jar gave me away. My mom took my brother and me to see *Willy Wonka and the Chocolate Factory* around this same time, which might have had something to do with my Ovaltine orgy. I am still crazy about that movie and the Roald Dahl book that inspired it.

When I was nine years old, I willed my way out of the chocolate allergy. I was always a skinny kid, and about this time I made a conscious decision to eat better so I would be stronger—and because I thought it might cure my allergy. Whether it was the change in diet or mind over matter I'm not sure, but one day at school I decided to have chocolate milk with my lunch. I remember saying to myself, "I'm going to have chocolate milk today and nothing's going to happen." I drank it and was fine—no hives. I have eaten chocolate ever since, on just about a daily basis.

My fascination with chocolate intensified after I saw chocolate being made at the Scharffen Berger and Ghirardelli factories in the Bay Area and at an El Rel factory in Venezuela. The process of taking bitter-tasting beans, roasting them, shelling and grinding them, and having chocolate as the end result—it seemed almost miraculous to me. Add to that the captivating and intoxicating aroma of chocolate that surrounds a chocolate factory, and you have exactly the inspiration a chocoholic pastry chef thrives on. The more I learn about chocolate and chocolate making, the more excited I am to work with it.

Chocolate is the common ground in the recipes that follow, sometimes acting as the focal point and other times working as a stage for other flavors, such as the cherries with wine in Black on Black (page 64) or the brown sugar, lime, and rum granita in CocoShok (page 53). There is a reason chocolate works well with so many flavors. Chemists have found more than five hundred different chemical compounds in chocolate, which give it an incredible range of flavors. This means that chocolate goes well with just about anything, from pears, bananas, oranges, berries, and nuts to cinnamon, cardamom, ginger, and basil.

If my allergy to chocolate ever reappears, I would have to find a way to get around it. I love chocolate too much to give it up.

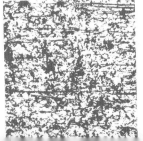

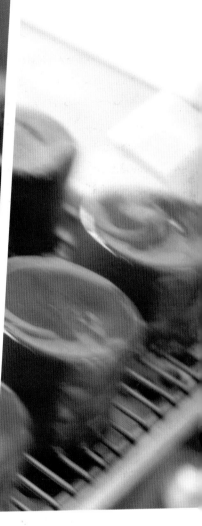

TIRAMISUSHI

cocoa roulade sponge cake, marsala mascarpone filling, mocha-rum dipping sauce, fruit ribbons, biscotti chopsticks

UP TO 2 DAYS BEFORE

➠ make the chopsticks

THE DAY BEFORE

➠ make the dipping
sauce

➠ make the cake
and leave it rolled
overnight

A FEW HOURS BEFORE

➠ fill the cakes and
reroll them

JUST BEFORE SERVING

➠ gently warm the dip-
ping sauce if you like

➠ make the fruit ribbons

➠ slice the cake rolls
and plate the dessert

MINIMALIST VERSION

Leave off the
chopsticks and
fruit ribbons.

serves **6**

I came up with this dessert while working as the pastry chef at Elka, one of the early Pacific Rim restaurants in San Francisco's Japantown. I wanted to make a tiramisu but with a Japanese aesthetic, and Tiramisushi seemed a natural way to combine the two traditions.

This dessert has been served at Citizen Cake over the years, but we continually switch it around, playing with the flavor of the sponge cake, the sauces, and the chopsticks and with the appearance of the sushi roll. Feel free to do the same, assembling your sushi plate with any components or flavors you like.

To Make the COCOA ROULADE SPONGE CAKE

Position a rack in the center of the oven and preheat the oven to 375°F. Butter a quarter sheet pan (9$\frac{1}{2}$ by 13 inches) and line with parchment paper.

Sift together the flour, cocoa powder, and baking powder into a small bowl. Set aside.

Bring a few inches of water to a simmer in a saucepan. Combine the eggs and granulated sugar in a heatproof bowl and place over (not touching) the simmering water (or use a double broiler). Whisk together for 2 to 3 minutes, or until the sugar melts and the mixture is warm to the touch. Pour the mixture into the bowl of a stand mixer fitted with the whip attachment (or a deep bowl that you can use with a handheld mixer). Add the salt and whip on medium to medium-high speed for 5 to 7 minutes, or until the mixture has tripled in volume and is cool.

In a small pan, melt the butter over medium heat. Add the water and remove the pan from the heat.

Add the flour mixture to the egg mixture and fold it in with a few gentle strokes of a spatula. Add the butter mixture and continue to fold in until smooth. Pour the batter onto the prepared pan and spread evenly with an offset spatula or the back of a spoon, taking care not to overwork the batter.

Cocoa Roulade Sponge Cake

$\frac{1}{2}$ cup (2$\frac{1}{2}$ ounces) all-purpose flour

$\frac{1}{4}$ cup plus 2 tablespoons (about 1 ounce)
unsweetened cocoa powder, preferably natural

$\frac{1}{4}$ teaspoon baking powder

3 (4$\frac{1}{2}$ ounces by weight) large eggs

$\frac{1}{2}$ cup (3$\frac{1}{2}$ ounces) granulated sugar

Pinch of kosher salt

2 tablespoons (1 ounce) unsalted butter

1 tablespoon water

Powdered sugar or unsweetened cocoa
powder for dusting

Bake the cake for 10 to 12 minutes, or until the center bounces back when lightly pressed.

Let the cake cool in the pan on a cooling rack for a few minutes. While it is cooling, cut a piece of parchment paper about the size of a half sheet pan (13 by 19 inches) and dust it with powdered sugar or cocoa powder.

Gently turn the cake out onto the dusted parchment, working carefully because both the cake and the pan will still be hot. Peel off and discard the parchment paper stuck to the cake. Cut the cake lengthwise down the middle, to yield 2 long rectangles. Slide each rectangle slightly away from the center, and cut the parchment paper down the middle so you can roll each cake separately, using the parchment to help roll.

Working from the long side of a cake half, slowly and gently roll the cake, along with the parchment, into a cylinder. The cake will want to unroll, so prop it against something to keep it tightly rolled, such as a wine bottle or the edge of a cutting board. Repeat with the remaining cake half. Let the rolls cool for 45 minutes to 1 hour, or until they are at room temperature.

To Make the BISCOTTI CHOPSTICKS

Biscotti means "twice-baked" in Italian, so you are going to make the dough, bake it, cut it into neat chopsticks, and bake it again. Position a rack in the center of the oven and preheat the oven to 350°F. Line a baking sheet with parchment paper.

In a small bowl, lightly beat the eggs until blended, then stir in the vanilla. In a large bowl, stir together the flour, granulated sugar, baking powder, sesame seeds, and salt. Pour the eggs into the dry ingredients, working the mixture into a dough with a wooden spoon or your hands.

Turn out the dough onto the prepared pan, sprinkle a little flour on top, and pat the dough into a rectangle about 7 by 5 inches and 1 inch high.

Bake for about 30 minutes, or until lightly golden. Remove from the oven and set the pan on a cooling rack. Reduce the oven temperature to 250°F. Let the baked dough cool in the pan for 10 minutes, transfer it to a cutting board, and trim all 4 sides of the rectangle to even them. Slice the rectangle lengthwise into cookies $1/4$ to $1/2$ inch wide. Now cut each slice in half lengthwise, so the cookies resemble oversized chopsticks.

Line the same pan with another sheet of parchment, place the chopsticks on top, and bake for 15 to 20 minutes, or until crisp. Let the chopsticks cool completely on the pan. You should have about 24 chopsticks, each 6 inches long. Once you plate the dessert, you will have lots of chopsticks left over, but that means you can handpick the best-looking ones for the dessert and reserve the others for dunking in your morning coffee, tea, or cocoa, or for dipping into a glass of sweet wine in the evening. They will keep in an airtight container at room temperature for up to 2 days.

Biscotti Chopsticks

3 ($4^1/2$ ounces by weight) large eggs

1 teaspoon pure vanilla extract

2 cups (10 ounces) all-purpose flour

$3/4$ cup ($5^1/4$ ounces) granulated sugar

$1^1/2$ teaspoons baking powder

2 teaspoons black sesame seeds

$1/2$ teaspoon kosher salt

To Make the MARSALA MASCARPONE FILLING

In a medium bowl, combine the mascarpone, powdered sugar, and Marsala and mix with a rubber spatula or wooden spoon just until the ingredients are evenly blended. Don't overmix. You should have about 1 cup.

To Form the "SUSHI ROLLS"

Make sure the cake rolls are completely cooled before you start. Cut 2 pieces of parchment paper about the size of a half sheet pan. Gently unroll 1 cake roll on a sheet of the parchment. Then, using an offset spatula, spread half of the mascarpone filling on the cake in an even layer. Using the parchment paper like a sushi mat, tightly roll up the cake again.

    Repeat with the remaining cake roll, filling, and parchment to make a second roll. Your cakes may crack slightly while you are rolling or unrolling them. But don't worry, because the filling will keep the rolls together. Place the parchment-wrapped cake rolls in the refrigerator to chill for at least 1 hour.

Marsala Mascarpone Filling

- 1 cup (8 ounces) mascarpone cheese, softened but still cool
- 1 tablespoon powdered sugar, sifted
- 1 tablespoon Marsala wine

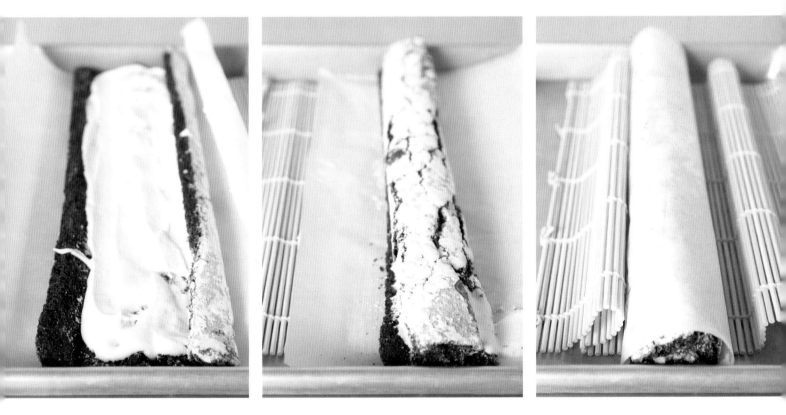

Mocha-Rum Dipping Sauce

1/2 cup heavy cream

1 tablespoon light corn syrup

1 tablespoon unsweetened cocoa powder, preferably natural

4 ounces bittersweet chocolate, coarsely chopped (scant 1 cup)

3 tablespoons piping-hot brewed espresso or strong coffee

2 tablespoons (1 ounce) unsalted butter

2 tablespoons dark rum

A few grains of *fleur de sel* or kosher salt

Fruit Ribbons

1 Asian pear, firm but ripe Bosc or Bartlett pear, mango, or cantaloupe

1 piece fresh ginger, 1 to 2 inches long, peeled

To Make the MOCHA-RUM DIPPING SAUCE

In a small saucepan, whisk together the cream, corn syrup, and cocoa powder over medium-high heat and cook, whisking, for about 3 minutes, or until the mixture comes to a simmer. Remove the pan from the heat.

Place the chocolate in a heatproof bowl and pour the hot espresso over it. Stir a few times to mix, and then add the hot cream mixture and stir until the chocolate is completely melted. Add the butter, rum, and salt, and stir until the butter has melted. You should have 1 1/2 cups of dipping sauce.

To Plate the Dessert

The fruit ribbons should look like the pickled ginger served with sushi. To make them, first peel the pear with a vegetable peeler, discarding the skin. Now draw the peeler across the flesh, letting a small mound of the fruit shavings pile up on each individual plate. (If using cantaloupe, cut it into quarters, slice away the rind, and then draw the vegetable peeler across the flesh the same way.)

Cut the filled cake rolls into rounds 1 to 2 inches thick, and stand 2 of these maki-like slices on each plate. Divide the dipping sauce among 6 small, shallow bowls, ideally the kind of bowl used for soy sauce on a sushi platter. With a Microplane, box, or ginger grater, grate a few teaspoons of ginger. Gather the ginger gratings into little knobs and rest a knob alongside each mound of fruit shavings. (These knobs should look like the little mound of wasabi that comes with a sushi platter.) Place 2 biscotti chopsticks on each plate.

THE REAL McCOY ICE CREAM SANDWICH

minty gelato, fudgy sandwich biscuits, dark chocolate sauce, basil-mint oil

UP TO 1 WEEK BEFORE

- make the gelato
- make the chocolate
  sauce
- bake the biscuits
- assemble the
  sandwiches, wrap,
  and freeze

A FEW HOURS BEFORE

- make the basil-
  mint oil

JUST BEFORE SERVING

- rewarm the
  chocolate sauce
- plate the dessert

MINIMALIST VERSION

Skip the chocolate
sauce and the basil-
mint oil.

serves 4

The fudgy biscuits for these sandwiches are similar to the biscuits used for the ice cream sandwiches you used to buy in the school cafeteria—only better, because our cookie is more chocolaty.

My friend Ann McCoy inspired this sandwich while I was still working at Rubicon. Ann, who is from Kentucky, has the greatest accent. So when she asked, "How come ya cain't get a good ice cream sandwich out heah?" she sounded like she was out on the verandah. I chose mint to go with the cookie because of the traditional Kentucky–mint julep connection, and because I like the combination. But you can make these sandwiches using any of the ice creams or sorbets in this book, or use store-bought ice cream if you are short on time. And if chocolate sauce doesn't suit you, use a fruit sauce (page 208) or a caramel sauce (page 210) instead.

I like to serve these sandwiches the day I make them, but they are sturdy and can be assembled ahead and kept in the freezer for a week. If you don't have time to make the basil-mint oil, you can skip it, but a few drops on each plate add a hint of flavor and color. If you like, you can substitute cilantro for the basil, but keep the mint either way.

To Make the MINTY GELATO

In a blender, combine the cream, milk, mint leaves, and spinach leaves. (The spinach leaves will make the ice cream a brighter green but won't add any flavor.) Pulse for 30 seconds, or until pureed. Let the mixture stand for 5 minutes, and then strain it through a fine-mesh strainer into a liquid measuring cup.

Wipe out the blender and pour 1 cup of the minted milk mixture back into the blender. Add the sugar, corn syrup, salt, guar gum, and milk powder and pulse for 30 seconds, or until slightly thickened. Add the peppermint extract, pulse for just a few seconds, and then pour in the remaining minted milk mixture and pulse to combine.

Pour the mint mixture into an ice cream maker and freeze according to the manufacturer's directions. Store in a covered container in the freezer for 1 to 2 hours before you plate the dessert. It will keep for 1 week. You should have about 3 cups.

Minty Gelato

- 1 cup heavy cream
- 1 1/2 cups whole milk
- 1 cup (about 1 ounce) firmly packed fresh mint leaves
- Generous handful of spinach leaves (optional)
- 1/4 cup (1 3/4 ounces) granulated sugar
- 1/4 cup (about 2 3/4 ounces by weight) light corn syrup
- 1/4 teaspoon kosher salt
- 1/2 teaspoon guar gum (see Secret Agent, page 140)
- 2 tablespoons (about 1/4 ounce) nonfat dry milk powder
- 1/4 teaspoon pure peppermint extract

Fudgy Sandwich Biscuits

5 ounces bittersweet chocolate, coarsely chopped (about 1 cup)

3/4 cup (3 3/4 ounces) all-purpose flour

2 tablespoons (about 1/4 ounce) unsweetened cocoa powder, preferably natural

1/4 teaspoon baking powder

1/2 teaspoon kosher salt

4 tablespoons (2 ounces) unsalted butter, softened but still cool

1/2 cup (4 1/4 ounces) firmly packed dark brown sugar

1/2 cup (3 1/2 ounces) granulated sugar

1 (1 1/2 ounces by weight) large egg

1/2 teaspoon baking soda

1 teaspoon water

2 ounces dark chocolate, coarsely chopped, for rolling the sandwich edges

To Make the FUDGY SANDWICH BISCUITS

Bring a few inches of water to a gentle simmer in a saucepan. Put the chocolate in a heatproof bowl and place over (not touching) the simmering water (or use a double boiler). Heat slowly, stirring occasionally, until about 90 percent melted, and then remove the bowl from the heat and whisk until smooth. Set aside.

In a small bowl, sift together the flour, cocoa powder, and baking powder. Stir in the salt and set aside.

In a bowl, using a stand mixer fitted with the paddle attachment or a handheld mixer, cream together the butter and brown and granulated sugars on medium speed for 3 to 4 minutes, or until light in color. Add the egg and beat until creamy, about 1 minute. Add the chocolate and mix just until combined.

In a small bowl or cup, stir together the baking soda and water and add to the chocolate mixture. With the mixer on low speed, add the dry ingredients in two additions, mixing after each addition until combined.

Divide the dough in half and turn out each half onto its own piece of plastic wrap. Using your fingers, flatten the dough slightly, so it will be easier to roll after chilling, and then wrap it well. Refrigerate for at least 2 hours or up to overnight.

Position racks in the upper third and lower third of the oven and preheat the oven to 350°F. Line 2 baking sheets with parchment paper.

Place half of the dough on a lightly floured work surface. If it doesn't look smooth, knead it once or twice, and then roll it out until about 1/4 inch thick. This dough is extremely forgiving and can be pushed back into place if it crumbles a little, but try not to overhandle it.

Using either a cookie cutter or a template and a sharp knife, cut out 4-inch rounds or squares. Place the cookies on the prepared pans, spacing them about 1 1/2 inches apart (they don't spread much). Prick each cookie three times with a fork. Repeat with the remaining dough.

Bake the cookies, rotating the pans after 5 minutes, for 10 minutes, or until they puff up and cracks appear on the top. Use your nose, too, in deciding when they are done. If you smell an intense chocolaty aroma, it is probably time to take the cookies out of the oven. Let cool on the pans on cooling racks. You should have eight to ten 4-inch cookies.

To Assemble the SANDWICHES

Take the gelato out of the freezer a few minutes before you are ready to assemble the sandwiches. It should be firm enough so that it doesn't drip, but not so hard that it is a challenge to scoop onto the biscuit. Have the roughly chopped chocolate ready on a sheet of parchment paper.

Set 1 biscuit, bottom side up, on a work surface. Top the biscuit with a scoop or two of gelato and place another biscuit on top, bottom side down.

Working over the parchment paper, press the chopped chocolate all the way around the ice cream. Repeat to make 3 more sandwiches. If you would like to freeze the sandwiches at this point, wrap each one separately in plastic wrap and place in the freezer.

To Plate the Dessert

I like to use a white plate to make the chocolate sauce and basil-mint oil stand out. Warm the chocolate sauce gently. Place 1 ice cream sandwich on each plate. Drizzle the warm chocolate sauce and the basil-mint oil around each sandwich.

About 1/4 cup Dark Chocolate Sauce (page 207)

2 to 3 teaspoons Herb Oil, basil version (page 220), optional

CAREMI, THAT MAY BE THE WORLD'S LARGEST REAL McCOY SANDWICH.

WHERE CAN I GET CHOCOLATE SPRAY PAINT?!#?

I WANT TO START TAGGING WITH CHOCOLATE. WOULDN'T THAT BE SUPERCOOL?

...BUILDINGS NABBED WITH CHOCOLATE...

*You can make some
components in advance:*

UP TO 1 WEEK BEFORE

→ make the
 chocolate sauce

UP TO 3 DAYS BEFORE

→ make the granita

UP TO 2 DAYS BEFORE

→ make the candy

THE DAY BEFORE

→ make the *panna cotta*

JUST BEFORE SERVING

→ rewarm the
 chocolate sauce

→ plate the dessert

MINIMALIST VERSION

The *panna cotta* and
the granita can each
be served on its
own, plain or with
any extras you like.

COCOSHOK

coconut panna cotta, dark chocolate sauce, walnut-caramel coconut candy,
venezuelan-spiced rum-and-lime granita

serves **6**

How do you make rich German chocolate cake with coconut icing appealing on a
hot day? CocoShok starts with the flavors of the classic cake and gives each one
its own (cool) spin. This dessert tastes so good on a warm evening that it has
become one of my best hot-weather offerings (it was 90 degrees in San Francisco
the day I created it).

I have traded in the traditional coconut icing for coconut-flavored *panna cotta*
that is light, refreshing, and almost translucent because it is made with milk
instead of cream. The granita was inspired by a trip to Venezuela, and it calls in
one of my favorite flavor combinations: rum, brown sugar, and lime. Venezuelan
rum tastes like liquid brown sugar; served on the rocks with lime, it's a fabulous
and dangerous concoction, especially on sultry tropical evenings.

To complete the homage to German chocolate cake, I put a schmear of dark
chocolate sauce on the plate and finish with some buttery, crunchy walnut-
coconut candy.

You may wonder why I call for chopping walnut halves, rather than starting
with less expensive pieces. Whenever I make any recipe that calls for nuts, I want
them to be fresh. Ideally, that means buying walnuts in their shells and cracking
them yourself. But if you don't have the time to shell nuts, buying walnut halves
is the next best option, because they retain a little more moisture and freshness
than pieces do.

Instead of using individual molds for the *panna cotta*, I prefer to pour the mixture into a single container, and then, when it has set, cut it with a knife or scoop
it onto the plate. But if you like your *panna cotta* molded, by all means allow it to
set in small ramekins, candy molds, or any other molds you like.

If you are making all the components for this dessert the same day you are
serving it, be sure to allow 4 hours for the *panna cotta* to set and at least 3 hours
of freezer time for the granita.

Venezuelan-Spiced Rum-and-Lime Granita

2 tablespoons (1 ounce) firmly packed dark
   brown sugar

1/4 cup (1 3/4 ounces) granulated sugar

1 1/4 cups water

1 slice fresh ginger, 1/4 inch thick, peeled

1 teaspoon coriander seeds

2 tablespoons coarsely chopped fresh cilantro

1 lime zest strip, about 2 inches long by
   1/2 inch wide

1/2 vanilla bean

6 tablespoons to 1/2 cup fresh lime juice
   (from about 4 large limes)

2 teaspoons dark rum

Walnut-Caramel Coconut Candy

1/2 cup (1 ounce) unsweetened large dried
   coconut flakes (see Resources)

1/2 cup (3 1/2 ounces) granulated sugar

2 tablespoons water

1 tablespoon light corn syrup

1 tablespoon (1/2 ounce) unsalted butter

1/4 teaspoon kosher salt

1 cup (4 ounces) coarsely chopped walnut
   halves or pieces

To Make the VENEZUELAN-SPICED RUM-AND-LIME GRANITA

In a small saucepan, combine the brown and granulated sugars, water, ginger, coriander, cilantro, and lime zest. Split the vanilla bean lengthwise and, with the tip of the knife, scrape the seeds into the saucepan, and then toss in the empty pod. Place over medium to medium-high heat and cook, stirring to dissolve the sugar, for about 5 minutes, or until the mixture comes to a boil. Remove the pan from the heat and let steep for 20 minutes.

Strain the mixture through a fine-mesh strainer into a large liquid measuring cup for ease of pouring. Stir in the lime juice to taste and then add the rum. Pour the mixture into a shallow freezerproof container that will hold at least 3 cups of liquid and won't react badly to scraping with a fork, such as a 9-inch square Pyrex dish. Place the container in the freezer.

After 1 1/2 hours, remove it from the freezer and rake it with a fork to break up the ice crystals, making sure to scrape the bottom and sides. Return the container to the freezer and then continue to rake the mixture every 20 minutes for 1 hour. Cover tightly with plastic wrap and store in the freezer until you are ready to plate the dessert. You can make it up to 3 days ahead, as long as the container is well sealed. Remove from the freezer about 20 minutes before plating and rake it once more to break up the granita. You should have about 3 cups.

To Make the WALNUT-CARAMEL COCONUT CANDY

Position a rack in the center of the oven and preheat the oven to 350°F. Spread the coconut flakes on a baking sheet or pie pan and toast in the oven for 3 to 5 minutes. It is easy to burn the coconut, so watch carefully and remove the pan from the oven as soon as the flakes begin to turn a light golden brown along their edges. Pour onto a plate and set aside.

Line a baking sheet with parchment paper or a nonstick baking mat. In a saucepan, combine the sugar, water, and corn syrup, cover, and place over high heat. Bring to a boil and cook for 2 minutes. Uncover and continue to cook, without stirring, for 2 to 3 minutes, or until the sugar begins to color.

As soon as the sugar has turned deep amber, add the butter, salt, walnuts, and toasted coconut. Mix with a wooden spoon just until the nuts and coconut are coated with the caramel, and then turn the mixture out onto the prepared pan. Use the spoon to spread the candy, which will be very hot and sticky, into a fairly even layer. Let stand for about 30 minutes, or until completely cool, and then chop it or break it into 1/2-inch chunks. Don't be precise—just give the candy a quick chop. Store the candy in an airtight container at room temperature for up to 2 days. You should have 2 1/2 cups.

To Make the COCONUT PANNA COTTA

In a heatproof bowl, sprinkle the gelatin over the water and set aside to soften while you heat the milk.

In a small saucepan, combine the milk and sugar, bring to a boil over medium heat, and cook, stirring constantly, for 3 to 4 minutes, or until the sugar dissolves. Pour the hot milk into the gelatin and stir until the gelatin dissolves. Add the coconut milk and stir to mix. At this point, you can cover the bowl and put it into the refrigerator to chill, or pour the mixture into a shallow container (or small ramekins if you prefer) and cover and refrigerate. The *panna cotta* will be fully set after about 4 hours. You should have about 1^1/$_2$ cups.

Coconut Panna Cotta

1^1/$_2$ teaspoons powdered gelatin

1 tablespoon water

^{3}/$_4$ cup whole milk

3 tablespoons (1^1/$_4$ ounces) granulated sugar

^{3}/$_4$ cup (6^3/$_4$ ounces by weight) coconut milk

To Plate the Dessert

Warm the chocolate sauce gently. With a spoon or offset spatula, make a fine line or a smudge of chocolate across each plate. Place a serving of *panna cotta* on top of the chocolate. Place a chunk or two of the coconut candy near the *panna cotta*. Place a quenelle (see page 37) or a scoop of granita on the other side.

^{1}/$_2$ cup Dark Chocolate Sauce (page 207)

You can make some
components in advance:

UP TO 2 MONTHS BEFORE

- make the tart dough

UP TO 1 WEEK BEFORE

- make the caramel
  sauce

- make the pecan
  praline

- make the chocolate
  sauce

UP TO 3 DAYS BEFORE

- make the ice cream

UP TO 2 DAYS BEFORE

- bake the tart shells

A FEW HOURS BEFORE

- make the cake batter

JUST BEFORE SERVING

- fill the tart shells
  and bake them

- rewarm the
  chocolate sauce

- plate the dessert
  while the tarts are
  warm

MINIMALIST VERSION

Serve the tarts on
their own, or serve
the ice cream topped
with warm caramel
sauce, with or without
the pecan praline.

A CHOCOLATE TART NAMED DESIRE

warm chocolate-caramel tart, mint julep ice cream, dark chocolate sauce,
pecan praline

serves 8

The name of this tart says it all. Who can resist the sex appeal of rich chocolate
cake atop a layer of caramel baked in a flaky tart shell? I developed this dessert
a decade ago, and I haven't really changed it. It is from the era when pastry chefs
were giving desserts provocative names like Death by Chocolate or Chocolate
Decadence. I love the surprise of warm caramel, and I wanted a name that carried
a little southern exposure.

The pastry dough recipe yields 16 tart shells, though you will need only
8 shells for this dessert. But you can store the leftover dough in the freezer for a
couple of months, where it will be ready when you need it.

To Make the MINT JULEP ICE CREAM

Working over a medium saucepan, tear the mint leaves into pieces with your
fingers, allowing them to drop in the pan. Pour in the cream and milk and
place over medium to medium-high heat. Heat the mixture for 5 to 7 minutes, or just until it comes to a boil (small bubbles will appear around the
edges of the pan). Remove the pan from the heat and let the mixture steep
for 20 minutes.

In a bowl, whisk together the egg yolks and sugar until smooth. If the
cream mixture has cooled, place it over medium heat for 1 to 2 minutes.
Whisk a few tablespoons of the hot cream mixture into the egg mixture.

Mint Julep Ice Cream

1/2 cup (about 1/2 ounce) firmly packed fresh
mint leaves

1 cup heavy cream

1 cup whole milk

6 (3 ounces by weight) large egg yolks

1/2 cup (31/2 ounces) granulated sugar

2 tablespoons bourbon

Pinch of kosher salt

Then, while whisking steadily, slowly add the rest of the hot liquid to the egg mixture.

Return the mixture to the saucepan. Cook over low heat, stirring constantly with a wooden spoon or heatproof spatula, for about 5 minutes, or until the custard begins to thicken. The custard is done when the trace of foam on the surface is gone and you can run your finger across the back of the spoon and the line holds.

Pour the custard through a fine-mesh strainer into a heatproof container. Stir in the bourbon and salt and let the mixture cool for 20 to 30 minutes, then cover and refrigerate for at least 1 hour or up to overnight.

Briefly stir the chilled custard, and then pour into an ice cream maker and freeze according to the manufacturer's directions. Store in a covered container in the freezer for 1 to 2 hours before you plate the dessert. It will keep for 1 week but will taste best if served within 3 days. You should have about 2¼ cups.

To Make the PECAN PRALINE

Position a rack in the center of the oven and preheat the oven to 350°F. Spread the pecan halves on a baking sheet and lightly toast in the oven for no more than 5 minutes. It is easy to burn nuts, so take them out as soon as the aroma of toasted pecans fills the air. While the nuts are toasting, place a nonstick baking mat or a piece of parchment paper on your work surface.

In a medium saucepan, combine the brown sugar, cream, and butter. Clip a candy thermometer onto the side of the pan, place over medium-high heat, and cook, stirring just once or twice to mix, for about 5 minutes, or until the syrup registers 240°F on the thermometer. Remove the pan from the heat, add the vanilla and salt, give the pan a good swirl, and then add the toasted pecans. Stir with a wooden spoon or heatproof spatula for about 15 seconds, or until the mixture looks somewhat creamy, and then turn the contents of the pan out onto the nonstick baking mat. Using the spoon, spread the mixture just slightly, and then let it cool for 20 to 30 minutes, or until cool and crystallized.

Break the pecan praline into slabs or chunks with a heavy knife. It will keep in an airtight container at room temperature for up to 1 week. You should have about 3 cups.

Pecan Praline

1 cup (4 ounces) pecan halves

1 cup (about 8½ ounces) firmly packed dark brown sugar

¼ cup heavy cream

2 tablespoons (1 ounce) unsalted butter

1 teaspoon pure vanilla extract

½ teaspoon kosher salt

To Make the DOUGH FOR THE TART SHELLS

In the bowl of a stand mixer fitted with the paddle attachment, stir together the flour, sugar, and salt. Add the butter and mix on medium speed just long enough to lightly combine the butter with the dry ingredients. Don't overmix it. The butter should be in dime-sized chunks. Add the egg yolk and cream and mix on low speed just until the dough begins to come together.

Scrape the dough out of the bowl onto a piece of plastic wrap, shape it into a slab, cut the slab in half, and wrap each half tightly in plastic wrap. Refrigerate for at least 1 hour or up to overnight. You will need to bake just 8 tart shells for this recipe, and the dough is enough for 16 tart shells, so you can either bake the extra shells for another use, wrap them gently in plastic wrap, and keep at room temperature for up to 2 days, or freeze the unused dough for up to 2 months. You should have a little more than 1 pound of dough.

To SHAPE AND BAKE THE TART SHELLS

Position a rack in the center of the oven and preheat the oven to 350°F. Have ready eight 3^{1}/2-inch tart rings or tart pans on a baking sheet.

Place half of the dough on a lightly floured work surface and roll out about ^{3}/16 inch thick. Using a round cookie cutter or a template and a sharp knife, cut out eight 4^{1}/2-inch rounds. (The largest round cutter in a standard set is about 4^{1}/4 inches, which works perfectly for 3^{1}/2-inch tart rings.) Set a round of dough in each ring, pressing it lightly into place. If you like, trim the dough with an offset spatula or knife so the edge is even with the rim, or pinch the dough to make an even top.

Line each tart shell with a small piece of aluminum foil or parchment and fill with dried beans or rice. (This prevents the dough from puffing up in the oven.)

Bake the tart shells for about 20 minutes, or until their edges are lightly browned. Remove the weights and foil and bake for another 6 to 8 minutes, or until dark golden brown. Let cool completely on the pan.

To Make the WARM CHOCOLATE CAKE BATTER

Bring a few inches of water to a gentle simmer in a saucepan. Combine the chocolate and butter in a heatproof bowl and place over (not touching) the simmering water (or use a double boiler). Heat slowly, stirring occasionally, until nearly melted, and then remove the bowl from the heat and whisk until smooth. Set aside.

In a medium bowl, combine the egg whites, salt, and 3 tablespoons (1^{1}/4 ounces) of the sugar and whisk until soft peaks form. Alternatively, use a stand mixer fitted with the whip attachment or a handheld mixer and beat on medium-high speed for about 3 minutes. Set aside.

Tart Shells

1^{1}/2 cups plus 2 tablespoons (8 ounces) all-purpose flour

^{1}/4 cup plus 1^{1}/2 teaspoons (about 2 ounces) granulated sugar

1 teaspoon kosher salt

12 tablespoons (6 ounces) unsalted butter, softened but still cool, cut into ^{1}/2-inch pieces

1 (^{1}/2 ounce by weight) large egg yolk

2 tablespoons plus 2 teaspoons heavy cream

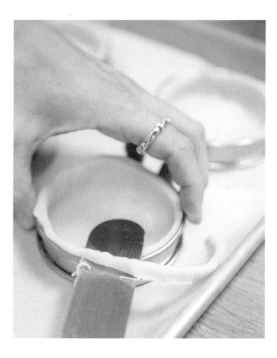

Warm Chocolate Cake Batter

8 ounces bittersweet chocolate, preferably 70% cacao, coarsely chopped (about 1^{1}/2 cups)

4 tablespoons (2 ounces) unsalted butter

3 (4^{1}/2 ounces by weight) large eggs, separated
Pinch of kosher salt

6 tablespoons (2^{1}/2 ounces) granulated sugar

3 tablespoons (about 1 ounce) all-purpose flour

In a large bowl, whisk together the egg yolks and the remaining 3 tablespoons sugar until blended, and then dribble in a few spoonfuls of the chocolate mixture and whisk until smooth. While whisking steadily, dribble in the remaining chocolate mixture and whisk until smooth. Alternatively, use the stand mixer fitted with the whip attachment and slowly dribble in the chocolate mixture while beating on medium speed for about 2 minutes.

Using a rubber spatula, gently fold in the egg whites. Sift the flour directly into the bowl, and then gently fold the flour in as well. The batter can be covered and refrigerated for up to 3 hours before you fill and bake the tart shells.

To Bake the Tarts

8 tablespoons Basic Caramel Sauce (page 210)

Position a rack in the center of the oven and preheat the oven to 350°F. Have the cooled tart shells nearby on their baking sheet.

Spoon 1 tablespoon of the caramel sauce into the bottom of each tart shell. Spoon the chocolate cake batter on top the caramel, using $2^{1}/_{2}$ to 3 tablespoons for each shell, and smooth gently. The tarts should be filled almost to the rim, and the batter should touch the tart shell all the way around to prevent the caramel from bubbling up.

Bake the tarts for just 10 minutes. The tops should still be gooey when you pull the tarts from the oven. Let cool on the pan for about 3 minutes before serving (begin plating the dessert while the tarts are baking and cooling). The chocolate filling will deflate slightly. It is best if you serve the tarts just after baking, but if you need to rewarm them, return them, on the baking sheet, to a 350°F oven for no more than 2 to 3 minutes.

To Plate the Dessert

$^{1}/_{4}$ cup Dark Chocolate Sauce (page 207)
Powdered sugar for dusting
Mint sprigs or leaves for garnish

Warm the chocolate sauce gently. Spoon it into a squeeze bottle or a pastry bag fitted with a fine plain tip and squeeze or pipe a grid pattern across each plate. (You can also use a spoon, though the lines won't be as uniform.) Place a warm tart slightly off center on top of the grid. Dust the top with powdered sugar. Balance a slab of the pecan praline on the edge of the tart. Put a quenelle (see page 37) or a small scoop of the ice cream alongside the tart, opposite the praline slab, and add another chunk or two of the praline if you like. Garnish with a mint sprig, or slice mint leaves into a thin chiffonade and drape a few mint ribbons on top of the ice cream.

You can make some
components in advance:

UP TO 1 WEEK BEFORE

➤ make the graham
  crackers (or buy
  them)

➤ make the caramel
  sauce

➤ make the
  marshmallows

THE DAY BEFORE

➤ make the chocolate–
  peanut butter cream

➤ make the peanut
  rice curry

JUST BEFORE SERVING

➤ make the hot
  chocolate

➤ melt the dark
  chocolate

➤ plate the dessert

MINIMALIST VERSION

It would be a mistake
to minimize this one.

S'MORE A PALOOZA

malted hot chocolate, chocolate–peanut butter cream, toasted marshmallows, crushed graham crackers, peanut rice curry

serves **6**

When every industrial food producer has a s'more flavor profile in its line, it is clear that s'mores have made a comeback. I did love s'mores as a kid, but I always felt they were too sweet. It wasn't until I became obsessed with dark chocolate that I gave the combination of chocolate and marshmallows another try. At Citizen Cake, years after the debut of our S'More Brownies (page 153), I came up with what I consider the end-all statement of this American classic, adding even more candy-bar influences and calling it S'More A Palooza.

You can use any kind of peanut butter you like—salted or unsalted, smooth or crunchy. Just make sure it is natural and contains no trans fats. The salted peanuts seemed to fit the candy bar theme, and the curry is here just because I love Indian flavors. This one is definitely over the top.

In the photo, you will see that I like to serve this with the marshmallow still burning. You can do this if you are feeling adventurous, but it's also fine to torch it in the kitchen and serve it with the marshmallow toasted but not flaming.

To Make the CHOCOLATE–PEANUT BUTTER CREAM

Choose a standard loaf pan or a 5-inch square baking dish or plastic container (give or take an inch; you can use any container that holds 13 liquid ounces). Line it with plastic wrap, allowing it to overhang the sides and smoothing out any wrinkles. You will pour peanut butter cream into the container, and once it sets, you will use the plastic wrap to lift it out in one piece.

In a heatproof bowl, combine the milk chocolate and bittersweet chocolate and set aside. In a small saucepan, heat the cream over medium heat for 4 to 5 minutes, or just until it comes to a boil (small bubbles will appear at the edge of the pan). Remove the pan from the heat, pour the hot cream over the chocolate, and stir until the mixture is smooth. Stir in the peanut butter.

Pour the mixture into the prepared container and refrigerate for about 30 minutes, or until set.

Chocolate–Peanut Butter Cream

2 ounces milk chocolate, coarsely chopped
  ($1/3$ to $1/2$ cup)

$1 1/2$ ounces bittersweet chocolate, preferably
  70% cacao, coarsely chopped (about $1/3$ cup)

$1/4$ cup heavy cream

$2 1/2$ tablespoons (about 1 ounce) peanut butter

To Make the PEANUT RICE CURRY

In a small bowl, stir together the peanuts, cereal, and curry powder and set aside. You should have about 1/3 cup.

To Make the MALTED HOT CHOCOLATE

In a small saucepan, stir together the chocolate sauce, malt powder, and milk. Place over medium-low heat and bring to a simmer. Keep warm over low heat. You should have about 1 1/2 cups.

To Plate the Dessert

Bring a few inches of water to a gentle simmer in a small saucepan. Put the chocolate in a small heatproof bowl and place over (not touching) the simmering water (or use a double boiler). Heat slowly until the chocolate is nearly melted, and then remove the bowl from the heat and whisk until smooth. Spread or drizzle the melted chocolate over each plate.

Apply the caramel sauce to the plates any way you like: you can smoosh it on with the back of a spoon, drizzle it, schmear it on with a knife—you decide. Make a pile of the crushed graham crackers on top of the chocolate. Using the plastic wrap, lift the chocolate–peanut butter cream out of its container. Cut into blocks and set a block on each plate. Set a marshmallow on top of each block and toast the marshmallows with a butane torch until they are done to your satisfaction. (You can also toast the marshmallows the old-fashioned way, spearing each one on a fork or skewer and holding it over the flame of a gas burner on your stove top, and then setting it on the block.)

Scatter a spoonful of the peanut rice curry across each plate. Pour the hot chocolate into 6 shot glasses or other small glasses and set a chunk of marshmallow on top of the hot chocolate. Place the glass on the plate or on the table next to the plate.

Peanut Rice Curry

1/4 cup (1 1/4 ounces) salted skinless roasted peanuts

2 tablespoons (scant 1/4 ounce) crisp rice cereal

1/4 teaspoon curry powder

Malted Hot Chocolate

1/2 cup Dark Chocolate Sauce (page 207)

1/4 cup plus 3 tablespoons (2 ounces) malt powder or Ovaltine

1 cup whole milk

1 ounce bittersweet chocolate, preferably 70% cacao, coarsely chopped (about 1/4 cup)

3 tablespoons Basic Caramel Sauce (page 210)

4 graham crackers, homemade (page 214) or store-bought, crushed with your fingers (don't turn these into powder but keep them in chunks)

12 marshmallows, made with gelatin (page 212) or xanthan gum (page 213)

FLAMING!

You can make some components in advance:

UP TO 2 MONTHS BEFORE
➥ make the cherries

UP TO 3 DAYS BEFORE
➥ make the ice cream

A FEW HOURS BEFORE
➥ make the *chibouste*

JUST BEFORE SERVING
➥ plate the dessert

MINIMALIST VERSION
Serve the *chibouste* with the cherries and skip the ice cream.

BLACK ON BLACK

chocolate chibouste, wine-soaked cherries, altoids liquorice ice cream

serves 4

Our wine director, John Mark, and I are both fond of Malcolm McLaren's *Paris* album, and this black cherries and chocolate dessert is named after some of the lyrics on the album. (Chef William Pilz thinks we should call this dessert Back in Black because it's pretty badass, but I'm sticking with the McLaren homage.)

Chibouste is a combination of pastry cream and Italian meringue, with the addition of chocolate here. It can be served as a mousse without further cooking, or it can be warmed, brûléed, or baked, as in this recipe. When it is baked, it develops a smooth, rich texture that is like a cross between a warm chocolate cake and a soufflé. There is too little *chibouste* to whip up properly in a stand mixer here, so I use a whisk or handheld mixer, and I try to find a friend to hold the bowl and beat while I drizzle in the syrup.

If you can't find Altoids Liquorice flavor, you can order them online (see Resources).

Altoids Liquorice Ice Cream

10 Liquorice Altoids
1 cup whole milk
1/3 cup (4 ounces by weight) unsulfured dark molasses
1 cup heavy cream

To Make the ALTOIDS LIQUORICE ICE CREAM

Crush the Altoids to a powder in a mortar with a pestle. (If you don't have a mortar and pestle, wrap the Altoids in several layers of plastic wrap and smash them with a hammer or mallet.)

In a saucepan, stir together the milk and powdered Altoids. Place over medium-high heat and cook for 4 to 6 minutes, or just until the mixture comes to a boil (small bubbles will appear along the edges of the pan). Remove the pan from the heat, add the molasses, and stir until dissolved. Pour in the cream, stir well, cover, and refrigerate for at least 2 hours or up to overnight.

Briefly stir the chilled mixture, and then pour into an ice cream maker and freeze according to the manufacturer's directions. Store in a covered container in the freezer for 1 to 2 hours before you plate the dessert. It will keep for up to 3 days. You should have about 2½ cups.

Chocolate Chibouste

8 ounces bittersweet chocolate, coarsely chopped (about 1¹/₂ cups)

¹/₄ teaspoon grated orange zest

¹/₄ cup plus 2 tablespoons (2¹/₂ ounces) granulated sugar

2 tablespoons water

2 (2 ounces by weight) large egg whites

³/₄ cup Pastry Cream (page 203)

To Make the CHOCOLATE CHIBOUSTE

Position a rack in the center of the oven and preheat the oven to 350°F. Have ready an ungreased 4¹/₂-cup soufflé dish.

Bring a few inches of water to a gentle simmer in a saucepan. Put the chocolate in a heatproof bowl and place over (not touching) the simmering water (or use a double boiler). Heat slowly, stirring occasionally, until nearly melted, and then remove the bowl from the heat and whisk until smooth. Stir in the orange zest.

In a small saucepan, combine the sugar and water and stir once or twice to mix. Clip a candy thermometer onto the side of the pan, place over high heat, and cook, without stirring, for 10 to 15 minutes, or until the mixture registers 240°F on the thermometer.

Meanwhile, in a medium bowl, whip the egg whites with a whisk or a handheld mixer on medium-high speed until they begin to hold soft peaks. When the syrup is ready, very slowly drizzle it into the whites while whipping steadily. Place a dish towel under the bowl to help keep it in place while you simultaneously whisk and dribble. When all the syrup has been added, you will have a seductively smooth Italian meringue.

In a medium bowl, whisk the pastry cream once or twice and then whisk in the melted chocolate until blended. In two or three additions, fold in the meringue, working gently to deflate it as little as possible. Pour the batter into the soufflé dish. Don't bother smoothing the top.

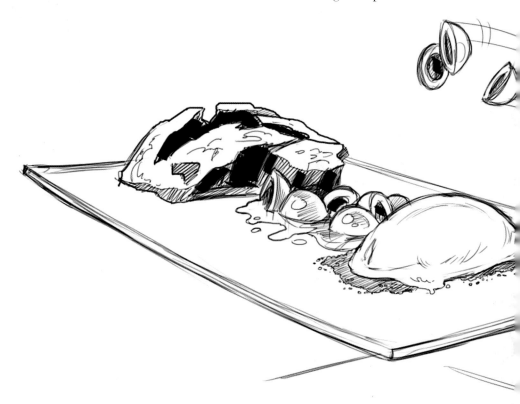

Bake the *chibouste* for 25 to 30 minutes, or until the center is slightly souffléd and the top shows some cracks. Let cool to room temperature, about 40 minutes. If the *chibouste* sticks to the pan, use a knife to gently set it free. Makes about 2 1/2 cups.

To Plate the Dessert

Spoon cherry halves and a little of the wine syrup onto the center of the plate. Place a spoonful of the chocolate *chibouste* next to the cherries. Put a small mound of ground espresso on the opposite side of the cherries. Put a quenelle (see page 37) or a small scoop of the ice cream on top of the espresso mound. Ideally, serve this while wearing black on black.

Wine-Soaked Cherries (page 209)

2 tablespoons finely ground espresso-roast coffee beans

THE CHOCOLATE CRAWL
FUN FOR KIDS
OF ALL AGES

FRUIT

Sometimes fruit is the only inspiration you need, but it doesn't hurt to have a person nearby who is equally awed by beautiful fruit. Chef Sara Ko and I remind each other which fruit season is coming up and toss out titles or talk about what we would like to make with Manila mangoes, Concord grapes, Adriatic figs (Figs in Space, Sara's title), or some other gems coming our way.

In Northern California, we are fortunate to have some of the best fruit in the world, and at Citizen Cake I am often able to buy directly from farmers. The chefs and I make frequent trips to the different farmers' markets in San Francisco,

Berkeley, and Marin to find fruit that inspires us. Most home cooks can do the same thing. Because of consumer interest in produce that has flavor and a heritage—as well as in meeting the people who actually grow it—farmers' markets are thriving in communities of all sizes, from the Greenmarket in Manhattan to the Klamath Falls Farmers' Market in central Oregon.

The first thing I do when I begin to create a plated dessert with fruit is to let go of any preconceived ideas. When I think of an apple, for example, a general taste immediately comes to mind. But Pink Pearl apples, which appear for about two weeks every year, have their own distinct flavor that reminds me of SweeTarts candy. For those two weeks, I make everything I can with Pink Pearls, and then I move on to a different variety and a whole new set of desserts. With apples, I might set out

SCAPES

to make a pie concept, but I let the flavor of the raw fruit guide me, suggesting pairings and cooking methods. I taste a Winesap or Jonathan or Golden Delicious, and then I consider what ingredients might work best with its unique flavor profile. Cinnamon? Nuts and butter? Brown sugar or honey? Blue cheese?

The characteristics of a fruit vary not only from variety to variety, but also from one crop to the next, even within the same orchard, depending on the weather, the soil, how long the fruit ripened on the tree or stem, and how it traveled to market. Every apple, tangerine, or peach is rich in detail, which is why it is so important to taste the raw fruit before you decide not only what ingredients to pair with it, but also how much sugar or acidity to add. For example, Suddenly Last Summer (page 92) calls for briefly sautéing peaches in honey and wine. The

sweeter the peaches, the less honey I will use, while if the peaches are tart or underripe, I will cut down on the wine to control the acidity.

Think of the ingredient measures as a starting point in these recipes and feel free to add more sugar, honey, lemon juice, or wine until your fruit tastes the way you like it. You can always sauté too-tart summer fruit in a little butter, sugar, and Grand Marnier (which is what I sometimes do when the berries aren't as ripe and juicy as I like for Citizen Shortcake, on page 97). And if you find amazing peak-season nectarines, Pluots, or Elephant Heart plums at the market, take my call to improvisation a step further and make your own signature homage to seasonal fruit.

lemon lovers =
LEMANIACS

You can make some components in advance:

UP TO 1 WEEK BEFORE
- make the caramel sauce
- make the lemon curd

THE DAY BEFORE
- make the shortbread cookies

A FEW HOURS BEFORE
- make the basil-mint oil

JUST BEFORE SERVING
- make the meringue
- plate the dessert

MINIMALIST VERSION

Spoon the lemon curd onto a plate, add a mound of meringue, and brown the meringue with a butane torch, or just serve the lemon curd with a few shortbread cookies.

LEMON MERINGUE PIE = LEMON DROP

eggless lemon curd, vanilla shortbread cookies, brandy caramel sauce, french meringue, basil-mint oil

serves **6** to **8**

At Citizen Cake, we use almost every fruit seasonally except lemons. Our customers can't get enough of lemon desserts, so lemons figure big all year long. We call these lemon lovers Lemaniacs, and this reinvented lemon meringue pie is made with them in mind. The traditional layers of the pie are all here—the browned meringue, the lemony center, the caramelly crust—but they have been pulled apart and modernized, and the flavors have been intensified, so each one stands out more clearly.

Most lemon curds and lemon meringue pies taste too eggy and not lemony enough for me. I fixed the problem by using agar agar, a gelling agent long used in Asian sweets (see Secret Agent, page 140), instead of eggs in the curd. Many people underbake shortbread cookies, so they taste raw or doughy and lack the snap of perfectly baked cookies. You will discover that the cookies taste better when the sugar and butter caramelize during baking, which means you need to leave the cookies in the oven until they are the color of light brown sugar.

I brown meringue with a butane torch, but I recently learned a trick from chef Yuko Fujii. She pipes meringues from a pastry bag fitted with a spaghetti tip onto a perforated pan set over hot water and bakes them in the oven, which steams and browns the meringues. What I love about cooking is that there are always new techniques to be discovered.

CAREMI, WHAT ARE YOU UP TO?

I'M MAKING THE WORLD'S LARGEST MERINGUE!

OH, I CAN'T WAIT TO SEE THAT...

Vanilla Shortbread Cookies

1 cup (5 ounces) all-purpose flour

1/4 cup plus 1 tablespoon (2 1/4 ounces) granulated sugar

1/2 teaspoon kosher salt

8 tablespoons (4 ounces) unsalted butter, softened but still cool, cut into 1/2-inch chunks

1/2 teaspoon pure vanilla extract

French Meringue

2 (2 ounces by weight) large egg whites

1/8 teaspoon cream of tartar

1/4 cup plus 1 tablespoon (2 1/4 ounces) granulated sugar

3/4 to 1 cup Eggless Lemon Curd (page 204)

1/4 cup Brandy Caramel Sauce (page 210)

2 to 3 teaspoons Herb Oil, basil version (page 220)

To Make the VANILLA SHORTBREAD COOKIES

In a medium bowl, toss together the flour, sugar, and salt. Scatter the butter over the flour mixture and work it in with your fingers until the mixture almost comes together in a dough. Add the vanilla and lightly push the mixture together into a block. Knead the block a couple of times in the bowl to form a cohesive dough. Transfer the dough to a work surface and shape it into a log about 9 inches long and 1 inch in diameter. Wrap it in plastic wrap and refrigerate for 30 minutes. If you don't have time, you can slice and bake it immediately, but chilling makes slicing the dough much easier.

Position a rack in the center of the oven and preheat the oven to 350°F. Line a baking sheet with parchment paper.

Cut the log into 1/4-inch-thick slices and arrange them about 1 inch apart on the prepared pan. Bake the cookies for 12 to 15 minutes, or until golden on top and slightly darker on the edges. Transfer to a rack and let cool. You should have about 3 dozen cookies. Store the extras in an airtight container, where they will keep for 2 weeks. Alternatively, you can bake just the number of cookies you need, wrap the remaining dough tightly in plastic wrap, and freeze the dough for up to 2 months.

To Make the FRENCH MERINGUE

Make the meringue just before you are ready to plate the dessert. In a bowl, using a stand mixer fitted with the whip attachment or a handheld mixer, beat together the egg whites and cream of tartar on high speed until foamy. Add the sugar a spoonful at a time and continue beating until stiff peaks form.

To Plate the Dessert

Set a large spoonful of meringue on each plate. If you like, form the meringue into tiny ski slopes, but don't overwork it, or it will lose all its air bubbles. Using a butane torch, sear the meringue just enough to brown the edges. Spoon a mound of the lemon curd (1 to 2 tablespoons) beside each meringue mound and add a stripe of the caramel sauce (1 to 2 teaspoons). Place 2 shortbread cookies on each plate, and finish with a couple of drops of the basil-mint oil.

WARM CHOCOLATE CAKE CROTTIN AND SALAD OF GIANDUJA AND CITRUS

warm chocolate crottin cakes, citrus, chocolate-hazelnut cream,
espresso vinaigrette

serves **6**

The heart of this dessert is a warm chocolate cake made to look like a goat cheese *crottin*, the kind used for the goat cheese salad found on countless restaurant menus in the 1980s. Just like the chèvre *crottin* on the salad menu, this *crottin* has a bread crumb and nut crust. But unlike the salad chèvre, this version is dressed with a sweet, zesty vinaigrette made from orange juice and dark, aromatic espresso.

A vinaigrette makes sense in a dessert because it is bright and fresh and the oil lingers in your mouth. Dessert vinaigrettes are generally sweeter than green salad vinaigrettes, to complement chocolate and other rich flavors. A suggestion for a sweet raspberry vinaigrette and a simple way to serve it appears in the variation on page 79, and the Karrot Keiki (page 85), with its honey-sweetened sesame vinaigrette, offers another example.

Freshly toasted hazelnuts—used to coat the cake and as a garnish—add a lot of flavor to this dessert; you will need about 1 cup (4½ ounces) total of whole toasted hazelnuts. For the chocolate-hazelnut cream, start with a hazelnut paste that contains only hazelnuts and sugar and nothing else (see Resources).

Chocolate Crottin Cakes

- 8 ounces bittersweet chocolate, coarsely chopped (about 1½ cups)
- 4 tablespoons (2 ounces) unsalted butter
- 4 (6 ounces by weight) large eggs, separated
- 2 tablespoons (1 ounce) granulated sugar
- 2 tablespoons (about 1 ounce) firmly packed brown sugar
- Pinch of kosher salt
- ⅓ cup (about 1 ounce) dried bread crumbs
- ⅓ cup (about 1½ ounces) coarsely crushed toasted hazelnuts (see page 157)

To Make the Batter for the CHOCOLATE CROTTIN CAKES

Bring a few inches of water to a gentle simmer in a saucepan. Combine the chocolate and butter in a heatproof bowl and place over (not touching) the simmering water (or use a double boiler). Heat slowly, stirring occasionally, until nearly melted, and then remove the bowl from the heat and whisk until smooth. Set aside.

In a large bowl, whisk together the egg yolks and granulated and brown sugars. In a separate bowl, using a stand mixer fitted with the whip attachment or a handheld mixer, whip together the egg whites and salt on high speed for about 5 minutes, or until soft peaks form. Or, use a clean whisk and whip by hand.

While the chocolate mixture is still warm, whisk it into the egg yolk mixture. Using a spatula, gently fold in the egg whites in three additions. Cover and refrigerate for at least 1 hour or for up to overnight. Reserve the bread crumbs and hazelnuts for using later.

Chocolate-Hazelnut Cream

2 ounces bittersweet chocolate, coarsely chopped (scant 1/2 cup)

2 ounces hazelnut paste (see headnote)

1/2 cup heavy cream

2 tablespoons (1 1/2 ounces) light corn syrup or honey

3 tablespoons (1/2 ounce) unsweetened cocoa powder, preferably natural

1/4 cup water

2 tablespoons (1 ounce) unsalted butter, at room temperature

1/8 teaspoon kosher salt

Citrus and Vinaigrette

4 tangerines or blood oranges, or a mixture

2 tablespoons freshly brewed espresso or strong coffee

2 teaspoons granulated sugar

Pinch of kosher salt

1 tablespoon fresh tangerine juice (reserved from slicing the tangerines)

1 teaspoon fresh lemon juice

2 tablespoons hazelnut oil (see Resources)

1/4 cup (1 1/2 ounces by weight) canola or olive oil, plus 1/2 teaspoon if needed

1 tablespoon honey (optional)

To Make the CHOCOLATE-HAZELNUT CREAM

Place the chocolate and hazelnut paste in a heatproof bowl. In a small saucepan, combine the cream and corn syrup, place over medium-high heat, and cook for about 5 minutes, or just until the mixture comes a boil. Remove the pan from the heat and pour the hot mixture over the chocolate and hazelnut paste. Let stand for 1 minute, and then stir until the chocolate melts and the mixture is smooth.

In another small saucepan, combine the cocoa powder and water, place over medium heat, and whisk for 2 to 3 minutes, or until a thick paste forms.

Pour about one-fourth of the chocolate mixture into the cocoa powder paste and whisk to combine. Then add the cocoa powder mixture to the remaining chocolate mixture, scraping the pan well, and whisk until blended. Whisk in the butter until melted, and then whisk in the salt.

You can make this sauce up to 1 week in advance and store it, tightly covered, in the refrigerator. It will be solid when you pull it out to use it, however. Heat it gently, either setting the sauce in its bowl in a warm water bath, or heating a portion of the sauce in the microwave using short bursts and then stirring it into the rest of the sauce.

To Prepare the CITRUS and Make the VINAIGRETTE

With a sharp knife, slice the top and bottom off each tangerine and/or blood orange. Cut away the peel and pith, and then slice each fruit into rounds. Pour off any juice that collects on your cutting board and save it for the vinaigrette.

To make the vinaigrette, in a small bowl, combine the espresso, sugar, salt, and tangerine and lemon juices and whisk to dissolve the sugar and salt. Add the hazelnut oil and canola oil one at a time, pouring them in a thin, steady stream and whisking continuously. This vinaigrette is "broken," or separated, and I like the way the oil and espresso look separated on a plate. If you want the vinaigrette to come together, whisk in the honey and an additional 1/2 teaspoon canola oil.

To Bake the CHOCOLATE CROTTIN CAKES

You want to serve the cakes warm, so don't put them into the oven until you are just about ready to plate. Position a rack in the center of the oven and preheat the oven to 350°F. Have ready a baking sheet lined with parchment paper. If you would rather bake these in ramekins, have ready 6 greased 4-ounce ramekins.

In a small bowl, stir together the reserved bread crumbs and crushed hazelnuts. Using an ice cream scoop, a large spoon, or even your fingers, scoop up about one-sixth of the batter and roll it in the bread crumb mixture gently until the entire surface is evenly coated. Place the coated ball on the baking sheet or in a ramekin. Repeat with the rest of the batter. If using ramekins, place them on a baking sheet.

Bake for 15 to 17 minutes, or until the chocolate is very fragrant but there is no hint of a burnt aroma. Remove the pan from the oven. If you have used ramekins, run a knife around the inside edge of the dish before inverting onto serving plates.

To Plate the Dessert

Place a warm *crottin* in the center of each plate and divide the citrus slices evenly among the plates, arranging them so they loosely circle the *crottin* but don't touch it. Scatter the whole or broken hazelnuts and candied orange peel around the citrus pieces and on the outer edge of the plate. Drizzle the plate with the vinaigrette, and finish with the chocolate-hazelnut cream. And about that chocolate-hazelnut cream: you can warm it and spoon it on as a sauce, you can chill it and make a quenelle (see page 37), or you can just smear it on! Don't worry, because it's good any way you do it.

2 tablespoons candied orange peel

12 to 16 hazelnuts, toasted and skinned (see page 157), and then left whole or lightly broken

UNTITLED II: CHOCOLATE WITH RASPBERRY AND FENNEL TONES

warm chocolate crottin cakes, shaved fennel, sweet raspberry vinaigrette, vanilla gelato

You can make some components in advance:

UP TO 3 DAYS BEFORE

➥ make the gelato

THE DAY BEFORE

➥ make the batter for the cakes

A FEW HOURS BEFORE SERVING

➥ shave the fennel

➥ make the vinaigrette

➥ toast the almonds

JUST BEFORE SERVING

➥ bake the cakes

➥ plate the dessert

MINIMALIST VERSION

Serve the shaved fennel with raspberry vinaigrette, raspberries, and a quenelle of vanilla gelato.

serves **6**

While writing about using vinaigrettes in desserts, I began thinking about how I might use raspberry vinaigrette and decided it was a good match with fennel. This might seem like an odd combination, but if you like fresh fennel, I bet you will like it in a dessert. And while I probably wouldn't serve just the citrus salad in the previous chocolate *crottin* cake recipe, I would definitely serve the shaved fennel and vinaigrette by itself or with gelato.

Fennel pollen is an unusual seasoning that tastes a little like ground toasted fennel seeds. If you can't find it, toast a few fennel seeds in a small, dry skillet on your stove top and grind them in a spice grinder or coffee grinder. Save a few of the prettier fronds from your fennel tops for a garnish.

Make the batter for the *crottins* and refrigerate as directed on page 74.

Chocolate Crottin Cakes (page 74)

To Shave the FENNEL

Have ready a bowl of ice water. Cut out the core from the fennel bulb. A flat edge will make it easier to handle the fennel, so slice off a small section if you are starting with a whole bulb. Place the flat edge against a mandoline and shave the fennel. Or, use a sharp knife to cut the shavings. Drop the shavings in the ice water so they stay cold and crisp.

½ large or 1 whole small fennel bulb, fronds reserved for garnish

To Make the RASPBERRY VINAIGRETTE

In a small bowl, whisk together the raspberry vinegar, sugar, salt, and lemon juice. Add the olive oil and canola oil one at a time, pouring them in a thin, steady stream and whisking continuously.

Raspberry Vinaigrette

1 tablespoon raspberry vinegar

2 teaspoons granulated sugar or honey

Small pinch of kosher salt

½ teaspoon fresh lemon juice

1 tablespoon olive oil

2 tablespoons canola oil

To Plate the Dessert

Just before you are ready to plate the dessert, coat and bake the *crottins* and unmold onto plates as directed on page 76. Drain the fennel and dry it with paper towels or a clean kitchen towel. Scatter the shaved fennel over each plate. Place a quenelle (see page 37) or a small scoop of gelato next to the cake. Drizzle vinaigrette over the fennel and scatter raspberries and almonds over the plate. Finish each plate with a few small fennel fronds and a very light dusting—less than ⅛ teaspoon—of the fennel pollen.

1 cup vanilla gelato, homemade (page 205) or store-bought

1½ cup (about 6 ounces) raspberries

½ cup (2¾ ounces) almonds, toasted (see page 157) and lightly broken

¾ teaspoon fennel pollen (see Resources)

UP TO 2 WEEKS BEFORE

➤ braise the pineapple

UP TO 3 DAYS BEFORE

➤ make the gelato

➤ make the coconut
   cream

THE DAY BEFORE

➤ make the cake

A FEW HOURS
BEFORE SERVING

➤ let the pineapple
   come to room
   temperature or
   gently warm it

➤ ready your garnishes

➤ cut the cake
   into cubes

JUST BEFORE SERVING

➤ plate the dessert

MINIMALIST VERSION

The star of this parfait
is the braised pine-
apple. If you make
just that and spoon
it over homemade or
store-bought gelato,
you will still have
very happy guests.

UPSIDE-DOWN PINEAPPLE PARFAIT

pineapple braised with brown sugar and star anise, vanilla mochi cake, coconut cream, vanilla gelato

serves 4

Braised in brown sugar and star anise, fantastic dark, rich pineapple makes this dessert a standout. I usually avoid the word *parfait* because it has been misused by fast-food places, but this tropical, exotic combination gives back to the parfait some of its original status. (And I am not the only chef who has an aversion to the name. Pierre Hermé, one of the most brilliant pastry chefs of our time, has been making beautiful parfaits at his shops in Paris and Tokyo for the last decade, but he calls them *les emotions*, while at other pâtisseries in France, *verrines*—parfait glasses filled with layers of sweet and savory—are all the rage.)

I love the architecture a clear glass presents, the beautiful layers of a parfait revealed. Sell those old fluted glass sundae dishes on eBay. They are too frilly and outdated for this pared-down and yet extravagant version of pineapple upside-down cake. A simple clear drinking glass shows off this dessert with more style and is easier to clean at the end of the evening.

This version of pineapple upside-down cake is cross-cultural. The cake can be thought of as either Japanese or Hawaiian in style, but it also has the beautiful fragrance of star anise, a classic ingredient of the Chinese pantry. Look for star anise in Asian markets and well-stocked grocery stores. If you can't find it, you can braise the pineapple without it, but it gives the fruit an irresistible aroma and subtle flavor.

Mochi cakes, made of glutinous rice, are popular in Japan. For centuries, making *mochi* has been a Japanese family tradition, with each family member taking a turn at pounding the freshly cooked rice with a large mallet until it is a soft, chewy dough. (The best comparison for Americans might be the old-fashioned hand-cranked ice cream makers packed with rock salt and ice, with every family member having a go at turning the crank.) In most of the United States, we see *mochi* surrounding an ice cream center, but in Hawaii many cakes are made of *mochiko*, a delicate flour milled from glutinous (sweet) rice. In that tradition, I have used rice flour in this cake, which makes it light and springy—and delicious when topped with the braised fruit and syrup.

You can make all of the components ahead of time. Once you have made the dessert a few times and have mastered it, try spooning some Passion Fruit Caramel Sauce (page 210) on top of the gelato along with the syrup from the braised pineapple. Parfait heaven.

Vanilla Mochi Cake

2 (3 ounces by weight) large eggs

1/2 cup (3 1/2 ounces) granulated sugar

1/4 cup whole milk

1/2 teaspoon pure vanilla extract

1 cup (5 1/4 ounces) *mochiko* (glutinous rice flour), see Resources

1/4 teaspoon kosher salt

1/2 teaspoon baking powder

3 tablespoons (1 1/2 ounces) unsalted butter, melted

Coconut Cream

2/3 cup (5 3/4 ounces) light or regular coconut milk

2 tablespoons (1 ounce) granulated sugar

1/4 teaspoon guar gum (see Secret Agent, page 140)

Pineapple Braised with Brown Sugar and Star Anise

1/2 pineapple, about 2 pounds

1/2 cup (4 1/4 ounces) firmly packed dark brown sugar

1 star anise pod

1 teaspoon fresh lime juice (reserve zest for garnish before juicing the lime)

2 teaspoons dark rum

1/2 vanilla bean

To Make the VANILLA MOCHI CAKE

Position a rack in the center of the oven and preheat the oven to 350°F. Butter and flour a 4 1/2 by 8 1/2 by 2 3/4-inch loaf pan (or similarly sized 1-pound loaf pan).

In a medium bowl, whisk together the eggs and sugar until blended. Whisk in the milk and vanilla. Add the rice flour and salt and sift in the baking powder. Whisk until the batter is smooth. Whisk in the butter until combined. Pour the batter into the prepared pan.

Bake the cake for 20 to 28 minutes, or until the edges are lightly golden and a skewer inserted into the center shows crumbs but is not wet with batter. Let the cake cool in the pan on a cooling rack for about 10 minutes, and then turn the cake out onto the rack and let cool completely.

To Make the COCONUT CREAM

In a blender, combine the coconut milk, sugar, and guar gum and process for 30 seconds, or until well blended and slightly thickened. The mixture will continue to thicken as it chills. Pour into a small bowl, cover, and chill until ready to use. You should have 2/3 cup.

To Make the PINEAPPLE BRAISED WITH BROWN SUGAR AND STAR ANISE

Peel the pineapple half and cut lengthwise into 4 equal wedges. Cut away the core from each wedge. Each wedge will be used for 1 serving, so if the amount of pineapple looks skimpy, cut a wedge or two off the other half of the pineapple and use as well.

In a medium saucepan or 10-inch skillet with a lid, combine the brown sugar, star anise, lime juice, and rum. Split the vanilla bean lengthwise and, with the tip of the knife, scrape the seeds into the saucepan, and then toss in the empty pod. Stir to make sure all of the sugar is moistened and evenly distributed in the bottom of the pan. The mixture will be grainy. Place the pineapple wedges on top the sugar mixture. Take care not to crowd the pineapple wedges in the pan. Give each wedge enough room to soak up the brown sugar.

Cover the pan and place over medium heat. Once you hear the sugar begin to bubble, after about 5 minutes, reduce the heat to medium-low. Cook for about 10 minutes, lift the lid, and turn the pineapple wedges over with tongs or a spatula. Cook for another 7 minutes, and then turn the wedges again, checking to make sure they are getting just a little color on every side. Cook for another 7 minutes, if needed, so that every side of each wedge is caramel colored.

With tongs or a slotted spoon, transfer the pineapple wedges to a heat-proof container. Strain the syrup in the pan through a fine-mesh strainer held over the container. Recover the vanilla bean pod and add it to the strained syrup. You should have about 1/3 cup syrup. Set the pineapple aside until you are ready to plate the dessert. If you braise the pineapple in advance, let it cool to room temperature, pour the syrup back over it, cover tightly, and refrigerate for up to 2 weeks, until ready to plate.

To Plate the Dessert

Position a rack in the center of the oven and preheat the oven to 350°F. Spread the coconut on a baking sheet or pie pan and toast in the oven for 3 to 5 minutes. It is easy to burn the coconut, so watch carefully and remove the pan from the oven as soon as the strips or flakes begin to turn a light golden brown along their edges. Pour onto a plate and set aside.

Have ready 4 clear glasses to hold the parfaits. Trim the cake of any brown edges and cut about half of the cake into 1-inch cubes. (Wrap up the rest of the cake and set it aside for another use.) Cut each pineapple wedge into 4 or 5 chunks and rest 2 or 3 chunks in the bottom of each glass. Place 2 cake cubes on top of the pineapple. Drizzle a few teaspoons of the pineapple syrup over the cake. Spoon on 1 tablespoon of the coconut cream and drop in several macadamia nuts. Add another 2 or 3 chunks of the pineapple and another spoonful of the coconut cream. Place a quenelle (see page 37) or a small scoop of the gelato on top, and garnish with the toasted coconut, lime zest, and chile powder. (Fresh chile powder only—if your cayenne or chile powder is more than a year old, skip it.)

1/2 cup (about 3/4 ounce) fresh coconut strips or unsweetened large dried coconut flakes (see Resources)

1/3 cup (about 1 1/2 ounces) whole macadamia nuts, toasted (see page 157)

About 1 cup Vanilla Gelato (page 205)

1 teaspoon grated lime zest (optional)

1/8 teaspoon ground Aleppo, Espelette, or cayenne pepper (optional)

You can make some components in advance:

THE DAY BEFORE

➤ make the vinaigrette

➤ make the cake

➤ mix the currants and cream cheese (but don't roll into balls yet)

A FEW HOURS BEFORE SERVING

➤ make the cream cheese balls

➤ cut the carrot *brunoise*

JUST BEFORE SERVING

➤ cut the cake into cubes

➤ make the pear ribbons

➤ plate the dessert

MINIMALIST VERSION

Serve the cake with the cream cheese balls and a sprinkling of coconut.

KARROT KEIKI

carrot caketons, cream cheese–currant–walnut balls, pear sesame salad, sesame vinaigrette

serves **6** to **8**

This is like a dessert salad: small squares of carrot cake and a cream cheese and walnut ball surrounded by thin ribbons of pear. Keiki takes carrot cake to a lighter, more refreshing place while keeping the flavors you love in the traditional version. Make this dessert when crisp, juicy Asian pears are available, from fall through early January. Bosc and Anjou pears also work in this recipe, as long as they are not too ripe.

The inspiration for the cheese ball comes from my childhood in suburban Los Angeles. My parents would buy the then-popular nut-covered port–Cheddar cheese balls for parties, and I always liked the contrast of the crunchy nuts and the soft wine-flavored cheese inside. My cheese and walnut balls are a cross between those old-fashioned nutty cheese globes and a schmear from a bagel shop.

I like to play up the carrot theme in this dessert with a *brunoise* of carrot as a garnish. *Brunoise*, the French term for an ingredient diced in precise, small squares, is one of those chef's tricks that is easy to do but makes home-cooked dishes look professional. The key to making a carrot *brunoise* is to slice a thin portion off four sides of a peeled carrot, leaving a long, even rectangle. (Watch your fingers and take it slowly the first time.) Next, slice the rectangle into thin julienne strips, and then cut across the strips to form tiny squares. Scattering these little carrot squares across the dessert plate adds just the right visual element in brilliant orange.

This dessert stretches to serve eight people if you increase the amount of each garnish. You will still have some carrot cake left over, but you will be glad to eat it as a late-night snack or a ready-to-go breakfast the next day.

KEIKI...I LIKE THAT NAME.
KEIKI SAN, ARIGATO GOZAIMASU.

Carrot Caketons

1/4 cup (1 3/4 ounces) granulated sugar

1/4 cup (2 ounces) firmly packed dark brown sugar

1/4 cup plus 3 tablespoons (3 ounces by weight) canola oil

1 (1 1/2 ounces by weight) large egg

1 1/2 cups (about 4 ounces) peeled, shredded carrot (from about 2 large carrots)

1/2 cup (2 1/2 ounces) all-purpose flour

1/2 teaspoon baking powder

1/4 teaspoon baking soda

1/2 teaspoon ground cinnamon

1/4 teaspoon kosher salt

Cream Cheese–Currant–Walnut Balls

1/4 cup (1 ounce) dried currants

2 tablespoons water

1 block (8 ounces) cream cheese, at room temperature

3/4 cup (3 ounces) walnut halves, coarsely chopped

Sesame Vinaigrette

1 teaspoon honey

1/8 teaspoon kosher salt

1 tablespoon fresh lemon juice

2 teaspoons rice vinegar

1 tablespoon canola oil

1/2 teaspoon toasted sesame oil

To Make the CARROT CAKETONS

Position a rack in the center of the oven and preheat the oven to 325°F. Butter and flour a 4 1/2 by 8 1/2 by 2 3/4-inch loaf pan (or similarly sized 1-pound loaf pan).

In a medium bowl, whisk together the granulated and brown sugars, oil, and egg until thoroughly combined. Whisk in the carrot. In a large bowl, sift together the flour, baking powder, baking soda, and cinnamon, and then add the salt. Whisk the wet ingredients into the dry ingredients just until combined. Pour the batter into the prepared pan.

Bake the cake for about 30 minutes, or until a skewer or toothpick inserted into the center comes out clean and dry. Let the cake cool in the pan on a cooling rack for 10 to 15 minutes, and then turn the cake out onto the rack and let cool completely.

To Make the CREAM CHEESE–CURRANT–WALNUT BALLS

You can do this on the stove top or in a microwave. On the stove top, combine the currants and water in a small saucepan over medium heat. When you notice small bubbles in the water, after about 1 minute, remove the pan from the heat and let cool for 20 minutes. The currants will soak up the water and plump up. If you prefer to use a microwave, put the currants and water in a microwave-safe container, cover with plastic wrap, and microwave for 40 seconds, then let stand for at least 20 minutes to allow the currants to absorb the water. (If you like, you can go ahead and make the sesame vinaigrette while you are waiting for the currants to plump.)

In a food processor (a small one if you have it), combine the currants and cream cheese and process until the currants are chopped and distributed throughout the cheese. (If you don't have a small food processor, just chop and mash the currants with a chef's knife on a cutting board and stir them into the cream cheese.) Cover and refrigerate for 30 minutes to 1 hour, or until the mixture is well chilled, or overnight.

Spread the walnuts on a plate. Roll the cheese mixture into 8 balls, each a little bigger than a golf ball, and then roll the balls in the chopped walnuts. Arrange on a plate and refrigerate until you are ready to plate the dessert. (Be sure to serve them the day they are made, as the walnuts will soak up moisture.)

To Make the SESAME VINAIGRETTE

In a small bowl, whisk together the honey, salt, lemon juice, vinegar, and canola and sesame oils. You should have about 3 tablespoons.

To Plate the Dessert

Trim the cake of any brown edges and cut half of the cake into 1- to 2-inch cubes. (Wrap up the rest of the cake and set it aside for another use, but be sure to eat it within a day or two.) Using a vegetable peeler, peel the pears. Then continue to "peel" the fruit, turning as you go to create ribbons of pear for the salad. Wider ribbons are better. Divide the pear ribbons evenly among the plates and drizzle a little vinaigrette over them. Place 3 cake cubes on each plate, spacing them well apart. Place a cheese ball in the center. Garnish the plate with a sprinkle of the carrot *brunoise*, coconut flakes, and black sesame seeds.

2 or 3 ripe but firm Asian, Bosc, or Anjou pears

3 to 4 tablespoons carrot *brunoise* (see headnote)

3 to 4 tablespoons unsweetened large dried coconut flakes (see Resources)

1 to 1½ tablespoons black sesame seeds

CAKETONS

LOVELOVA (PERSIAN STRAWBERRY AND SAFFRON PAVLOVA)

saffron meringues, cardamom cream, rose-water berries, rose petals, pistachios

serves 4

Australians and New Zealanders each still claim their country invented the Pavlova, the meringue-based dessert named after Russian ballerina Anna Pavlova. This version is laced with Persian flavors: strawberries tossed with rose water and black pepper, saffron in the meringue, and sparks of cardamom in the whipped cream. Vivid green pistachios and a drizzle of pistachio oil finish the plate. If you don't have time to track down pistachio oil (see Resources), use a spicy extra virgin olive oil instead.

Start with whole cardamom pods (look for them in well-stocked supermarkets and in Middle Eastern or Indian shops). The freshly crushed seeds guarantee bursts of flavor in the cream that you won't get with even the most fragrant ground cardamom.

Don't be tempted to add sugar to the berries or the whipped cream. The natural sweetness of the berries and the distinctiveness of each spice are all you need; plus, the sugar in the pale gold meringues carries the plate.

Finally, play around with how you slice the strawberries. Cutting them into tiny cubes, rounds, or arrowheads adds style to the cloud-shaped meringue with its smaller cloud of whipped cream, plus the berries feel more interesting in your mouth.

To Make the SAFFRON MERINGUES

Position a rack in the center of the oven and preheat the oven to 400°F. Line a baking sheet with parchment paper.

In a small bowl, combine the saffron threads and vinegar. Set aside. In another small bowl, sift together the granulated and powdered sugars. Set aside.

In a large bowl, using a stand mixer fitted with the whip attachment or a handheld mixer, beat together the egg whites and salt on medium speed for about 3 minutes, or until soft peaks form. Gradually add the combined sugars while continuing to whip until all the sugar has been added. Switch to high speed and whip for 3 to 5 minutes, or until stiff peaks form and the mixture is glossy.

Using a spatula, fold the cornstarch and then the saffron-vinegar mixture into the egg whites. Spoon the meringue onto the prepared pan,

Saffron Meringues

1/2 teaspoon saffron threads

1 teaspoon white wine vinegar or Champagne vinegar

1/4 cup plus 1 tablespoon (2 1/4 ounces) granulated sugar

1/2 cup (2 ounces) powdered sugar

4 (4 ounces by weight) large egg whites
Pinch of kosher salt

1 tablespoon cornstarch

forming 4 well-spaced ovals each 5 to 6 inches long. Don't worry about precision. Just make 4 cloud puffs of meringue.

Lower the oven temperature to 250°F. Bake the meringues for 1 hour. Turn off the oven and, without opening the door, allow the meringues to dry for another hour. (It's fine if they sit in the turned-off oven for up to 2 hours.) They may still feel wet to the touch, but as soon as they come to room temperature, they will feel dry. The meringues should be pale gold, not brown, and lightly crisp on the outside.

To Make the CARDAMOM CREAM

Cardamom Cream

3 to 4 whole cardamom pods

1 cup heavy cream

2 tablespoons (1 ounce) crème fraîche (page 221) or sour cream

In a mortar, lightly crush the cardamom pods with a pestle and pull away the green-brown, papery husk. Crush the seeds and measure out 1/4 teaspoon. If you don't have a mortar and pestle, you can wrap the cardamom pods in plastic wrap and crush them lightly with a rolling pin, then discard the pods and lightly crush the seeds.

In a bowl, using a stand mixer fitted with the whip attachment or a handheld mixer, beat together the cream and crème fraîche on medium speed for 3 to 4 minutes, or until soft peaks form. Gently fold in the cardamom. Cover and refrigerate until serving.

To Make the ROSE-WATER BERRIES

Rose-Water Berries

2 cups (about 12 ounces) strawberries

2 teaspoons rose water

2 teaspoons fresh orange juice

2 cranks on a pepper mill of black pepper

2 tablespoons pistachio oil or extra virgin olive oil

1/4 cup (about 1 ounce) shelled pistachio nuts

1/2 cup organic red or pink rose petals (from about 2 large roses), cut into narrow ribbons

Hull the strawberries and cut into any variety of shapes you like. In a bowl, toss the berries with the rose water, orange juice, and pepper.

To Plate the Dessert

Place a saffron meringue on each plate. Spoon some of the cardamom cream on top of each meringue. Spoon on the berries. Drizzle the pistachio oil around the edge of the plate. Sprinkle the plate with the pistachio nuts and garnish with the ribbons of rose petals.

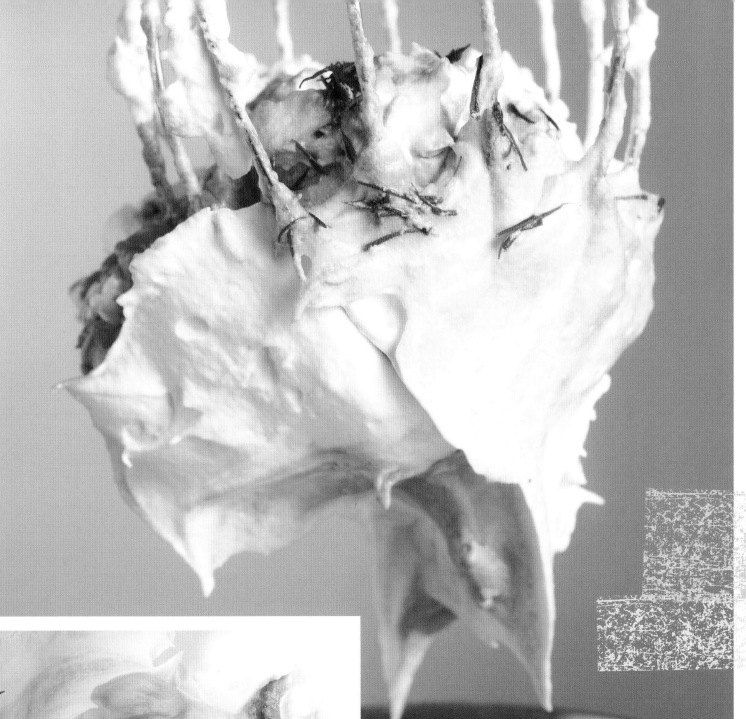

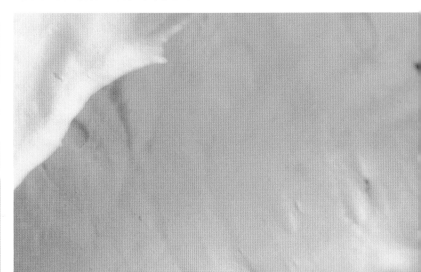

You can make some
components in advance:

UP TO 2 WEEKS BEFORE

➤ make the streusel

THE DAY BEFORE

➤ make the cream
  reduction

➤ make the filo crisps

JUST BEFORE SERVING

➤ sauté the peaches

➤ plate the dessert

MINIMALIST VERSION

Serve just the peaches
and cream reduction.

SUDDENLY LAST SUMMER

peaches sautéed in wine and honey, walnut-thyme streusel, sweet cream
reduction, olive oil filo crisps

serves 4 to 6

I made this dessert in my third year as pastry chef at Rubicon, just when I had
decided to break out, do my own thing, and open a pâtisserie. I had been coming
up with some great titles and found that I didn't need to list the elements with
this dessert—the name alone sold it. It conjures up not just the end of summer
but the end of an era for me.

The peaches are important here, so look for the most gorgeous, softly fuzzed
yellow-gold peaches you can find. I leave the skins on for this dessert, but if
you prefer, you can peel them with a vegetable peeler before sautéing. I top the
peaches with streusel and light, crisp shards of filo and finish the dish with
thickened cream.

Here, the filo crisps are made with olive oil and ground pistachios (though
in a pinch you can omit the nuts). A simpler version, used for The M Word
(page 137), calls for melted butter. You can switch the crisps between the two
desserts, depending on whether you are in the mood for olive oil or butter.

This dessert goes together quickly with the exception of the cream reduction,
which needs to chill for at least 4 hours. And if you like, you can make a parfait
from this dessert by layering the components in a clear, simple glass instead of
using a plate.

To Make the SWEET CREAM REDUCTION

Sweet Cream Reduction

2 cups heavy cream

2 teaspoons granulated sugar

In a deep saucepan, combine the cream and sugar, bring to a simmer over
medium heat, and cook for 25 to 30 minutes, or until the mixture is reduced
by half. (The mixture will boil up, so don't choose a pan that is too small. If
you put a ladle in the pan, it will help draw off some of the heat and prevent
the cream from boiling over.) The bubbles should stay small and low, so watch
closely, stir occasionally, and reduce the heat to medium-low if the mixture
begins to boil vigorously. When the cream is ready, pour it into a heatproof
container, let cool to room temperature, and then cover and refrigerate for
at least 4 hours or up to overnight. You should have about 1 cup.

Olive Oil Filo Crisps

2 tablespoons (1 ounce) turbinado sugar

1/2 cup (2 ounces) ground pistachio nuts (see page 157)

1 teaspoon ground cinnamon

1/2 teaspoon kosher salt

4 sheets filo dough, each 9 by 14 inches (see Help with Filo Dough, opposite)

1/4 cup (1 3/4 ounces by weight) olive oil

About 2 tablespoons powdered sugar

Walnut-Thyme Streusel

Streusel (page 218)

1/2 cup (2 ounces) chopped walnuts

1 teaspoon chopped fresh thyme

Peaches Sautéed in Wine and Honey

4 perfectly ripe peaches or nectarines (about 1 3/4 pounds)

1 tablespoon (1/2 ounce) unsalted butter

2 tablespoons (1 1/2 ounces by weight) honey

1/4 cup (1 1/2 ounces by weight) muscat wine

1/4 teaspoon fresh lemon juice

1/4 cup (scant 3 ounces by weight) honey

To Make the OLIVE OIL FILO CRISPS

Position a rack in the center of the oven and preheat the oven to 350°F. Lightly brush a baking sheet with olive oil and line it with parchment paper. Brush the parchment lightly with olive oil.

In a small bowl, stir together the turbinado sugar, pistachios, cinnamon, and salt. Lay 1 sheet of filo dough on the parchment-lined pan. Brush the filo with some of the olive oil, coating it lightly. Sprinkle the filo with about one-fourth of the nut-sugar mixture. Lay a second sheet of filo on top, brush with more olive oil, and sprinkle with another one-fourth of the nut-sugar mixture. Repeat with the remaining 2 filo sheets and nut-sugar mixture, ending with the nut-sugar mixture.

Bake the filo stack for 10 to 12 minutes, or until the filo is golden brown. Watch the filo closely, as the color will change quickly and the nuts on the top can become too dark. Let cool completely on the pan on a cooling rack and then sprinkle with the powdered sugar. If you are making the crisps in advance, cover gently with plastic wrap and don't sprinkle with the powdered sugar until just before you plate.

To Make the WALNUT-THYME STREUSEL

Combine the ingredients for streusel as directed, omitting the vanilla. When the mixture is the consistency of gravel, stir in the walnuts and thyme, then bake as directed. You should have about 2 cups.

To Make the PEACHES SAUTÉED IN WINE AND HONEY

Don't sauté the peaches until you are ready to plate the dessert. You can leave the peach skins in place, or you can peel the peaches with a vegetable peeler. (Another option is to blanch them in boiling water for about 10 seconds, plunge them immediately into cold water, and then slip off the skins.) Halve and pit the peaches and cut each half into 3 or 4 slices.

In a large sauté pan, melt the butter over medium-high heat, adding the honey before the butter is completely melted. The honey will bubble. When the butter is completely melted, add the wine and lemon juice and reduce the heat to medium. Cook, stirring constantly, for about 3 minutes, or until the mixture has reduced to syrup. Add the peaches, stir them gently to coat them with the syrup, and cook for 2 to 3 minutes, or until they start to exude their juices.

To Plate the Dessert

Divide the peaches among individual serving plates or bowls, spooning a little of the syrup from the pan into each dish. Sprinkle a few spoonfuls of the streusel alongside the peaches. Spoon a few tablespoons of the cream reduction on top of the peaches. Break the filo into large pieces and place a few shards above the peaches. Drizzle each serving generously with the honey.

help with filo dough

Greek filo (sometimes spelled fillo or phyllo) is a paper-thin unleavened dough best known in the United States for its use in honey-and-nut-laden baklava. Similar doughs that go by other names are found in Turkish, Serbian, Albanian, Bosnian, and other kitchens in what was once the Ottoman Empire.

Making homemade filo is close to impossible unless you have a Greek grandmother to walk you through it. Luckily, ready-made frozen filo is easy to find in most grocery stores. Athens and Apollo are widely available brands, though I particularly like the organic dough packaged by the Fillo Factory (see Resources). Here are some tips to keep in mind when using filo for the recipes in this book:

- Filo sheets are sold primarily in two sizes, 13 by 18 inches (20 sheets in a 1-pound box) and 9 by 14 inches (40 sheets in a 1-pound box). You can use either size to make the filo shards in Suddenly Last Summer (page 92) and The M Word (page 137). The recipes are written for 9 by 14-inch sheets, so if you have bought the larger sheets, cut them to size with a sharp knife.

- Precision isn't all that important when making filo shards. As long as you are brushing on enough butter or olive oil to keep the sheets from cracking (but not so much that you drench them), you can use any size sheets you like and nearly any amount of sugar and nuts.

- You can keep filo in your freezer for months or in your refrigerator for up to 4 weeks. If your box of filo is in the freezer, move it to the refrigerator at least a day or two before you plan to use the dough, so the sheets have time to thaw completely.

- When you are ready to work with the filo, open the package, set the stack of sheets on a work surface, and immediately cover the stack with a kitchen towel that has been lightly spritzed with water. This will keep the sheets from drying out.

- If a filo sheet does crack, you can either pull a new sheet from the stack, or you can piece the broken sheet together and brush it with oil or butter to seal the crack. You are going to break the stack of baked filo sheets into shards anyway, so don't worry too much about perfection.

- Use a pastry brush to coat the filo sheets lightly with oil or butter, and don't miss any sections. The coating is what keeps the dough from cracking until you are ready to break or cut the sheets yourself. I have found that silicone brushes don't work as well as old-fashioned bristle brushes for this task.

You can make some
components in advance:

UP TO 1 WEEK BEFORE

→ make the syrup

A FEW HOURS BEFORE

→ make the biscuits

→ make the whipped
    crème fraîche

JUST BEFORE SERVING

→ sauté the berries
    if needed

→ plate the dessert

MINIMALIST VERSION

This dessert is simple,
so don't omit anything.
If you find peak-season
berries, you can skip
the sautéing step.

CITIZEN SHORTCAKE

shortcake biscuits, berries, black pepper–tarragon syrup, whipped crème fraîche

serves 4

I haven't modernized this classic summer dessert except for the addition of
an intensely flavorful simple syrup. Just that one touch—a line of clear syrup
encircling the biscuit—gives the shortcake a more interesting look and a blast
of flavor. You can use any fresh, ripe, juicy fruit with this shortcake, and you can
infuse the simple syrup with any flavor you like. Taste the fruit that you plan to
use with the shortcake and then decide which simple syrup you would like to
make (see page 215).

Don't worry if your fruit isn't as sweet as you expected or is slightly past its
prime. I have included directions on how to heighten its flavor with a quick sauté
in butter and just a little sugar and Cointreau.

To Make the BLACK PEPPER–TARRAGON SYRUP

In a small saucepan, combine the sugar, water, and corn syrup and place
over medium to medium-high heat. Heat, stirring to dissolve the sugar, for
about 5 minutes, or until the mixture comes to a boil. Then turn down the
heat to low and simmer for 1 minute. Remove the pan from the heat, add
the peppercorns, tarragon, and lemon zest, and let steep for 10 minutes.

Pour the syrup through a fine-mesh strainer into a clean container. Add the
lemon juice, and then taste and adjust with more lemon juice if needed. Let
cool, cover, and refrigerate until ready to serve. The syrup will keep for 1 week.

Black Pepper–Tarragon Syrup

1 cup (7 ounces) granulated sugar

1 cup water

1/2 cup (about 5 3/4 ounces) light corn syrup

1 teaspoon black peppercorns

2 sprigs tarragon

1 lemon zest strip, 2 inches long and 1/2 inch wide

2 or 3 drops fresh lemon juice, or to taste

To Make the SHORTCAKE BISCUITS

Position a rack in the center of the oven and preheat the oven to 350°F.
Line a baking sheet with parchment paper.

In a large bowl, stir together the flour, baking powder, baking soda,
1/2 teaspoon salt, and 2 tablespoons sugar. Scatter the butter over the flour
mixture and work it in with your fingers. Flatten out some of the butter
cubes but don't overwork them. You want to see dime-sized disks of butter
still visible in the mixture.

In a small bowl, stir together the buttermilk, milk, and cream. Pour the
buttermilk mixture into the flour-butter mixture and stir just until the two
mixtures come together. Don't overmix.

Turn out the dough onto a floured work surface. Dip your hands into
flour and gently flatten the dough into a rectangle about 12 by 8 inches.
Lightly dust the rectangle with flour. As if closing a book, fold the dough

Shortcake Biscuits

1 cup (5 ounces) all-purpose flour

1 teaspoon baking powder

1/8 teaspoon baking soda

1/2 teaspoon plus 1/8 teaspoon kosher salt

2 tablespoons (1 ounce) granulated sugar, plus
    about 1 teaspoon for sprinkling

4 tablespoons (2 ounces) cold unsalted butter,
    cut into 1/2-inch cubes

1/4 cup (2 1/4 ounces by weight) buttermilk or
    (2 ounces) low-fat or nonfat plain yogurt

2 tablespoons cold whole milk

2 tablespoons cold heavy cream

1 (1 1/2 ounces by weight) large egg

2 teaspoons water or whole milk

in half, creating a 6 by 8-inch rectangle. Fold the dough over one more time, again as if you are closing a book, creating a 6 by 4-inch rectangle. Each time you fold, you are adding a layer of air and flakiness to the biscuit dough. Cut the dough into 4 equal triangles or rectangles (or make them round if you like them round), and place the biscuits on the prepared pan.

To make an egg wash, in a small bowl, whisk together the egg, water, and the 1/8 teaspoon salt. Brush the tops of the biscuits with the wash, and then sprinkle each biscuit with about 1/4 teaspoon sugar. Bake the biscuits for 22 to 25 minutes, or until golden brown. Transfer to a rack and let cool.

To Make the WHIPPED CRÈME FRAÎCHE

In a medium bowl, combine the cream and crème fraîche and whisk until soft peaks form. Alternatively, use a stand mixer fitted with a whip attachment or a handheld mixer and beat on medium-high speed for about 3 minutes.

To Prepare the BERRIES

If the berries (or other summer fruits) are at their peak of flavor, you can just stem and cut as needed. If the berries look perfect but don't taste perfect once you get them home, it is easy to boost their flavor and juices. In a sauté pan, melt the butter over high heat and add the sugar. Add the berries and Cointreau and sauté for about 2 minutes but no longer, as the berries need just a little time over the heat to coax out their flavor.

To Plate the Dessert

Using a serrated knife, cut each biscuit in half horizontally. There should be a natural line between the dough layers that you can follow as you cut. Set each biscuit on a plate, lift off the top, and spoon about 1 cup of the fruit onto the bottom half. Dollop on a large spoonful of whipped crème fraîche, and lightly replace the top half of the biscuit. Drizzle the black pepper–tarragon syrup around the biscuit, encircling it. Lightly dust the shortcake with powdered sugar.

Whipped Crème Fraîche

1/2 cup cold heavy cream

1/2 cup (4 ounces) cold crème fraîche (page 221)

Berries

4 cups (about 1 pound) raspberries, olallieberries, blackberries, blueberries, or halved or quartered strawberries, or a combination, or sliced peaches and/or other summer fruits

2 tablespoons (1 ounce) unsalted butter (optional)

2 tablespoons (1 ounce) granulated sugar (optional)

Splash of Cointreau or Grand Marnier (optional)

Powdered sugar for dusting (optional)

You can make some
components in advance:

UP TO 1 MONTH BEFORE

➤ make the puff pastry

UP TO 1 WEEK BEFORE

➤ make the caramel
sauce

JUST BEFORE SERVING

➤ roll out the dough
and cut into rounds

➤ peel and slice
the apples

➤ assemble and
bake the galettes

➤ whip the crème
fraîche

➤ rewarm the
caramel sauce

➤ plate the dessert
while still warm

APPLE GALETTES

thinly sliced apples on blitz puff pastry with almond paste and apricot glaze

serves 5

Apple galettes have been one of my signature desserts for more than a decade.
I served them with whipped crème fraîche, a little caramel sauce, green apple
sorbet, and spun sugar. Here, I have left off the spun sugar (too complicated) and
the green apple sorbet (because it requires a restaurant-style juicer), replacing
them with a spoonful of crème fraîche and a drizzle of caramel sauce that keep
this dessert classically beautiful.

If you find Pink Pearl apples, which appear in late August to mid-September,
use them. These bright, fragrant, sweet-tart apples make the galettes sing. Otherwise pippins, Jonathans, Granny Smiths, or other tart baking apples work well. I
peel apples, cut them in half, and then cut out the core, which seems the fastest,
easiest way to prepare them for baking. I make paper-thin apple slices using an
inexpensive mandoline from Japan. You can cut your apples with a knife, especially if you have excellent knife skills like Iron Chef Morimoto, but it is worth
investing in a mandoline to make slices quickly.

This recipe makes enough dough for 10 pastries. I recommend wrapping half
of the dough and freezing it for the next time you want puff pastry. Allow 12 hours
for the dough to thaw in the refrigerator. See Puff Pastry (page 201) for another
way to use the leftover dough.

MINIMALIST VERSION

Make simpler French apple strip tarts instead of galettes. Cut the puff pastry into
strips, each about 4 inches wide by 7 inches long, and form a line of marmalade,
almond paste, and apple slices down the center of each strip. Bake at 400°F for
25 to 30 minutes, or until the edges of the pastry and the apples are golden.
Reduce the oven temperature to 350°F and continue to bake for 5 to 8 minutes
longer, or until the apples lose some of their moisture. This makes a lovely breakfast or teatime pastry.

Blitz Puff Pastry

2 cups (10 ounces) all-purpose flour

2 teaspoons kosher salt

Pinch of granulated sugar

12 tablespoons (6 ounces) cold unsalted butter, cut into 1-inch cubes

2 tablespoons (1 ounce) crème fraîche (page 221) or heavy cream

2/3 to 3/4 cup ice-cold water

To Make the BLITZ PUFF PASTRY

In a large bowl, stir together the flour, salt, and sugar. Scatter the butter over the flour mixture and work it in with your fingers. Flatten out some of the butter cubes but don't overwork them. You want to see dime-sized disks of butter still visible. Make a well in the flour-butter mixture and pour in the crème fraîche and 2/3 cup of the water. With a fork, a rubber spatula, or your hands, gently work the wet ingredients into the flour mixture. Don't overwork it. The mixture should look a little ragged. Don't worry if it looks dry or if you have some dry ingredients at the bottom of the bowl. Only if it really seems like there isn't enough moisture, add the rest of the water. Scoop up the dough and dry ingredients at the bottom of the bowl, and slip it all into a plastic bag or wrap in plastic wrap and refrigerate for at least 1 hour or up to overnight. The flour will continue to soak up the water while it chills.

Turn out the chilled dough onto a lightly floured work surface and bring it together a bit with your hands before you begin rolling it. Then, roll out the dough into a rectangle measuring about 6 by 12 inches and 1/2 inch thick. Work quickly, being careful not to overwork the dough. Fold the dough over onto itself into thirds, as if folding a business letter. Fold it in half lengthwise once more, wrap well, and refrigerate for 1 hour.

Remove the dough from the refrigerator and repeat the rolling and the folding, first in thirds and then in half. Cut the dough in half and wrap each half well. Place one half in the freezer for future use; it will keep for up to 1 month. Chill the other half in the refrigerator for 1 hour. Each half should weigh about 11 ounces.

To Shape the GALETTES

Line a baking sheet with parchment paper. Remove the dough from the refrigerator, place it on a floured work surface, cut in half, and set one half aside. Roll out the other half 1/4 inch thick. Using a 4-inch round cutter or a paring knife and a template, cut out two 4-inch rounds. Repeat with the other half of the dough, then gather up the scraps and cut out 1 more round. Prick each round a few times with a fork, then set the rounds, upside down and well spaced, on the prepared pan. (Turning them upside down allows air to circulate beneath the punctures, keeps juice from escaping during baking, and coaxes a little more rise.)

Slide the pan into the refrigerator to chill for 10 to 15 minutes while you prepare the apple slices.

To Slice the APPLES

5 Pink Pearl or 3 pippin, Jonathan, or Granny Smith apples

Peel the apples and cut them in half from the stem down. Cut off the very top and bottom and core each half. Using a mandoline or sharp knife, slice each half as thinly as possible.

Galette Topping

1 (1$\frac{1}{2}$ ounces by weight) large egg

1 teaspoon water

5 teaspoons apricot marmalade or jam

4 teaspoons almond paste

$\frac{1}{2}$ lemon

1 tablespoon granulated sugar

$\frac{1}{4}$ cup Basic Caramel Sauce (page 210), optional
Powdered sugar for dusting

$\frac{1}{4}$ to $\frac{1}{2}$ cup (2 to 4 ounces) cold crème fraîche (page 221), whipped with a whisk to soft peaks

To Finish and Bake the Galettes

Position a rack in the center of the oven and preheat the oven to 400°F.

In a small bowl, lightly beat together the egg and water. Brush each pastry round with the egg wash.

Place 1 teaspoon of the marmalade in the center of each pastry round and spread it out, leaving a $\frac{1}{4}$-inch border uncovered. Separate the almond paste into 5 equal pieces and flatten each piece to about the size of a lima bean. Place 1 piece in the center of each galette.

Starting at the outer edge of each pastry round, arrange the apple slices, overlapping them, encircling the almond paste, and creating a kind of domed pyramid. You will use 12 to 15 apple slices per galette. Squeeze a few drops of lemon juice over each galette, and sprinkle the tops with the granulated sugar.

Bake the galettes for 25 to 30 minutes, or until the edges of the pastry and the apples are golden. Lower the oven temperature to 350°F and continue to bake for 5 to 8 minutes longer, or until the apples lose some of their moisture and the pyramid shrinks. I bake these galettes until the tips of the apples are dark or even almost burnt.

To Plate the Dessert

Spoon a pool of caramel sauce onto one side of each plate. Place a galette in the center of the plate and dust the top of the galette with the powdered sugar. Place a dollop of the whipped crème fraîche alongside the galette.

You can make some components in advance:

UP TO 1 WEEK BEFORE
→ make the balsamic-apple reduction

UP TO 3 DAYS BEFORE
→ make the ice cream

UP TO 2 DAYS BEFORE
→ make the crumbles
→ prepare the apples

JUST BEFORE SERVING
→ rewarm the balsamic-apple reduction
→ plate the dessert

MINIMALIST VERSION
Nope. Don't do it.

APPLE OF MY EYE

tarte tatin apples, cheddar crumbles, cinnamon ice cream, balsamic-apple reduction

serves 4

I can never choose what sort of apple pie I like best. There is a French galette with thinly sliced apples on puff pastry (page 99), and a French *tarte Tatin* with caramelized apples and a spoonful of crème fraîche on a short-pastry crust or puff pastry. American apple pie often has chunks of apple with cinnamon and nutmeg in a flaky crust, and sometimes a slab of sharp Cheddar cheese melted on the top. Each one balances the acidity of the apples with sugar, but they take off in different directions after that.

This altered apple pie lets me combine my favorite aspects of each type. I have always been put off by the thick, doughy crust and too-sweet filling of most diner apple pies, so I like the restraint here: a few apple cubes, their tartness underscored by a subtle burnt caramel flavor; a sprinkling of streusel-like Cheddar crumbles; cinnamon-spiced ice cream; and a drizzle of balsamic. The ice cream is Philadelphia-style, which means it contains no egg yolks. Yet it is rich and satisfying, and I especially like how it contrasts with the Cheddar.

While preparing the apples, you might be tempted to flip them instead of just letting them sit there, soaking up the caramel in peace. Resist the urge. And don't worry if some apples are very brown and almost translucent while others are pale and still have some crunch to them.

To Make the CINNAMON ICE CREAM

Set up an ice bath by half filling a large bowl with ice and water. Have ready a heatproof storage container or bowl that fits in the ice bath.

In a saucepan, combine the milk, turbinado sugar, maple syrup, and cinnamon and place over medium heat. (Keep the cream in the refrigerator until you are ready to use it, so it stays chilled.) Heat, stirring occasionally, for 6 to 8 minutes, or just until the mixture starts to bubble and the sugar is dissolved. Add the cream, vanilla, and salt, stir to mix, and pour into the container. Nest the container in the ice bath. When the mixture is completely cool, cover and refrigerate for at least 1 hour or up to overnight.

Briefly stir the mixture to redistribute any cinnamon that has settled to the bottom, and then pour into an ice cream maker and freeze according to the manufacturer's directions. Store in a covered container in the freezer for 1 to 2 hours before you plate the dessert. It will keep for 1 week but will taste best if served within 3 days. You should have about 2¼ cups.

Cinnamon Ice Cream
1 cup whole milk
¼ cup (2 ounces) turbinado sugar
¼ cup (3 ounces by weight) pure maple syrup
1 teaspoon ground cinnamon
1 cup heavy cream
½ teaspoon pure vanilla extract
½ teaspoon kosher salt

Cheddar Crumbles

1 cup (5 ounces) all-purpose flour

½ cup plus 2 tablespoons (2½ ounces) cornstarch

¼ cup (1 ounce) powdered sugar

1 teaspoon kosher salt

¼ teaspoon freshly ground pepper

¼ teaspoon paprika

12 tablespoons (6 ounces) cold unsalted butter, cut into ½-inch pieces

½ cup (2 ounces) coarsely chopped pecans

4 ounces sharp white Cheddar cheese, grated (about 2 cups)

Tarte Tatin Apples

½ cup (3½ ounces) granulated sugar

2 tablespoons water

1 tablespoon fresh lemon juice

2 large, crisp apples such as Granny Smith (about 1 pound), peeled, cored, and cut into ¾- to 1-inch cubes

½ teaspoon pure vanilla extract

¼ teaspoon kosher salt

To Make the CHEDDAR CRUMBLES

Position a rack in the center of the oven and preheat the oven to 350°F. Line a large baking sheet with parchment paper.

In a large bowl, stir together the flour, cornstarch, powdered sugar, salt, pepper, and paprika. Using your fingers, 2 knives, or a pastry blender, work in the butter until the mixture resembles gravel. Scatter the pecans and cheese over the top and toss together to mix evenly.

Dump the mixture onto the center of the prepared pan. Using your fingers, gently distribute the mixture to the edges of the parchment so the crumbles bake evenly. Slide the pan into the oven. After about 10 minutes, use a spatula to flip the crumbles over. Continue to bake for 15 to 20 minutes longer, or until the crumbles are golden and any bits of cheese are crisp. The crumbles should not be blond and doughy. Just like when you are toasting nuts, you want them toasted but not burned.

Let the crumbles cool completely on the pan on a cooling rack. To store them, transfer them to an airtight container. The crumbles will keep for 4 days but taste best if used within 2 days. You should have about 2½ cups. (You won't need all the crumbles. Put the extra in a bowl and serve with cocktails.)

To Make the TARTE TATIN APPLES

In a 10-inch skillet, combine the granulated sugar, water, and lemon juice over high heat. Heat, without stirring, until the sugar dissolves, then slowly tilt the pan back and forth several times, allowing the sugar to caramelize evenly until it is a dark amber. This will take 4 to 5 minutes. (I tell new cooks at Citizen Cake to cook the sugar until it is the color of an Anchor Steam beer.)

Remove the pan from the heat and carefully add the apples, arranging them in a single, even layer. *Do not stir the apples now or at any point during the process.* Place the pan over medium heat and let the caramel simmer and bubble around the apples for 5 minutes. At first, it will seem as if nothing is happening—that you have nothing more than apples cubes sitting on dark caramel. But slowly the apples will begin to darken as they release their juices and then reabsorb their own liquid along with the caramel.

Remove the pan from the heat and sprinkle the apples with the vanilla and salt. Resist the temptation to stir or move the apples in any way. They will begin to look like beautiful jelly cubes—like beautiful *tarte Tatin* apples. Let the apples sit, undisturbed, for 10 to 15 minutes, or until all of the caramel has been absorbed back into the apples. (You can begin making the balsamic-apple reduction the moment you remove the apples from the heat.)

To Make the BALSAMIC-APPLE REDUCTION

In a small saucepan, combine the apple juice, vinegar, and granulated sugar and set over medium heat. As soon as the mixture begins to bubble slightly, reduce the heat to medium-low or low and cook for about 20 minutes, or until the liquid is reduced by half. Remove from the heat. You should have about 1/4 cup. If you have made this in advance, let it cool to room temperature, cover tightly, and refrigerate for up to 1 week.

To Plate the Dessert

You can use plates, bowls, or even drinking glasses to plate this dessert. Whichever option you choose, divide the apples evenly among them. Place a quenelle (see page 37) or a small scoop of the ice cream next to the apples. Sprinkle some of the crumbles (about 1/4 cup per serving) around the apples and ice cream. Drizzle the balsamic-apple reduction along the edge of the plate or bowl, or directly over the ice cream if you have opted to serve in a glass, parfait-style.

Balsamic-Apple Reduction

1/2 cup apple juice

2 tablespoons balsamic vinegar

2 tablespoons (1 ounce) granulated sugar

A VEIL OF VANILLA

tarte tatin apples, point reyes blue cheese crumbles, pecan caramel sauce, honey semifreddo, pomegranate

serves **6**

This dessert starts with the same apples used in Apple of My Eye, but then it zooms off into its own realm. I created it for an autumn James Beard dinner, and I wrote a short poem to introduce it on the menu:

> It opens in Point Reyes.
> On a currant-studded cliff.
> A veil of vanilla,
> *Et soudain* apple confit, pomegranate gelée
> Ineluctable sticky-sweet
> Lingering red rubies.

Inspired by the mysterious and achingly lonely stretch of Pacific coast near Point Reyes and my love for Manka's Inverness Lodge and my friend Margaret Grade, (the chef-owner of this famous old hunting lodge and restaurant), this dessert called for something different than the Cheddar cheese often served with apples. I substituted a famous blue made in Point Reyes, created an ethereal *semifreddo*, and then added components as if I was possessed. When I had finished making the dessert, it seemed like something from a French film: the veil—the *semifreddo*—is the moment just before the mystery is revealed. The apple is the main character in the story, the caramel is the rich, sultry sidekick, and then—in the last reel—the red rubies of pomegranate, resting in the bottom of the glass like something a jewel thief would steal.

Choose straightforward, clear glasses—nothing frilly—for serving this parfait-style dessert. The easy-to-make *semifreddo* is a good match for the apples' tartness, while the ruby red pomegranate delivers color and counterbalances the sweetness of the caramel sauce and the saltiness of the pecans. (For this recipe, I removed the pomegranate gelée and use only fresh pomegranates, but if you want an even more over-the-top dessert, add the gel from page 219.) Making this dessert takes time, of course, but you will have something incredible to show for your effort. After you have made it once, you will make it again, though only in fall when apples and pomegranates are in season—and ideally after a long drive along a foggy, deserted coastline.

To Make the HONEY SEMIFREDDO

Honey Semifreddo

2 tablespoons (about 1¹/₂ ounces) honey

1 cup heavy cream

¹/₂ cup (4 ounces) crème fraîche (page 221)

¹/₃ cup (2³/₄ ounces by weight) egg whites (about 3 large egg whites)

¹/₂ cup (3¹/₂ ounces) granulated sugar

Put the honey and a splash of the cream in a small cup and heat in the microwave for 15 seconds, or until hot. If you would rather do this on the stove top, use an especially small saucepan or a butter warmer set over medium heat. Let cool completely.

In a bowl, using a stand mixer fitted with the whip attachment or a handheld mixer, beat together the remaining cream and the crème fraîche on medium-high speed for about 2 minutes, or until soft peaks form. Using a spatula or a whisk, fold the cooled honey mixture (the mixture must be fully cooled or it will deflate the cream mixture) into the cream mixture just until combined.

In another bowl, with the clean whip attachment, beat the egg whites on medium speed for about 1 minute, or until foamy. Gradually add the granulated sugar while continuing to beat for 5 to 7 minutes, or until soft peaks form. Using a spatula, fold the egg whites into the cream mixture in two additions.

Cover the *semifreddo* with waxed paper or plastic wrap, smoothing the paper against its surface, and freeze for 4 hours. You have some leeway with the freezing time, but 2 hours is not enough time and at 6 hours the *semifreddo* begins to lose its silkiness.

To Make the BLUE CHEESE CRUMBLES

Position a rack in the center of the oven and preheat the oven to 325°F. Line a baking sheet with parchment paper.

In a large bowl, stir together the flour, cornstarch, powdered sugar, salt, and pepper. Using your fingers, 2 knives, or a pastry blender, work in the butter until the mixture resembles gravel. Crumble the cheese into 1/4- to 1/2-inch chunks into the bowl and work it in lightly with your fingers until the mixture has the texture of granola. Don't add the currants until after baking, or they will burn and taste bitter.

Dump the mixture on the center of the prepared pan. Using your fingers, gently distribute the mixture to the edges of the parchment so the crumbles bake evenly. Slide the pan into the oven. After about 10 minutes, use a spatula to flip the crumbles over. Continue to bake for 15 to 20 minutes longer, or until the crumbles are golden and any bits of cheese are crisp. The crumbles should not be blond and doughy. Just like when you are toasting nuts, you want them toasted but not burned.

Remove the pan from the oven and sprinkle the currants evenly over the crumbles. Let cool completely on the pan on a cooling rack. To store them, transfer to an airtight container. The crumbles will keep for 3 days but taste best if used within a day or two. You should have about 2 1/2 cups.

To Make the PECAN CARAMEL SAUCE

Before you begin making this sauce, see Basic Caramel Sauce on page 210 for tips on making caramel sauces. In a heavy saucepan, stir together the sugar and water and place over medium heat. Cook, without stirring, for 2 to 3 minutes, or until the sugar has dissolved. Increase the heat to medium-high and let the sugar boil vigorously (without stirring!) for 5 to 6 minutes, or until the mixture is a dark amber.

When the color looks good, remove the pan from the heat, add the butter, and then slowly add the cream (be careful, as the mixture will bubble up when you add it). Return the pan to low heat and stir slowly and carefully (the mixture will still be boiling) for about 2 minutes, or until all the ingredients come together. Add the honey and molasses, stir until dissolved, and bring to a boil. Remove from the heat, add the vanilla, salt, pink pepper,

Point Reyes Blue Cheese Crumbles

1 cup (5 ounces) all-purpose flour

1/2 cup plus 2 tablespoons (2 1/2 ounces) cornstarch

1/4 cup (1 ounce) powdered sugar

1 teaspoon kosher salt

1 crank on a pepper mill of black pepper

12 tablespoons (6 ounces) cold unsalted butter, cut into 1/2-inch pieces

4 ounces Point Reyes or Wisconsin blue cheese, cold

2/3 cup (3 ounces) dried currants

Pecan Caramel Sauce

1/2 cup (3 1/2 ounces) granulated sugar

2 tablespoons water

1 tablespoon (1/2 ounce) unsalted butter

1/2 cup heavy cream

2 tablespoons (about 1 1/2 ounces) honey

1 tablespoon unsulfured blackstrap molasses

1 drop pure vanilla extract

1/2 teaspoon kosher salt

2 cranks on a pepper mill of pink peppercorns (see Resources), or a pinch of freshly ground pink peppercorns ground in a mortar (optional)

1 cup (4 ounces) pecan halves or pieces, lightly toasted (see page 157)

and pecans, and stir to mix. Set the caramel sauce aside to cool slightly before you plate the dessert. If made ahead, it will keep tightly covered in the refrigerator for up to 3 days. You should have about 1 1/2 cups.

To Plate the Dessert

Use clear glasses to show off all the layers. Drop a spoonful of pomegranate seeds into each glass. Spoon in a large chunk or scoop of *semifreddo.* Pour a generous spoonful of the caramel sauce on top the *semifreddo.* Spoon in 4 or 5 apple cubes. Resist the temptation to add more apples; restraint is everything here. Finish with a small handful of the blue cheese crumbles.

Tarte Tatin Apples (page 106)

60 to 70 pomegranate seeds

CONSIDER THE ART OF RESTRAINT...

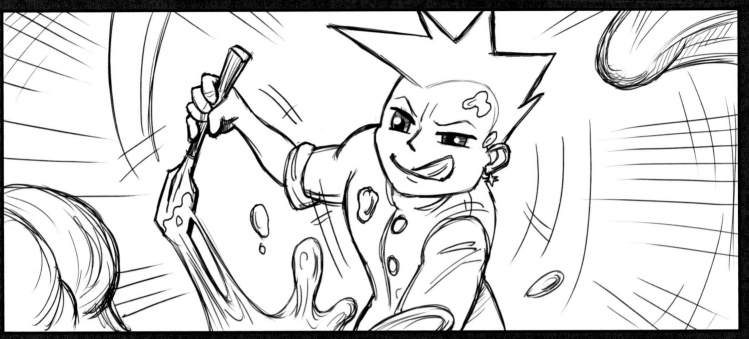

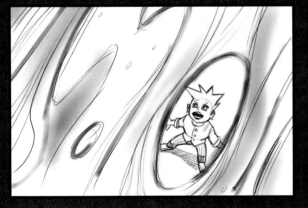
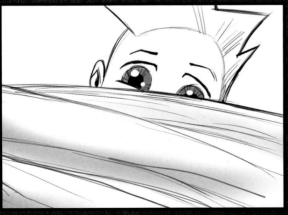

CON-STRUCTION ZONE

this chapter—and really, my entire approach to desserts (and life)—is about demolishing stereotypes and then rebuilding something different and exciting. Cheesecake is a good example. You probably have a specific image of cheesecake in mind, but when you turn to the next page, you will see a version that's entirely new. The name of the dessert, Waking Up in a City That Never Sleeps, conjures up a New York state of mind and is the first indication to expect a different kind of cake. The custard stands on its own, the blueberries take an unexpected form, and the whole dessert looks nothing like the cheesecake you are used to, yet the flavors you love are still there.

I have always felt that a traditional banana split is overwhelming to look at, much less to eat. But take apart the flavors and reassemble them in scaled-down form, and you have Bananas Foster Cane Split (page 133), a light, interesting, refined take on the ice cream parlor classic. And at Citizen Cake, we rarely stop at one interpretation, since part of the fun is making a dish a little differently every time we put it on the menu. I have made more gingerbread houses than I can count, but the version in this chapter (page 117) breaks down the walls (so to speak), giving you a soft, spicy gingery cake with the architecture on the side.

You will find the same spirit on the savory portion of our menu, where steak gives us room to play. Ice cream may not pop into your head when you consider accompaniments to beef, unless you think of ice creams as what they are: frozen sauces. We keep coming up with new flavors—horseradish ice cream and candy cap mushroom ice cream to name just two—as a fantastic finishing touch to a rib eye or a strip cut. We call it Citizen Steak.

You can make some
components in advance:

UP TO 1 WEEK BEFORE

— make the graham
   crackers (or buy
   them)

UP TO 3 DAYS BEFORE

— make the sorbet

THE DAY BEFORE

— make the
   blueberry paper

— make the
   cheesecake custard

JUST BEFORE SERVING

— make the graham
   cracker powder

— cut some of the
   blueberries in half

— plate the dessert

MINIMALIST VERSION

Serve the cheesecake
custard surrounded
by fresh blueberries.

WAKING UP IN A CITY THAT NEVER SLEEPS

cheesecake custard, sour cream sorbet, graham cracker powder, blueberry paper

serves **6**

If you are imagining the standard cheesecake, envision something lighter: an airy custard gently surrounded by finely ground homemade graham crackers. And instead of a thick layer of blueberries, think blueberry paper, a sort of thin fruit leather but softer and sexier, with a texture reminiscent of suede. The typical sour cream layer on the top is gone, too, replaced with a refreshing sour cream sorbet.

I have always leaned toward Italian-style cheesecakes made with ricotta, rather than New York–style cheesecakes, but this version calls for both cream cheese and ricotta cheese. The custard needs time to chill and the paper needs to set, so begin making this dessert at least seven hours before you plan to serve it.

To Make the BLUEBERRY PAPER

Position a rack in the center of the oven and preheat the oven to 250°F. Line a baking sheet with a nonstick baking mat. (If you don't own a mat, you can use parchment paper, but the blueberry peels off of a mat much more easily.)

In a medium saucepan, combine the blueberries, sugar, and the 1 tablespoon water over medium heat. Cook for 3 to 4 minutes, or until the sugar dissolves, the blueberries darken, and the water comes to a boil.

While the blueberries are heating, in a small bowl, stir together the 1 teaspoon water and the cornstarch to form a slurry. When the blueberries reach a boil, add the slurry and stir constantly for 1 to 2 minutes, or until the mixture comes to a rapid boil. Remove the pan from the heat and let cool to room temperature. Transfer the cooled berry mixture to a stand blender and process until smooth, or scrape into a bowl and process with an immersion blender until smooth.

Using an offset spatula, the back of a spoon, or a rubber spatula, spread the blueberry puree on the prepared pan. Form as thin a layer as you can. Holes may or may not form as the paper dries; either way is fine. The paper sheet should measure about 10 by 8 inches.

Bake the paper for 10 minutes, and then turn off the oven. Without opening the oven door, let the paper dry for at least 6 hours or up to

Blueberry Paper

1/2 cup (about 2 1/2 ounces) blueberries
2 tablespoons (1 ounce) granulated sugar
1 tablespoon plus 1 teaspoon water
1 teaspoon cornstarch

Cheesecake Custard

1 block (8 ounces) cream cheese, at room temperature

1/2 cup (4 ounces) whole-milk ricotta cheese or *fromage blanc*

1/3 cup (3 ounces) Crème Anglaise (page 202)

1/4 cup plus 3 tablespoons (3 ounces) granulated sugar

1/2 teaspoon pure vanilla extract

1/2 vanilla bean or 1/2 teaspoon pure vanilla extract (optional)

Sour Cream Sorbet

1 cup (8 ounces) sour cream

1 cup (8 ounces) Greek-style nonfat or low-fat plain yogurt

2/3 cup (7 ounces by weight) Simple Syrup (page 215)

1 tablespoon honey

3 tablespoons water

1 tablespoon fresh lemon juice

Graham Cracker Powder

4 graham crackers (about 3 1/2 ounces), homemade (page 214) or store-bought

2 tablespoons (1 ounce) turbinado sugar

2 tablespoons (1 ounce) unsalted butter, melted

3/4 cup (about 4 ounces) blueberries, half left whole and the remaining berries cut in half

---

overnight. To store the paper, keep it on the mat on the baking sheet, cover the pan with plastic wrap, and leave it at room temperature. Try to keep the plastic from touching the blueberry paper.

To Make the CHEESECAKE CUSTARD

In a bowl, using a stand mixer fitted with the paddle attachment or a handheld mixer, beat the cream cheese on medium speed for about 1 minute. Using a rubber spatula, stir the ricotta into the whipped cream cheese just until combined. Stir in the crème anglaise and the sugar. If using a half vanilla bean, split the bean with a sharp knife and scrape the seeds into the bowl with the knife's tip. If using vanilla extract, pour it in now. Stir just until combined. You can pour the custard into anything you like: a soufflé mold, a Tupperware container, or a large bowl. Cover and refrigerate for at least 4 hours or up to overnight. You should have about 2 cups.

To Make the SOUR CREAM SORBET

In a blender, combine the sour cream, yogurt, simple syrup, honey, water, and lemon juice and process until smooth. Transfer to a container, cover, and refrigerate for at least 2 hours or up to overnight.

Pour the sour cream mixture into an ice cream maker and freeze according to the manufacturer's directions. Store in a covered container in the freezer for 1 to 2 hours before you plate the dessert. It will keep for 1 week but will taste best if served within 3 days. You should have about 3 cups.

To Make the GRAHAM CRACKER POWDER

With your hands, roughly break up the graham crackers over a mortar or the bowl of a food processor. Add the turbinado sugar and crush with a pestle or pulse 4 or 5 times, until the crumbs are fairly even. Add the butter and mix until the mixture resembles coarse, moist sand. Pour the powder into a bowl, cover, and set aside until you are ready to plate the dessert. You should have about 1/2 cup.

To Plate the Dessert

Sprinkle a spoonful of the graham cracker powder in the center of each plate. If you can, make a quenelle (see page 37) of cheesecake custard and gently place it on top of the powder. If the custard is too soft to form a quenelle, shape a neat spoonful and put it on the powder. Lightly sprinkle more of the powder on the sides and top of the custard. Make a quenelle or a small scoop of the sorbet and place it next to the custard. Scatter 2 tablespoons of whole and halved blueberries on each plate. Cut the blueberry paper into 6 squares (or triangles or strips, whatever you like) and stand a piece of the paper between the custard and the sorbet.

You can make some
components in advance
(and you have to make
the icing for the shards
in advance):

UP TO 1 WEEK BEFORE

- make the royal icing
  and the shards
- make the
  pomegranate gel

UP TO 3 DAYS BEFORE

- make the sorbet

THE DAY BEFORE

- make the
  gingerbread

JUST BEFORE SERVING

- plate the dessert

MINIMALIST VERSION

Serve the warm
gingerbread with
pear slices and softly
whipped cream.

GINGERBREAD BAUHAUS

chipotle gingerbread, pear sorbet, pomegranate gel, royal icing shards

serves 6

I like nothing better than building structures from gingerbread, but I am also a big fan of soft, spicy gingerbread cake. Bauhaus tears down the gingerbread house and gives you instead a cake spiced with ginger and chipotle chile, with the icing on the side. And it is all set off by a not-too-sweet pear sorbet made with fresh pears and pear brandy.

I like my gingerbread with a pronounced ginger flavor, so I use both ground ginger and crystallized ginger, in addition to smoky, spicy ground chipotle chile. Of course, you can use other ground chiles, such as ancho or *pimentón de la Vera*, in place of the chipotle, but the flavor of chipotle works especially well. I bought my vibrantly colored chile powder in little cellophane bags at my local farmers' market, where it is always fresh.

Make the royal icing shards a couple of days ahead so they have time to dry. The longer the icing dries, the crisper your shards will be, so make it as long as a week ahead if you like. You can make the pear sorbet a few days ahead and the cake a day ahead if you like (although the cake is really good served warm from the oven).

To Make the ROYAL ICING SHARDS

Make the royal icing at least 2 days before you plan to serve the dessert. To shape it into shards, line the bottom of a half sheet pan (13 by 19 inches) with parchment paper. Drop the icing by large spoonfuls onto the prepared pan. Using a rubber spatula or a small offset spatula, spread the icing thinly but not paper-thin. You want it thick enough so it will harden firmly (thinner than a chocolate bar but much thicker than a sheet of waxed paper). It should cover an area of about 9 by 10 inches. Let the sheet dry in a warm, dry spot for at least 2 days.

Cover and refrigerate the rest of the icing, then pull it out of the refrigerator an hour or so before you are ready to plate the dessert. If the icing is too stiff, whisk in 1 teaspoon milk or warm water.

When the icing sheet has hardened, break it into 18 large shards, place them in an airtight container or cover them in plastic wrap, and store in a dry spot until you are ready to plate the dessert.

Royal Icing (page 216) for royal icing shards and for plating

1 teaspoon milk or water, if needed

Pear Sorbet

1 pound Bartlett, Comice, or Anjou pears (about 2 pears), chopped into 1-inch chunks with their skin and seeds

1/4 cup plus 3 tablespoons (3 ounces) granulated sugar

1 1/2 cups water

1 tablespoon fresh lemon juice

2 tablespoons pear brandy

Chipotle Gingerbread

2 tablespoons (1 ounce) unsalted butter

1/4 teaspoon ground chipotle chile

1 cup (5 ounces) all-purpose flour

1 tablespoon baking powder

1 tablespoon minced crystallized ginger

1 teaspoon ground ginger

1/2 teaspoon kosher salt

1/4 teaspoon ground cinnamon

1/4 cup (1 1/2 ounces by weight) canola oil

1 (1 1/2 ounces by weight) large egg

1/4 cup plus 1 tablespoon (2 1/4 ounces) granulated sugar

2 tablespoons (about 1 ounce) firmly packed dark brown sugar

1 1/2 tablespoons unsulfured blackstrap molasses

1 1/2 tablespoons honey

1/4 cup (2 1/4 ounces by weight) buttermilk

Pomegranate Gel (page 219)

To Make the PEAR SORBET

In a large saucepan, combine the pears, sugar, and water and place over medium-high heat. (Because you will strain this mixture after cooking, it is okay to chop the pears with the skin and seeds left in place.) Heat for about 5 minutes, or until the mixture comes to a boil. Remove from the heat and let cool in the pan for 15 to 20 minutes.

Transfer the pear mixture to a blender and process until smooth, or leave in the pan and process with an immersion blender until smooth. Strain through a medium-mesh strainer into a bowl and stir in the lemon juice and pear brandy. Cover and refrigerate for at least 2 hours or up to overnight.

Pour the pear mixture into an ice cream maker and freeze according to the manufacturer's directions. Store in a covered container in the freezer for 1 to 2 hours before you plate the dessert. It will keep for 1 week but taste best if served within 3 days. You should have about 2 1/2 cups.

To Make the CHIPOTLE GINGERBREAD

Position a rack in the center of the oven and preheat the oven to 350°F. Butter and flour a 4 1/2 by 8 1/2 by 2 3/4-inch loaf pan (or similarly sized 1-pound loaf pan).

In a small saucepan, melt the butter over medium heat. Stir in the chipotle chile, remove the pan from the heat, and set aside.

In a medium bowl, stir together the flour, baking powder, crystallized ginger, ground ginger, salt, and cinnamon. In a large bowl, whisk together the canola oil and egg until blended. Add the granulated and brown sugars, molasses, and honey to the oil mixture and stir just until combined. Then stir in the buttermilk and the butter-chile mixture. Pour the wet ingredients into the dry ingredients and whisk just to combine. Pour into the prepared pan.

Bake the cake for 25 to 30 minutes, or until a skewer inserted into the center comes out clean. Let cool in the pan on a cooling rack for 10 minutes, then turn the cake out onto the rack and turn the cake upright. If you have baked the cake ahead of time, cover it with plastic wrap once it is completely cool. Don't cut the cake until you are ready to plate the dessert.

To Plate the Dessert

Cut the gingerbread into 12 or more blocks. They don't need to be equal—in fact, I like it better when the blocks are uneven. Set 2 or 3 shards of the icing on each serving plate. Set a few blocks of gingerbread on the plate. Spoon a little pomegranate gel onto each plate, either on top of a shard or to one side. Rest a shard of icing on one of the gingerbread blocks or, if your shards are small, slide it into the gingerbread so it juts out of the top. Make a quenelle (see page 37) or a scoop of pear sorbet and place it on one of the icing shards. Finish the plate with a spoonful of royal icing, placed either on top of one of the gingerbread blocks or on the plate.

gingerbread houses i have known

I love gingerbread displays and try to build something every holiday season. I have never made a Hansel and Gretel house, but I have made *The Brady Bunch* house, urban buildings that I have tagged with my airbrush, cityscapes, and a cave with crevices through which you could see prehistoric gingerbread scenes drawn on the cavern walls inside.

The cave was one of my favorite creations. I made it in my girlfriend's apartment over a three-week period, and it looked like an ancient site at the North Pole—like something Mulder and Scully would have uncovered. It appeared to be a large block of ice, but I included small cracks in the outer walls to look through. When you peered inside, you saw white stalactites meeting red stalagmites and turning into the world's first candy canes, all made out of pulled sugar. I glued Egyptian-style gingerbread people on the inside walls, and I used cinnamon sticks and gnarled lengths of fresh ginger around the outside base of the cave to give it a lean, vegetal look. They also made it extremely aromatic when you leaned close to see inside.

In 1993, I created an elaborate Japanese tea garden for San Francisco's Miyako Hotel. The hotel engineers built me a clear plastic table with a trough. I put lakes and other waterways between biscotti teahouses, filled them with blue aspic, and lit the table from underneath.

For years, I've taken part in a gingerbread-house event put on by Beth Casey at Bubba's Diner in San Anselmo and later at the Lark Creek Inn. The event benefits Whistlestop, a terrific charity that delivers meals to homebound seniors. Beth has slabs of gingerbread ready to go, and then assigns each chef to a group. All the other groups cheerfully build their houses in the open, while I always drag my group into a huddle in the corner so we can make our house undercover. The first thing I suggest is tossing the standard floor plan and cutting up the gingerbread planks; initially this idea makes my group nervous, but once they abandon the conventional gingerbread house, the door opens for all kinds of unconventional construction, and everyone brings their own great ideas to the building.

These days my holiday creations at Citizen Cake are more sculptural than houselike. And it always seems like there is one new cook on the staff who comes out of the kitchen, spots the eccentric monolith, and stands there, baffled, gazing at this huge gingerbread thing. Suddenly, light dawns and you can tell he or she is thinking, "Whoa. Cool." That's just one more thing to love about my job.

Our very talented cookie designer, Sean Knox, makes the most amazing, detailed cookies year-round. This is his version of the "painted ladies" Victorian houses in San Francisco.

UP TO 3 DAYS BEFORE

➥ make the ice cream

➥ make the grape sorbet if you are feeling ambitious (see page 125)

➥ make the caramel corn

UP TO 2 DAYS BEFORE

➥ make the *panna cotta*

➥ make the tapioca

JUST BEFORE SERVING

➥ have the grapes ready for garnish

➥ plate the dessert

MINIMALIST VERSION

Two options are possible. You can serve the *panna cotta* with Concord grapes (a few cut in half), or you can serve the grape sorbet (see headnote) with caramel corn and a schmear of peanut butter.

CONCORD EXPRESS

concord grape tapioca, buttermilk panna cotta, peanut butter ice cream, caramel corn

serves **6**

This dessert comes down to Concord grapes. When they are in season, I have to make something creative with them. I first tasted Concord grapes when I was working at Masa's. They amazed me then and they still amaze me. I am a tapioca fan, too, and one day it occurred to me that it would be cool to make tapioca look like grapes. This idea was partly due to the influence of my good friend pastry chef Pichet Ong, who has worked for Jean-Georges Vongerichten at Spice Market and at 66, and who now has his own shop, P*Ong, in New York. Pichet showed me how to make tapioca pearls the way you would make gnocchi, but with a dough made from steamed kabocha squash and tapioca starch. He also soaks fresh water chestnuts in pandan juice or grenadine and then tosses them with tapioca starch before blanching them for his signature dessert, Thai Jewels.

Pichet's creations inspired me to experiment with different ways to cook tapioca. For this dessert, you boil large Asian pearl tapioca just like you would pasta. Scout out the tapioca in Asian markets (or see Resources). I use pearl tapioca from Thailand, which is white, lumpy, and about 3/8 inch in diameter. Don't try to make this with the usual large, smooth tapioca beads sold in most supermarkets.

The peanut butter is a subtle component. You might think the combination of peanut butter and jelly in a dessert would be popular, but it is not. We have tried lots of variations at Citizen Cake over the years, and they don't usually sell well. When you think PB&J, you automatically imagine a slab of bread, a thick layer of nut butter, and a coating of bright purple jelly—too filling and cloying for a dessert. But here, the combination is salt, sweet, and tart: salty peanut butter, sweet grapes, and tangy buttermilk *panna cotta*. The combination is energizing and refreshing at the same time, and you don't feel the need to drink a lot of milk with it. If you want one more hit of purple, you can make one of the grape sorbets on page 125 and add it to the layers, after the *panna cotta*.

Caramel corn is important to me because my maternal grandfather always made it when we visited him. He caught fish and hunted quail, but he didn't cook them. My grandmother did all the cooking except for caramel corn and peanut brittle. My grandfather would disappear into the kitchen and suddenly reappear with a big bowl of warm caramel corn made with lots of Spanish peanuts. My grandparents were fanatical about Spanish peanuts and had bags and bags of them in their house. It's no mystery where I got my taste for them.

Peanut Butter Ice Cream

2 cups whole milk

1/2 vanilla bean

3 (1 1/2 ounces by weight) large egg yolks

1/4 cup plus 3 tablespoons (3 3/4 ounces) granulated sugar

1 cup heavy cream

1/4 cup (1 3/4 ounces) salted or unsalted, creamy or chunky peanut butter

Concord Grape Tapioca

3 cups water

2 teaspoons kosher salt

1/2 cup (about 3 ounces) large tapioca pearls

2 cups Concord grape juice

3 tablespoons (about 1 1/4 ounces) granulated sugar

To Make the PEANUT BUTTER ICE CREAM

Set up an ice bath by half filling a large bowl with ice and water. Have ready a heatproof storage container or bowl that fits in the ice bath and a fine-mesh strainer or chinois.

Pour the milk into a saucepan. Split the vanilla bean lengthwise and, with the tip of the knife, scrape the seeds into the saucepan, and then toss in the empty pod. Place over medium heat. In a medium bowl, whisk together the egg yolks and sugar.

After 4 to 5 minutes, when the milk mixture just begins to boil (small bubbles will appear around the edges of the pan), remove the pan from the heat. Whisk a few tablespoons of the hot liquid into the egg mixture. Then, while whisking steadily, slowly add the rest of the hot milk to the egg mixture. Pour the mixture into the saucepan and place over medium-low heat. Cook, stirring constantly but gently with a wooden spoon or heatproof spatula, for 3 to 4 minutes, or until the custard begins to thicken. The custard is done when the light lacy foam on the surface vanishes or when you run your finger across the back of the spoon and the line holds.

Pour the custard through the strainer into the heatproof container. Stir in the cream, nest the container in the ice bath, and let cool for at least 30 minutes, or until completely cooled. Pour into a blender, add the peanut butter, and process until smooth.

Pour the custard into an ice cream maker and freeze according to the manufacturer's directions. Store in a covered container in the freezer for 1 to 2 hours before you plate the dessert. It will keep for 1 week but will taste best if served within 3 days. You should have about 4 cups.

To Make the CONCORD GRAPE TAPIOCA

In a saucepan, combine the water and salt and bring to a boil over high heat. Add the tapioca pearls, reduce the heat to medium-low, and simmer uncovered, stirring occasionally, for 45 minutes. Add more water if at any point the tapioca is not completely covered by water. When the tapioca is ready, it should have a translucent exterior through which you see a white interior. If you taste a pearl, it should feel a little firmer than al dente pasta.

Drain the tapioca, return it to the pan, and add the grape juice and sugar. Bring to a simmer over medium-low heat and cook uncovered, stirring gently every 5 minutes or so, for 15 to 20 minutes, or until the tapioca is slightly softer than al dente pasta. The pearls should still have some white in their centers. Watch closely to make sure the tapioca does not boil vigorously. Remove the pan from the heat and let stand for 5 minutes.

Pour the tapioca and any liquid into a heatproof container, let cool to room temperature, cover, and refrigerate for at least 1 hour. It will keep in the refrigerator for up to 1 week, though the starch will continue to absorb the liquid. You should have about 1 1/2 cups.

Buttermilk Panna Cotta

1 teaspoon powdered gelatin

2 tablespoons water

1 cup heavy cream

3 tablespoons (1¼ ounces) granulated sugar

   1-inch piece vanilla bean

1 cup (about 9 ounces by weight) buttermilk

Caramel Corn

  4 cups popped popcorn

¼ cup (1¼ ounces) salted roasted peanuts, preferably Spanish

   Pinch of kosher salt (only if you have used unsalted peanuts)

½ cup (3½ ounces) granulated sugar

  2 tablespoons water

  2 teaspoons unsulfured dark molasses

  1 tablespoon honey

  1 tablespoon (½ ounce) unsalted butter

¼ teaspoon baking soda

   Cluster of Concord grapes or any dark, pretty, flavorful grapes, half left whole and the remaining grapes cut in half

To Make the BUTTERMILK PANNA COTTA

In a small bowl or cup, sprinkle the gelatin over the water and set aside to soften for 3 to 5 minutes.

In a saucepan, combine the cream and sugar. Split the vanilla bean lengthwise, scrape the seeds into the saucepan, and then toss in the empty pod. Place over medium heat for about 2 to 3 minutes, or just until the mixtures comes to a boil. Remove the pan from the heat, add the gelatin mixture, and stir until the gelatin is dissolved. Let cool for 10 minutes, remove and discard the vanilla pod, and stir in the buttermilk.

Pour the mixture into a heatproof container, let cool completely, cover, and refrigerate for at least 2 hours and preferably for 4 hours. It will keep for up to 3 days. You should have about 2 cups.

To Make the CARAMEL CORN

Line the bottom of a large baking sheet with a nonstick baking mat, or line it with parchment paper and butter the paper.

In a large bowl, mix together the popcorn and peanuts. (Add a pinch of salt if you use unsalted peanuts.) In a large saucepan, combine the sugar, water, molasses, honey, and butter and stir once or twice. Clip a candy thermometer onto the side of the pan and place over medium-high heat. Bring to a boil, then cook, without stirring, for 7 to 9 minutes, or until the mixture registers 250°F on the thermometer. Remove the pan from the heat and add the baking soda. The mixture will foam up and then the foam will recede. Whisk just once, and then count off 5 seconds. Pour the mixture over the popcorn and peanuts and toss to distribute evenly, being careful not to burn yourself.

Turn the mixture out onto the prepared pan. Using a heatproof spatula, gently spread it evenly over the bottom. Let cool to room temperature. You should have about 6 cups. It will keep in an airtight container or covered with plastic wrap for 3 days. This makes more caramel corn than you need for this dessert, but once people taste it, the leftovers disappear quickly.

To Plate the Dessert

You can assemble the dessert as a parfait in tall glasses or you can serve it on plates. Divide the tapioca and its liquid evenly, spooning it into the bottom of each glass or onto the center of each plate. Add a scoop of the *panna cotta*. The grape juice from the tapioca will rise up a little in the glass. Gently add a scoop of the ice cream to each glass or plate, as well as 4 or 5 Concord grapes, some whole and some halved. Finish with a cluster of caramel corn.

PB&J

peanut butter ice cream, concord grape sorbet

You can make some components in advance:

UP TO 3 DAYS BEFORE
- make the ice cream
- make the sorbet

JUST BEFORE SERVING
- have the grapes ready for garnish
- plate the dessert

serves 6

I created a grape sorbet as an extra kick for Concord Express, but here I've paired it with just the peanut butter ice cream, for PB&J purists. It's a dark, intensely purple sorbet that is especially good when made with Concord grapes. They aren't the easiest grapes to find, but for a short period every fall they are available in high-end markets and some farmers' markets. I have given you two recipes for the sorbet, one that calls for fresh Concord grapes and a really, really easy one made from bottled Concord grape juice, the backup plan if you can't find grapes in the market.

To Make GRAPE SORBET from CONCORD GRAPES

In a saucepan, combine the grapes, sugar, and water and place over medium-high heat. Heat, stirring once or twice, for 5 to 8 minutes, or until the mixture comes to a boil. Remove from the heat and let cool to room temperature.

Transfer the cooled mixture to a stand blender and process until smooth, or process in the pan with an immersion blender until smooth. Be careful not to overblend. If you beat the grape seeds into small pieces, they will give the sorbet a bitter, peppery flavor.

Pour the puree through a fine-mesh strainer into a bowl and stir in the lemon juice. Cover and refrigerate for at least 1 hour or up to overnight.

Pour the grape mixture into an ice cream maker and freeze according to the manufacturer's directions. Store in a covered container in the freezer for 1 to 2 hours before you plate the dessert. It will keep for 1 week but will taste best if served within 3 days. You should have about 3³/4 cups.

Grape Sorbet from Concord Grapes

2 cups (1 pound) Concord grapes, stems removed

¹/2 cup (3¹/2 ounces) granulated sugar

1 cup water

1 tablespoon fresh lemon juice

To Make GRAPE SORBET from GRAPE JUICE

In a bowl, stir together the grape juice, sugar, and lemon juice until the sugar has dissolved. Cover and refrigerate for at least 1 hour or up to overnight.

Pour the grape juice mixture into an ice cream maker and freeze according to the manufacturer's directions. Store as directed for the sorbet made with grapes. You should have about 3³/4 cups.

Grape Sorbet from Grape Juice

3 cups bottled Concord grape juice

¹/2 cup plus 1 tablespoon (4 ounces) granulated sugar

1 tablespoon fresh lemon juice

To Plate the Dessert

Make a quenelle (see page 37) or a small scoop of the ice cream and place it on a plate. Make another quenelle or small scoop of the sorbet and rest it next to the ice cream. Garnish with Concord grapes, some whole and some cut in half.

Peanut Butter Ice Cream (page 122)

Cluster of Concord grapes or any dark, pretty, flavorful grapes

You can make some components in advance:

UP TO 2 MONTHS BEFORE
➥ make the cherries

UP TO 3 DAYS BEFORE
➥ make the ice cream

THE DAY BEFORE
➥ make the grits

JUST BEFORE SERVING
➥ pop the popcorn
➥ plate the dessert

MINIMALIST VERSION
If you don't have time to make the ice cream, serve the cherries and the grits and maybe a handful of popcorn.

CHERRIES OF THE CORN

creamy grits, wine-soaked cherries, sweet corn ice cream, popcorn, fleur de sel

serves 4 to 6

Chef Roger Feeley, who worked at Citizen Cake for a few years, wanted to make a dessert from corn and cherries. Chef Sara Ko and I told him, "Blueberries, yes. But corn and cherries?" "Cherries," Roger insisted, and that is how this combination of creamy grits, Cabernet-soaked cherries, and sweet corn ice cream came to be. It is finished with popcorn and *fleur de sel*, which takes the whole concept over the top.

I can't take credit for this dessert's great name. One day, while walking upstairs to the Citizen Cake offices, I heard Sara and wine director John Mark laughing hysterically. Sara had come up with the name Cherries of the Corn, and John had printed it on the dessert menu in a spooky font. That was a great moment, because it made me realize that my coworkers got it when it came to naming our desserts.

Which grits you use will make a difference. Avoid buying packages marked "instant" or "precooked." We use the amazing Anson Mills grits at the restaurant, and I also lean toward Bob's Red Mill grits, which are reassuringly labeled "Organic Corn Grits also known as Polenta" (see Resources). You can also use good-quality polenta.

When cherries are at their peak, I make many batches of the red wine–soaked cherries because they keep for so long. I love having them ready to go any time I want this dessert or Black on Black (page 64).

To Make the SWEET CORN ICE CREAM

Set up an ice bath by half filling a large bowl with ice and water. Have ready a heatproof storage container or bowl that fits in the ice bath and a fine-mesh strainer or chinois.

Cut the kernels off the corn cob. (You won't use the kernels in the ice cream, so store them in your fridge for another use.) Break the cob in half, and put it in a medium saucepan with the milk and cream. Place over medium heat and cook for about 5 minutes, or until the mixture just comes to a boil. Remove from the heat and let the cob halves steep in the hot milk mixture for 20 minutes. Remove the cob halves, letting any excess liquid run back into the pan, and discard them. Return the milk mixture to medium-low heat to warm gently.

Sweet Corn Ice Cream

1 ear corn, husk and silk removed

1 cup whole milk

1/4 cup heavy cream

3 (1 1/2 ounces) large egg yolks

2 tablespoons (1 ounce) granulated sugar

1/4 teaspoon kosher salt

In a bowl, whisk together the egg yolks and sugar until blended. Whisk a few tablespoons of the hot milk mixture into the egg mixture. Then, while whisking steadily, slowly add the rest of the hot milk mixture to the egg mixture. Return the mixture to the saucepan and place over medium-low heat. Cook, stirring constantly but gently with a wooden spoon or heatproof spatula, for 3 to 4 minutes, or until the custard begins to thicken. The custard is done when the light lacy foam on the surface vanishes or when you run your finger across the back of the spoon and the line holds.

Pour the custard through the strainer into the heatproof container. Stir in the salt, nest the container in the ice bath, and let cool for about 20 minutes, or until completely cooled. Cover and refrigerate for at least 2 hours or up to overnight.

Pour the custard into an ice cream maker and freeze according to the manufacturer's directions. Store in a covered container in the freezer for 1 to 2 hours before you plate the dessert. It will keep for 1 week but tastes best if served within 3 days. You should have about 1^1/$_4$ cups.

To Make the CREAMY GRITS

Creamy Grits

2^1/$_2$ cups water

^{1}/$_2$ cup (2^1/$_2$ ounces) corn grits (see headnote) or polenta

2 teaspoons kosher salt

3 tablespoons (1^1/$_2$ ounces) unsalted butter

^{1}/$_4$ cup (2 ounces) mascarpone cheese or crème fraîche (page 221)

1 tablespoon honey

Small pinch of ground cinnamon

Have ready a sheet of parchment paper. In a saucepan, heat the water over medium-high heat for about 3 minutes, or until lukewarm. Whisk in the grits, add the salt and butter, lower the heat to medium-low, and cook, stirring every 4 to 5 minutes, for 30 minutes. Keep the mixture at a simmer and reduce the heat to low if the grits begin to boil.

After 30 minutes, taste the grits. They should be cooked through but al dente. If they are too hard, simmer for another 10 minutes. Remove from the heat, stir in the mascarpone, honey, and cinnamon and cover the surface with the parchment paper. If you are plating the dessert right away, let the grits stand for 5 minutes, to cool slightly. If you have made the grits ahead of time, rewarm them over medium-low heat, stirring constantly, just before plating. You should have about 2^1/$_2$ cups.

To Plate the Dessert

Wine-Soaked Cherries (page 209)

Fleur de sel for sprinkling

^{1}/$_2$ cup freshly popped popcorn or lightly crushed CornNuts

Evenly divide the warm grits among plates or bowls. Spoon cherry halves over each mound of grits, along with a drizzle of the syrup from the cherries. Make a quenelle (see page 37) or a scoop of the ice cream and set it either off to the side or in the center of the grits. Garnish the ice cream with a few grains of *fleur de sel* and scatter the popcorn around the plate.

CHERRIES OF THE CORN

You can make some components in advance:

UP TO 3 MONTHS BEFORE

➥ make the *membrillo*

UP TO 2 DAYS BEFORE

➥ make the churro dough and refrigerate it

JUST BEFORE SERVING

➥ make the *gastrique*

➥ toss the almonds with the *pimentón*

➥ cook the churros

➥ plate the dessert

MINIMALIST VERSION

Serve Manchego cheese and the *membrillo* with the almonds. If you want to focus on making the churros, you can buy great quince paste in Latin groceries and many well-stocked supermarkets.

SPANISH QUINCITION

manchego churros, membrillo, paprika almonds, sherry gastrique

serves **6**

In Spain, the combination of Manchego cheese, the dark, fruity quince paste known as *membrillo*, and crunchy Marcona almonds, served with sherry, is a fixture in tapas bars. I knew I wanted those flavors—Manchego, quince, almonds, and sherry—but in a different form. I decided to make the cheese into little savory churros that are crispy outside and very tender inside—perfect paired with the quince paste and popped into your mouth while still warm. The dough for the churros is based on a classic *pâte à choux* recipe; the same recipe, but doubled and minus the cheese and pepper, can be used for cream puffs and profiteroles (page 200). You can make the dough a day or two ahead if you like and keep it refrigerated until 30 minutes before heating the oil.

This homemade quince paste is softer than store-bought *membrillo*—closer to the consistency of apple sauce—and a gorgeous rose color. It keeps for months in the refrigerator, too, although its color will fade over time.

To Make the MEMBRILLO

In a medium saucepan, combine the quinces, 2 cups (14 ounces) of the sugar, the ¼ cup lemon juice, and the water and place over medium-high heat. Heat for 5 to 7 minutes, or until the mixture comes to a boil. Reduce the heat to medium-low and simmer uncovered, adjusting the heat as needed to maintain a gentle simmer, for 30 to 40 minutes, or until the quinces are tender when pierced with a knife tip. Drain the quinces, reserving the liquid. Reserve the pan.

Let the quinces cool for 10 minutes, then put the fruit in a blender. Measure 1½ cups of the reserved liquid, add it to the blender, and process until smooth. (The mixture will still be hot, so take care and hold the blender lid, covered with a kitchen towel, firmly in place.) Pour the puree back into the saucepan, add the remaining 1 cup (7 ounces) sugar, the 2 tablespoons lemon juice, and the lemon zest. Clip a candy thermometer onto the side of the pan, place over medium-high heat, and cook, stirring constantly, for about 20 minutes, or until the mixture registers 180°F on the thermometer. You can see the water slowly evaporating from the quince paste as it takes on its rosy color. Pour the quince paste into a heatproof dish and allow it to cool to room temperature. Leave it at room temperature if you will be plating the dessert the same day. Or, cover and refrigerate for up to 3 months.

Membrillo

2 pounds quinces (about 3 quinces), peeled, quartered, cored, and coarsely chopped

3 cups (21 ounces) granulated sugar

¼ cup plus 2 tablespoons fresh lemon juice (from about 2 lemons)

4 cups water

½ teaspoon finely grated lemon zest

Sherry Gastrique

2 tablespoons (1 ounce) granulated sugar

4 tablespoons water

1 teaspoon honey

1 tablespoon sherry

1 tablespoon sherry vinegar

Manchego Churros

1/2 cup water

2 tablespoons (1 ounce) unsalted butter

1 teaspoon granulated sugar

1/4 teaspoon kosher salt

1/4 cup plus 3 tablespoons (about 2 ounces) all-purpose flour

2 (3 ounces by weight) large eggs

1 1/2 cups (about 3 1/2 ounces) grated Manchego cheese

1 crank on a pepper mill of black pepper

Canola oil for deep-frying

To Make the SHERRY GASTRIQUE

In a small saucepan, combine the sugar, 1 tablespoon of the water, and the honey, stirring to dissolve the sugar. Place over medium-high heat and cook, without stirring, for about 4 minutes, or until the mixture turns a light amber. Remove from the heat. Working carefully because the mixture will splatter, pour in the sherry, vinegar, and the remaining 3 tablespoons water. Some of the ingredients will seize up, or form clumps. Return the pan to medium-high heat and bring the mixture to a rolling boil to melt the clumps. As soon as the mixture is lump free, pour it into a heatproof container and set aside. You should have about 1/4 cup.

To Make the MANCHEGO CHURROS

In a medium saucepan, combine the water, butter, sugar, and salt and place over high heat. Heat for 2 to 3 minutes, or until the butter is melted and the mixture comes to a boil. Remove from the heat, immediately add the flour all at once, and stir the mixture with a heatproof spatula or wooden spoon until a thick dough forms. Return the pan to medium heat and continue to stir the dough, being careful to scrape the bottom and sides of the pan, for about 2 minutes, or until the dough comes together in a mass and you can smell the aroma of cooked flour.

Transfer the dough to the bowl of a stand mixer fitted with the paddle attachment, or to a large bowl if using a handheld mixer. With the mixer on medium speed, add the eggs one at a time, beating well after each addition until incorporated. This will take about 3 minutes total. Stir in the cheese and pepper. The dough can be stored in the refrigerator (covered in a bowl, or in the pastry bag you will use when it is time to fry the churros) for up to 2 days.

Preheat the oven to 250°F. Line a baking sheet with paper towels and place it near the stove top.

Pour canola oil to a depth of 3 to 4 inches into a deep 2-quart pot. Clip a candy thermometer onto the side of the pan and heat over medium-high heat until the oil registers 350°F on the thermometer. If you don't have a thermometer, heat the oil for about 10 minutes and then drop in a nugget of the dough; if it sizzles vigorously and begins to color immediately, the oil is ready. While the oil heats, spoon the dough into a pastry bag fitted with a 1/4- to 1/2-inch plain or star tip. If you don't have a pastry bag, have a large spoon ready for spooning the batter into the oil.

When the oil is ready, pipe the batter into the hot oil, slicing off segments about 2 inches long and being careful not to crowd the pot. (If you are having trouble slicing off the dough sections, try dipping your knife into the hot oil before cutting.) The churros will sink in the oil and then slowly float to the top as they cook. Cook for 2 to 3 minutes, or until golden brown on the underside, and then flip them with a slotted spoon or tongs. Cook

for 2 to 3 minutes longer, or until golden brown on the second side. Using the slotted spoon or tongs, transfer the churros to the prepared pan to drain and slip the pan into the oven to keep them warm. Working in batches, repeat with the remaining dough. As soon as the last churro is cooked, be ready to plate the dessert. You should have about 2 dozen 2-inch churros.

To Plate the Dessert

¹/₄ cup (about 1¹/₂ ounces) Marcona almonds or roasted almonds

¹/₂ teaspoon *pimentón* (see Resources)

Manchego cheese for grating

Toss the almonds with the *pimentón*. Place 4 or 5 churros on each plate. Make a quenelle (see page 37) of *membrillo* if freshly made, or cut a wedge if made in advance, and place a few inches from the churros. Drizzle the *gastrique* on the plate around the *membrillo* and scatter a few almonds around the plate. To finish, lightly dust the churros with grated Manchego, preferably from a Microplane grater.

You can make some
components in advance:

UP TO 2 WEEKS BEFORE
- make the streusel

UP TO 1 WEEK BEFORE
- make the gel

UP TO 3 DAYS BEFORE
- make the sorbet

A FEW HOURS BEFORE
- make the cilantro-
  mint oil

JUST BEFORE SERVING
- slice the pineapple
- make the straw-
  berry *brunoise*
- melt the chocolate
- make the bananas
  Foster
- plate the dessert

MINIMALIST VERSION

Rather than making
a minimalist version
of this, think about
which banana split
flavors you want to
emphasize and create
your own version.

BANANAS FOSTER CANE SPLIT

pineapple sashimi, strawberry sorbet, strawberry brunoise, bananas foster with rum, cacao nib streusel, vanilla gel, melted chocolate, cilantro-mint oil, brandied cherries

serves **6** to **8**

You would never think a banana split could be refreshing, but this one is. Light, striking, and playful, this dessert has nine components, but every one of them is quick to make.

We have done lots of riffs on the banana split at Citizen Cake. I regularly give out an assignment to our pastry chefs, asking them to take apart and reassemble a classic dessert, with a banana split often the test. Some chefs think pineapple is important, while others insist that chocolate, banana, or even the cherry makes a split or breaks it. Citizen Cake chef Yuko Fujii made a version of a banana split with brioche beignets fried around a chunk of banana, and then injected with caramel and plated with vanilla whipped cream, chocolate agar noodles, straw-berry-ginger sorbet, dehydrated strawberry chips, and asparagus foam. Pairing strawberries and asparagus may sound strange, but the greenness of the aspara-gus flavor and the sweet-and-hot sorbet work beautifully together. The traditional elements of a banana split are all there but remodeled into striking textures.

Run any direction you like with your banana split. This recipe is just one way to go. For the rum, I have used 10 Cane, which is a flavorful white rum, but a dark rum of the Venezuelan persuasion would also be a knockout. You can make your own brandied cherries by soaking sour cherries in sugar and eau-de-vie, but you can also buy good ones (see Resources).

To Make the STRAWBERRY SORBET

In a saucepan, combine the strawberries, sugar, and water over medium heat and bring just to a boil, stirring occasionally. Remove from the heat and let the strawberries cool in the syrup for about 30 minutes. Transfer the berry mixture to a blender and process until smooth, or process in the pan with an immersion blender until smooth. Strain the puree through a medium- or fine-mesh strainer into a bowl and stir in the lemon juice, Coin-treau, and salt. I like to recover some of the strawberry seeds caught by the strainer—just a small amount—and add them back to the mixture, but you can decide whether you want a hint of seeds or a perfectly smooth sorbet. Cover and refrigerate the puree for at least 2 hours or up to overnight.

Briefly stir the mixture to redistribute any seeds that have settled to the bottom, and then pour into an ice cream maker and freeze according to the

Strawberry Sorbet

- 2 cups (12 ounces) hulled and quartered strawberries
- 1/4 cup plus 1 tablespoon (2 ounces) granulated sugar
- 1 cup water
- 1 tablespoon fresh lemon juice
- 1 tablespoon Cointreau
- Pinch of kosher salt

manufacturer's directions. Store in a covered container in the freezer for 1 to 2 hours before you plate the dessert. It will keep for up to 1 week but will taste best if served within 3 days. You should have about 2³/4 cups.

To Make the PINEAPPLE SASHIMI

Pineapple Sashimi

¹/2 pineapple, about 2 pounds

Peel the pineapple half, and cut lengthwise into 4 equal wedges. Cut away the core from each wedge. Cover and refrigerate until ready to plate.

To Make the STRAWBERRY BRUNOISE

Strawberry Brunoise

1 cup (6 ounces) strawberries, hulled

Brunoise is a method of cutting a food into small, even squares. Cut the strawberry into thin slices. (Watch your fingers here.) Cut the slices into thin julienne strips, and then cut across the strips to form tiny strawberry squares. Set the squares aside until you are ready to plate the dessert. You should have about ³/4 cup.

To Make the BANANAS FOSTER WITH RUM

Bananas Foster with Rum

¹/2 cup (6¹/2 ounces by weight) Basic Caramel Sauce (page 210)

¹/4 cup good rum

2 large bananas (about 1 pound total), peeled and cut into ¹/2-inch-thick slices

1 tablespoon fresh lime juice

The bananas cook quickly, so don't begin this step until you are ready to plate the dessert. Pour the caramel sauce into a 10-inch sauté pan or skillet and place over high heat. When you see small bubbles, rotate the pan once or twice so the caramel sauce heats evenly. As soon as all the caramel sauce is hot, remove the pan from the heat and add the rum. Place the pan back on the heat, tilting it slightly so the rum ignites and taking care to stand back because the rum will flame up. If you have an electric stove, use a long match to ignite the rum—again being very careful. When the flame has subsided, add the banana slices and lime juice. Gently turn the bananas so they are coated with the caramel. You should have about 1³/4 cups.

To Plate the Dessert

2 ounces bittersweet chocolate, melted
Vanilla Gel (page 219)

³/4 cup Cacao Nib Streusel (page 218)

¹/4 cup Herb Oil, cilantro version (page 220)

6 to 12 brandied cherries (see headnote; optional)

I like to use long, narrow plates—and ultramodern are better—but choose any serving plates you like. Make a thin line or scroll of chocolate down the length of one side of each plate. With a sharp knife, cut each pineapple wedge into very thin slices—like sashimi—and fan a few of the slices across one end of each plate. Nearby, make a small, loose nest of the strawberry *brunoise*, with more on the edges and less in the center. Place small wedges or scoops of vanilla gel at either end of the plate. Divide the bananas Foster evenly among the plates, spooning the banana slices and their sauce down the center. Sprinkle a little streusel on each plate. Make a quenelle (see page 37) or a small scoop of strawberry sorbet and place it on the *brunoise* nest. Drizzle a little cilantro-mint oil on the pineapple. Add 1 brandied cherry to each plate.

You can make some
components in advance:

UP TO 3 DAYS BEFORE

→ make the ice cream

THE DAY BEFORE

→ make the filo shards

JUST BEFORE SERVING

→ have the garnishes
ready

→ grill the figs

→ plate the dessert

MINIMALIST VERSION

Serve a quenelle of ice
cream with the grilled
figs and the garnishes
if you like, and forget
about the filo shards.

THE M WORD

grilled figs, mastic ice cream, filo shards

serves 4

This is probably the most unusual dessert in the book because Americans don't often see mastic, an amazing old-world gum that has been used in pastry and confectionary for centuries (see Secret Agent, page 140). Many modern chefs, both American and European, are afraid of mastic or don't like its flavor. But I love its resiny taste, especially for ice cream. It reminds me of retsina, the old-school Greek wine. (Just as mastic is used less frequently in cooking today, Greek wine-makers are shying away from retsina in favor of milder wines, which is too bad.) Mastic tastes the way fresh pine needles smell and is great with other Greek ingredients, such as figs, honey, oranges, olive oil, filo, pistachios, rosemary, and lavender. You can use lavender or rosemary to flavor the ice cream if you don't have mastic, but the mastic adds body and texture to the ice cream that the herbs can't match.

While Sabrina and I were in Athens, we ducked into a little café for ice cream. We ordered plain vanilla, but when we tasted it, I realized that it had been made with mastic. To find an ingredient that is considered new and exotic at home in an everyday bowl of ice cream in Greece made me think of all the flavors in the world that I haven't yet had the chance to try.

Mastic, which is sold in packets or tins (see Resources), looks like small crystals of rock sugar. The crystals come in three sizes: small, medium, and large tears. Any size works for this dessert because you grind the sticky crystals in a mortar. If you don't have a mortar, wrap the crystals in plastic wrap and gently smash them with a hammer. Begin making the ice cream at least 6 hours before you plan to serve it; a day or two ahead is even better.

A note about the filo shards: Here they are made with butter and a quick mix of cinnamon and sugar. In the recipe for Suddenly Last Summer (page 92), the shards are made with ground pistachios and olive oil. Either will work in this recipe.

Mastic Ice Cream

1 teaspoon ground mastic gum, or 2 teaspoons dried, crushed lavender flowers or finely chopped fresh or dried rosemary

2 cups whole milk

1/4 cup (1 3/4 ounces) granulated sugar

1/4 cup (3 ounces) honey

1 cup heavy cream

1 tablespoon nonfat dry milk powder

1/4 teaspoon kosher salt

Filo Shards

3 sheets filo dough, each 9 by 14 inches (see Help with Filo Dough, page 95)

2 tablespoons (1 ounce) unsalted butter, preferably clarified (page 217), melted

1 1/2 tablespoons turbinado sugar

1/4 teaspoon ground cinnamon

Grilled Figs

6 Black Mission or Adriatic figs, halved lengthwise

4 tablespoons (1 3/4 ounces by weight) olive oil

Pinch of kosher salt

1 tablespoon fresh lemon juice

2 tablespoons (1 1/2 ounces by weight) honey

To Make the MASTIC ICE CREAM

Set up an ice bath by half filling a large bowl with ice and water. Have ready a heatproof storage container or bowl that fits in the ice bath.

In a medium saucepan, combine the mastic, milk, sugar, and honey and place over medium heat. Heat, stirring to dissolve the sugar and the mastic as much as possible, for 7 to 8 minutes, or just until the mixture comes to a boil (small bubbles will appear around the edges of the pan). The mastic won't dissolve completely and may even clump up, but don't worry about this. Remove the pan from the heat and stir in the cream, milk powder, and salt. Pour the custard into the heatproof container, nest the container in the ice bath, and let cool completely, stirring occasionally. Cover and refrigerate for at least 2 hours or up to overnight.

Briefly stir the custard and then pour into an ice cream maker and freeze according to the manufacturer's directions. Store in a covered container in the freezer for 1 to 2 hours before you plate the dessert. It will keep for 1 week but will taste best if served within 3 days. You should have about 3 cups.

To Make the FILO SHARDS

Position a rack in the center of the oven and preheat the oven to 350°F. Lightly brush a baking sheet with butter and line with parchment paper. Brush the parchment lightly with butter.

In a small bowl, stir together the turbinado sugar and cinnamon. Lay 1 sheet of filo dough on the parchment-lined pan. Brush the filo with some of the butter. Sprinkle the filo with about one-third of the sugar mixture. Lay a second sheet of filo on top, brush with more butter, and sprinkle with half of the remaining sugar mixture. Repeat with the remaining filo sheet, butter, and sugar mixture.

Bake the filo stack for 10 to 12 minutes, or until the filo is golden brown. Watch the filo closely, as the color will change quickly. Let cool completely on the pan on a cooling rack. If you are making the shards in advance, cover gently with plastic wrap.

To Grill the FIGS

Preheat a gas or charcoal grill, a grill pan, or a griddle to medium-high. (If using a charcoal grill, the fire should be hot but the coals should be covered with ash, not flaming.)

In a bowl, toss the figs with 2 tablespoons of the olive oil, using your fingers to coat the figs evenly with the oil. Place the figs cut side down on the grill or pan and grill for 2 to 4 minutes, or until the surface has lightly caramelized and grill marks are visible. Turn the figs over and grill for 1 minute more. Remove the figs from the heat.

In a medium bowl, stir together the salt, lemon juice, honey, and the remaining 2 tablespoons olive oil. Add the warm figs and toss lightly to coat.

To Plate the Dessert

Break the filo into shards and dust with powdered sugar. Divide the warm fig halves among plates or bowls. Garnish each serving with an equal amount of the pine nuts and with drizzles of honey. Make a quenelle (see page 37) or a scoop of the ice cream and set it in the center of each plate. Finely grate some orange zest over the figs and the ice cream, preferably with a Microplane grater. Place a filo shard on each plate next to the ice cream. Drizzle olive oil around the edge of the plate and follow the oil with a few drops of balsamic vinegar. Serve while the figs are still warm.

About 1 teaspoon powdered sugar for dusting

About 2 tablespoons (1/2 ounce) pine nuts, toasted (see page 157)

About 1/4 cup honey for drizzling

1 orange with a bright, fresh peel for grating

About 1 tablespoon extra virgin olive oil for drizzling

About 2 teaspoons balsamic vinegar for sprinkling

secret agent

The more I experiment with gelling agents, the more excited I become about the different properties of these gums and hydrocolloids and how they allow me to play with texture. These ingredients thicken, emulsify, and stabilize foods easily. You can use your blender to whip guar gum, blueberries, and water into a beautiful, thick fruit sauce in a few seconds (page 208). A tiny amount of xanthan gum used in place of gelatin produces marshmallows that are light and airy with much less effort (page 213). And a mixture gelled with agar agar, which will set up at room temperature (unlike gelatin, which needs to be refrigerated), doesn't melt when warmed or in tropical or humid environments.

Most gelling agents come from natural sources. Guar gum comes from a tree native to India. Mastic gum is the resin from a tree that grows on a Greek island. Xanthan gum, which is produced from fermented corn, was discovered in the 1950s as a by-product of cornstarch manufacturing. These are just some of the gums I have worked with, and each has its own characteristics. For information on where to buy them, see Resources.

Agar agar

Called *kanten*, Japanese gelatin, or simply agar, agar agar is made from dried seaweed and is sold in chunks, powder, flakes, and strands. There is no hint of fishiness or seaweed to its taste, and in fact, I think it tastes cleaner than gelatin. I mostly use the flakes or the powder, but you can try the other forms, too. Agar agar has a strong gelling action, so you use much less of it than you would gelatin. You can use agar agar with warm foods because it can set at temperatures up to 105°F, and once set it won't melt until it reaches 172°F.

Carrageenan

Extracted from red seaweed, carrageenan has been used for hundreds of years as a thickener, emulsifier, and stabilizer. Because carrageenan molecules are highly flexible, they can form gels of various viscosities at room temperature.

Guar gum

This powdered gelling agent comes from the seeds of a legume tree that grows only in India. Guar gum is especially good for stabilizing ice cream (it keeps ice cream smooth by preventing any water from crystallizing) and for thickening vegetarian dishes and gluten-free foods.

Locust bean gum

You can use locust bean gum, which is extracted from the seeds of the carob tree, on its own, but I typically use it with xanthan gum (see opposite). It forms a gelling platform that lets the xanthan perform better.

Mastic gum

Mastic, which looks like crystals of rock sugar, comes from a tree in the pistachio family that grows mainly on the Greek island of Chios. It doesn't have the strong gelling properties of other gums, but it has been used since ancient times and has a unique flavor similar to that of retsina, the popular Greek wine. See The M Word (page 137) for my favorite way to use this ingredient.

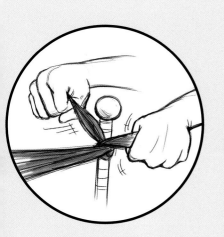

Xanthan gum

Xanthan gum holds on to water molecules better than gelatin and other gums, which means that it won't "perspire," or leak out water, so foods keep a particularly juicy taste and texture. The source of xanthan gum differs around the world, but in the United States it is primarily a by-product of cornstarch manufacturing. A bacterium, *Xanthonomonas campestris*, produces the gum as a result of fermentation. This may sound alarming, but this is a good bacterium, just like the bacteria that cause bread to rise or wine to ferment.

You can make some
components in advance:

UP TO 2 WEEKS BEFORE

- make the streusel

UP TO 1 WEEK BEFORE

- make the ganache

- make the ice cream
  (if using version 2)

UP TO 2 DAYS BEFORE

- make the shortbread

- make the raspberry
  sauce

- make the truffles

- make the ice cream
  (if using version 1)

JUST BEFORE SERVING

- make the cake

- plate the dessert

MINIMALIST VERSION

Serve the warm cake
with the raspberry
sauce and raspberries
and/or the streusel.

BATTLESHIP POTEMKIN

warm white chocolate cake with a dark chocolate center, odessa steps chocolate
shortbread, chocolate ice cream, bloodshed raspberries

serves 6

Inspiration comes from many sources: fiction and nonfiction, people, places, songs and lyrics, films, and architecture. In 1992, when I became the pastry chef at Elka in the Miyako Hotel, this was the first dessert that I presented to my wait staff. I told them that it was inspired by a scene in *The Battleship Potemkin*, a 1925 silent film by Sergei Eisenstein that forever changed both cinematography and film editing. I explained that the story takes place during the Russian Revolution of 1905, and that it depicts the crew of the battleship *Potemkin* rising up against their cruel officers. I described the heart-wrenching scene on the Odessa Steps in which scores of civilians are slaughtered. I showed them how I had made small Odessa Steps out of chocolate shortbread, with raspberry sauce–covered raspberries representing the bloodshed of the victims. When I was done talking, all seven of them stood staring at me, mouths hanging open. None of them said a word, but I could tell they were thinking, "What planet did *she* come from?" Finally one of them asked, "You want us to *say* that to our customers . . . about the bloodshed on the Odessa Steps?" "Yes," I told him. "I do."

To get the dark center in the white cake, you will need to drop a ganache truffle into the batter before baking. Unlike classic truffles, these are rolled in cocoa powder, not dipped in dark chocolate and then rolled.

I have given you two recipes for the chocolate ice cream. I prefer the first one, but it is more delicate and is best used within a day or two. If you want to make the ice cream a week ahead, use the second version. You have options with the shortbread cookies as well. You can make your own Odessa Steps from the cookies or, to plate the dessert more quickly, simply crush the cookies and make a small nest of crumbs for the ice cream.

Dark Chocolate Ganache (page 206)

Make the ganache as directed. You will use some for making the ice cream, some for making the truffles, and some for building the steps. Set aside ¹/₂ cup of the warm chocolate ganache to make the ice cream, and then spoon the remaining ganache into a pastry bag fitted with a ¹/₄-inch plain tip (or into a plastic bag) and refrigerate. Remove the ganache from the refrigerator 30 minutes before making the truffles.

Dark Chocolate Ice Cream Version I

¹/₂ cup (4³/₄ ounces) still-warm dark chocolate ganache

1 cup (9 ounces) Crème Anglaise (page 202)

Pinch of kosher salt

Splash of Cognac

To Make the DARK CHOCOLATE ICE CREAM VERSION 1

While the ganache is still warm, in a bowl, combine the ¹/₂ cup ganache with the crème anglaise. Stir in the salt and the Cognac. Cover and refrigerate for at least 2 hours or up to overnight.

Pour the ganache mixture into an ice cream maker and freeze according to the manufacturer's directions. Store in a covered container in the freezer for 1 to 2 hours before you plate the dessert. This makes a classic custard-based ice cream that is delicious but won't keep for more than a day or two. If you want an ice cream that lasts longer, make the following version. You should have about 1¹/₄ cups.

Dark Chocolate Ice Cream Version II

¹/₂ cup (4³/₄ ounces) still-warm dark chocolate ganache

1 cup (9 ounces) Crème Anglaise (page 202)

Pinch of kosher salt

Splash of Cognac

2 tablespoons (about ¹/₄ ounce) unsweetened cocoa powder, preferably natural

2 tablespoons (1¹/₂ ounces by weight) light corn syrup

¹/₄ teaspoon guar gum (see Secret Agent, page 140)

1 cup whole milk

To Make the DARK CHOCOLATE ICE CREAM VERSION 2

While the ganache is still warm, in a bowl, combine the ¹/₂ cup ganache with the crème anglaise. Stir in the salt and the Cognac. Set aside.

In a small bowl, stir together the cocoa powder, corn syrup, and guar gum until a thick paste forms. Add to the ganache custard and stir in the milk. Cover and refrigerate for at least 2 hours or up to overnight.

Pour the ganache mixture into an ice cream maker, and freeze according to the manufacturer's directions. Store in a covered container in the freezer for 1 to 2 hours before you plate the dessert. It will keep for 1 week but will taste best if served within 3 days. You should have about 3 cups.

Odessa Steps Chocolate Shortbread

¹/₂ cup plus 2 tablespoons (3 ounces) all-purpose flour

¹/₄ cup plus 2 tablespoons (1 ounce) unsweetened cocoa powder, preferably natural

¹/₄ teaspoon kosher salt

6 tablespoons (3 ounces) unsalted butter, softened but still cool

¹/₄ cup plus 1 tablespoon (2¹/₄ ounces) granulated sugar

¹/₂ teaspoon pure vanilla extract

To Make the ODESSA STEPS CHOCOLATE SHORTBREAD

In a medium bowl, stir together the flour, cocoa powder, and salt and set aside. In a large bowl, using a stand mixer fitted with the paddle attachment or a handheld mixer, beat together the butter and sugar on medium speed for 1 to 2 minutes, or until creamy and smooth. Beat in the vanilla. Add the flour mixture to the butter mixture in two additions, stirring after each addition until combined. The mixture will look dry at first, but it will come together if you continue to stir.

Cover and refrigerate for at least 30 minutes or up to overnight. If you refrigerate the dough for more than 2 hours, remove it from the refrigerator about 30 minutes before you plan to make the shortbread, kneading the dough once or twice after it warms slightly.

Position a rack in the center of the oven and preheat the oven to 350°F. Line a baking sheet with parchment paper.

On a lightly floured work surface, roll out the dough into a rectangle about 6 by 7 inches and ¼ inch thick. Cut the dough into rectangles about the length of your finger, 3 inches long by 1 inch wide, to make 24 steps that are more or less equal. You can use a ruler to make precise steps, but you don't have to go that far. Arrange on the prepared pan.

Bake the shortbread for 8 to 10 minutes, or until the aroma of chocolate fills your kitchen and the cookies are crisp. Let the cookies cool completely on the pan on a cooling rack. The shortbread rises as it bakes, but it sinks as it cools. The cookies will stay crisp for a few days in an airtight container at room temperature.

To Make the BLOODSHED RASPBERRIES

In a saucepan, combine the raspberries, sugar, and water and place over high heat. Bring to a boil, stir once, reduce the heat to low, and simmer for 2 to 3 minutes, or until the sugar has melted and the fruit has begun to break down. Remove from the heat and let cool completely.

Transfer the berry mixture to a blender and process until smooth. Pour through a fine-mesh strainer into a bowl. Cover and refrigerate the sauce for at least 2 hours or up to 2 days.

Bloodshed Raspberries

1 cup (about 4 ounces) raspberries

3 tablespoons (1¼ ounces) granulated sugar

¼ cup water

To Make the DARK CHOCOLATE GANACHE TRUFFLES

Line a plate or pie pan with parchment paper. If you have stored the ganache in a plastic bag, cut off a corner to make a ¼-inch hole. Pipe out 6 truffles, each about ¾ inch in diameter, onto the prepared plate. Refrigerate for about 30 minutes.

Pour the cocoa powder into a small bowl or saucer. One at a time, set the truffles in the cocoa, roll to coat evenly, and return them to the plate. Set the plate aside while you make the cake batter. Reserve the remaining ganache in the pastry bag for building your steps.

Dark Chocolate Ganache Truffles

Dark chocolate ganache

2 tablespoons (about ¼ ounce) unsweetened cocoa powder, preferably natural

To Make the WHITE CHOCOLATE CAKE

Position a rack in the center of the oven and preheat the oven to 350°F. Butter six ½-cup ramekins, nonstick standard muffin-tin cups, or ½-cup cake molds. (The ramekins work best.) If using ramekins or molds, place them on a baking sheet to bring them out of the oven more easily.

Bring a few inches of water to a gentle simmer in a saucepan. Combine the white chocolate and butter in a heatproof bowl and place over (not touching) the simmering water (or use a double boiler). Heat slowly, stirring occasionally, until nearly melted, and then remove the bowl from the heat and stir until smooth. Set aside.

Sift the flour into a large bowl and lightly stir in the almond meal and salt. Set aside. Whisk the sugar into the melted chocolate, and then whisk in

White Chocolate Cake

8 ounces white chocolate, coarsely chopped (about 1⅔ cups)

2 tablespoons (1 ounce) unsalted butter

½ cup plus 2 tablespoons (3 ounces) all-purpose flour

1 cup plus 1 tablespoon (4 ounces) almond meal (see Resources)

½ teaspoon kosher salt

3 tablespoons (1¼ ounces) granulated sugar

3 (4½ ounces by weight) large eggs

¼ teaspoon pure vanilla extract

the eggs and vanilla until smooth. Add the flour mixture to the white chocolate mixture and whisk until the batter is smooth. Divide the batter evenly among the prepared ramekins, using a liquid measuring cup to pour if you like. Set a chocolate truffle in the center of each cake and gently push it to the bottom of the batter with your finger.

Bake the cakes for 12 minutes, or until pale brown around the edges. Remove from the oven and let cool for 5 minutes, and then turn them out of the molds onto a cooling rack or a plate while they are still hot. Plate the desserts while the cakes are still warm.

Dark chocolate ganache

About 2 ounces bittersweet chocolate, melted

Unsweetened cocoa powder, preferably natural, for dusting

1 cup (about 4 ounces) raspberries

3 tablespoons Cacao Nib Streusel (page 218) or cacao nibs (see Resources)

To Plate the Dessert

Make six 2-step staircases—or add more steps to each if you like—out of the shortbread by stacking the cookies with a slight overhang and cementing them in place with the reserved ganache. Place a set of steps on one side of each plate. Using a small offset spatula, make a Rodchenko-style stripe of melted chocolate across each plate. If you need to rewarm the chocolate, the microwave is the easiest way to do it. Place the warm white chocolate cake beside the steps, slightly off center, and dust the top with cocoa powder. Arrange some of the raspberries on the steps and on the plate and then drizzle a little raspberry sauce over each berry. Make a small nest of streusel next to the cake to hold the ice cream. Make a quenelle (see page 37) or a scoop of ice cream and place it on the streusel nest.

DESSERT AS A GESTURE LANGUAGE MOVEMENT

You can make both components in advance:

UP TO 3 MONTHS BEFORE

➥ candy the kumquats

UP TO 3 DAYS BEFORE

➥ make the rice pudding

JUST BEFORE SERVING

➥ ready the garnishes

➥ plate the dessert

MINIMALIST VERSION

Every component is simple, so I wouldn't eliminate any of them.

NORCAL (AN HOMAGE TO LAURA CHENEL)

chèvre rice pudding, dates, candied kumquats, pistachios, honey

serves 4

I am not a big fan of rice pudding, but this version is different because of its use of fresh goat cheese and its method: you cook the rice; make a crème anglaise; stir together the still-warm rice, crème anglaise, and goat cheese; and the pudding is ready. No extra cooking and the result is light, fluffy, and creamy.

The components of this dessert sound Mediterranean, but to me they are more Northern Californian. That's because when I make it, every ingredient—the goat cheese, the honey, the dates, the rice—is from California. Even the kumquats, tangy little citrus fruits that are in season in winter when all the other citrus fruits are in the market, are from California. If you can't find kumquats, you can candy orange slices or orange peel instead.

While writing this book, I read that Laura Chenel had sold her cheese company. Laura was the first person to make and sell French-style goat cheeses in California, and she played an important part in the state's organic food revolution, inspiring a whole generation of chefs and home cooks. I typically use Laura Chenel's chèvre for this recipe, but if you don't see it in your grocery store and don't have time to order it (see Resources), you can use any soft fresh goat cheese.

To Make the CANDIED KUMQUATS

When you cut the kumquats, make the slices about the size of a quarter. Don't go crazy trying to get rid of every seed, but do discard any large seeds that pop out as you cut. In a medium saucepan, bring 2 cups of the water to a boil over high heat and add the salt. Carefully slide the kumquat slices into the boiling water and blanch for 30 seconds. Drain the kumquats, discarding the liquid, and set the kumquat slices aside on a plate.

Pour 2 cups of the water into the same pan and add 1 cup (7 ounces) of the sugar. Bring to a boil over high heat, stirring to dissolve the sugar. Add the kumquats, reduce the heat to low, and simmer for 30 minutes. Drain the kumquats, discarding the liquid, and set the kumquat slices aside on a plate.

Pour the remaining 1 cup water into the same pan and add the remaining 1 1/2 cups (10 1/2 ounces) sugar. Bring to a boil over high heat, stirring to dissolve the sugar. Add the kumquats, reduce the heat to low, and simmer for 30 minutes. Remove the pan from the heat and let the kumquats cool to room temperature in the syrup. You should have a generous 1/2 cup fruit

Candied Kumquats

- 1 cup (8 ounces) sliced kumquats (about 20 kumquats)
- 5 cups water
- 1/2 teaspoon kosher salt
- 2 1/2 cups (17 1/2 ounces) granulated sugar

and 1¹/₄ cups syrup. Transfer the candied kumquats and their syrup to an airtight container and refrigerate until ready to plate the dessert or up to 3 months.

To Make the CHÈVRE RICE PUDDING

In a saucepan, combine the milk, rice, sugar, and salt and place over high heat. Bring the mixture to a boil, reduce the heat to low, cover, and cook, adjusting the heat as needed to keep the rice at a constant low simmer, for 20 minutes, or until the rice is cooked but still slightly firm. Remove from the heat and stir in the goat cheese, orange flower water, and crème anglaise while the rice is still warm. Serve right away, or let cool, cover, and refrigerate for at least 2 hours or up to 3 days. You should have about 1¹/₂ cups.

To Plate the Dessert

Spoon a mound of rice pudding—either hot or chilled—into each bowl. Divide the dates evenly among the bowls. Scatter a few candied kumquats over each pudding and sprinkle with the pistachios. Drizzle each pudding with honey.

Chèvre Rice Pudding

1 cup whole milk

¹/₃ cup (about 2 ounces) jasmine rice

1 tablespoon granulated sugar

¹/₂ teaspoon kosher salt

2 ounces (about ¹/₄ cup) soft fresh goat cheese

2 or 3 drops orange flower water (see Resources)

1 cup (9 ounces) Crème Anglaise (page 202)

4 to 6 large dates, preferably Medjool, pitted and chopped

¹/₄ cup (about 1 ounce) shelled pistachio nuts

2 tablespoons honey

CITIZEN CAKE

CLASSICS

If you look at our desserts from the beginning, certain themes emerge. I have always thought of our desserts as art pieces—like paintings—and just as a painter explores new territory while keeping some recurring themes, so have we expanded our repertoire while staying true to a few original concepts: our often unorthodox use of ingredients, our desire to try new things, our twisted sense of humor.

The recipes in this chapter are a few of Citizen Cake's most popular pâtisserie desserts. Each illustrates one aspect of my approach to baking. Viewed as a body of work, they show the themes and ideas that have inspired us from the beginning.

Start with the traditional—but then go your own way. I love brownies of all persuasions, especially brownies made from rich, dark chocolate. Soon after we created our homemade marshmallows, the idea for the ultimate brownie came to me: add the marshmallows to a dark chocolate brownie with graham cracker shards and chunks of Venezuelan milk chocolate. S'More Brownies have been one of the most popular items at Citizen Cake for a decade.

Take desserts seriously—but not too seriously. As soon as most people see the Retro Tropical Shag cake at our pâtisserie, they laugh, which I consider the ideal frame of mind for tasting a dessert. The coconut-topped Shag has been one of our best-liked cakes—both on a small scale and as a wedding cake—since the first day we made it. I think that's not just because it is a fabulous combination of flavors and textures, but also because it is endearing, amusing, and has a great name.

Find a place for simplicity. The simple but incredible Mexican Wedding Cookies represent a milestone for me because they were my introduction to baker-extraordinaire Marion Cunningham, who wrote to me to ask for the recipe. This cookie is based on a centuries-old recipe that appears to have been carried from the Ottoman Empire through the Mediterranean and on to Latin America. The Sammysnaps, too, are very simple rolled ginger cookies.

No frosting or powdered sugar—just an unadorned cookie the exact color of a dachshund I once knew.

Use unusual ingredients—or usual ingredients but in imaginative ways. When I created Rose Petal Crème Brûlée, which appears here in a slightly different form as Rosebud, I flavored the custard with rose water, which wasn't yet popular among American bakers. Turning people on to ingredients that are new to me is a thrill. And it can be just as exciting to step back from familiar ingredients and reconsider how they might be used in a different way. You can transform fruit into paper (page 115), add saffron to meringues (page 89), or flavor ice cream with breath mints (page 64)—or with anything you like, from curry powder to Parmesan cheese to lemongrass.

At Citizen Cake, as the recipes in chapter 4 illustrated, we like to take a classic dessert and rethink it. But we also like to take our own combinations—even those that have become signature dishes—and reconfigure them in our ongoing search for the perfect interpretation. So today's Rosebud might become tomorrow's Snowglobe, with rose-petal ice cream encased in a blown-sugar bubble, or something even more fantastic.

You can make some
components in advance:

UP TO 1 WEEK BEFORE

- make the graham
  crackers
- make the
  marshmallows

S'MORE BROWNIES

makes about **16** 2¹/4 x 3¹/4-inch brownies

There is something magical about the combination of dark chocolate, marshmallows, and graham crackers. Homemade marshmallows are one reason why these brownies are so popular. Don't be intimidated by the idea of making your own marshmallows and graham crackers. If you can make chocolate chip cookies, you can make these brownies. If the recipe feels a little daunting, just make the graham crackers and the marshmallows ahead of time.

I cut the marshmallows into large chunks or slices for this recipe, so that when you cut the pan into squares, no two brownies look identical. I like that about these brownies—that every square has its own personality.

Position a rack in the center of the oven and preheat the oven to 350°F. Have ready an ungreased 9 by 13-inch baking pan.

Bring a few inches of water to a gentle simmer in a saucepan. Combine the bittersweet chocolate and butter in a heatproof bowl and place over (not touching) the simmering water (or use a double boiler). Heat slowly, stirring occasionally, until nearly melted, and then remove the bowl from the heat and whisk until smooth. Add the granulated and brown sugars and stir until blended. Add the eggs all at once and stir to combine.

In a bowl, sift together the flour and baking powder. Using a whisk or rubber spatula, gently whisk or fold the flour mixture into the chocolate mixture just until combined. Fold in the milk chocolate, graham crackers, and half of the marshmallows. Pour the batter into the prepared pan. Dot the surface of the batter evenly with the remaining marshmallows.

Bake for about 30 minutes, or until slightly souffléed but still wet in the center. The marshmallows will puff up and be a light golden brown and the chocolate surface will crack a little. Let cool in the pan on a cooling rack for about 45 minutes, or until completely cool.

Cut into squares, as big or small as you like. For neater squares, dip your knife into hot water and wipe the blade dry before each cut.

These brownies are very moist and will keep well for up to 2 days if stored at room temperature in an airtight container or tightly wrapped in plastic wrap. But good luck keeping them around that long.

10 ounces bittersweet chocolate, preferably 70% cacao, coarsely chopped (about 2 cups)

1¹/4 cups (10 ounces) unsalted butter, cut into ¹/2-inch pieces

1 cup plus 2 tablespoons (8 ounces) granulated sugar

1 cup plus 2 tablespoons (8 ounces) firmly packed dark brown sugar

5 (7¹/2 ounces by weight) large eggs

1 cup (5 ounces) all-purpose flour

1¹/2 teaspoons baking powder

4 ounces milk chocolate, coarsely chopped (²/3 cup)

4 to 6 Graham Crackers (page 214), broken into large pieces

8 to 10 marshmallows, made with gelatin (page 212) or xanthan gum (page 213)

MEXICAN WEDDING COOKIES

makes about 4 dozen cookies

This cookie was on the cookie plate at Rubicon, and I have always felt it has been blessed by the amazing baking guru-godmother Marion Cunningham. After Marion tasted it, she sent me a letter asking for the recipe. I gave it to her and it was published in her column in the *San Francisco Chronicle*. Marion described the cookie perfectly, saying, "rolling the dough in granulated and powdered sugar before baking creates a thin, delicious layer of icing around the cookie." I will never forget what a good friend and trusted advisor Marion has been throughout my career.

I have updated this recipe since Marion first tasted it by adding cornstarch, which makes the cookie even more tender.

2 cups (8 ounces) powdered sugar, sifted, plus $1/2$ to $3/4$ cup (2 to 3 ounces) for coating the cookies

$1/2$ cup ($3^1/2$ ounces) granulated sugar

1 cup (8 ounces) unsalted butter, softened but still cool

2 teaspoons pure vanilla extract

$1^1/2$ teaspoons water

2 cups (10 ounces) all-purpose flour, sifted

1 cup (4 ounces) cornstarch

1 teaspoon kosher salt

1 cup (4 ounces) finely ground toasted pecans (see page 157), from about $1^1/4$ cups pecan halves

Position racks in the upper third and lower third of the oven and preheat the oven to 350°F. Line 2 baking sheets with parchment paper.

Pour $1/2$ cup of the powdered sugar for coating into a shallow bowl or plate and pour the granulated sugar into another shallow bowl or plate. Set them aside until you are ready to coat the dough.

In a large bowl, using a wooden spoon, cream together the butter and the 2 cups powdered sugar for about 3 minutes, or until smooth and fluffy. I can be lazy about pulling out my stand mixer, so I usually do this by hand. But if you use a stand mixer fitted with the paddle attachment or a hand-held mixer, beat on medium speed for about 1 minute. Add the vanilla and water and stir just until combined. Add the flour, cornstarch, salt, and pecans and stir for 3 to 4 minutes, or until the mixture resembles coarse crumbs (see photo below).

Here comes the only trick to making this cookie: use a light touch when shaping the dough. Lightly press the crumbly chunks of dough together between your palms to form balls the size of walnuts, being carefully not to compact them. Don't try to form perfect, smooth little globes. You want to push the dough together just enough so the balls hold their shape. The looser the dough balls, the lighter the cookie. As the balls are formed, set them aside on a baking sheet or tray.

When all of the balls have been formed, roll each ball first in the granulated sugar and then in the powdered sugar and place on the prepared pans, spacing them about 1/2 inch apart. Don't throw away the powdered sugar yet, because you will give the cookies one final roll in it after they have been baked and cooled.

Bake the cookies, rotating the pans after about 7 minutes, for 14 to 18 minutes, or until lightly golden and just beginning to show cracks. While the cookies are baking, clean any dough crumbs out of your bowl of powdered sugar. If the powdered sugar seems low, add the remaining 1/4 cup to the bowl. You will have powdered sugar left over in the bowl when you finish, but having a good amount will make it easier to give the cookies the final coat.

When the cookies are done, let them cool completely on the pans on cooling racks. Some people like to transfer the cookies to racks, but I generally just let the cookies cool on the parchment. If you feel the cookies might be a little overbaked, you can slide the parchment onto the rack so the cookies cool a little faster. When they are completely cool, roll them gently in the powdered sugar one last time.

These cookies have the best texture the day they are made. They are fragile, so store them covered on a plate instead of in a cookie jar, and eat them within 24 hours.

toasting and grinding nuts

I usually toast nuts before using them as an ingredient because it brings out their flavor. Toasting is easy. You can either spread out the nuts on a baking sheet and place the pan in a 350°F oven for 10 to 12 minutes, or you can toast them in a small skillet on the stove top over low heat, tossing them constantly, for 6 to 8 minutes. Either way, keep an eye on them because they toast quickly and burn easily. They are ready as soon as you can smell their aroma. If you cut a nut in half, you will see the outside is a pale brown, darker than the inside of the nut.

If you are toasting hazelnuts, wrap the still-warm nuts in a clean towel and rub vigorously until the skins peel away. Don't be concerned if all the skin doesn't fall away from the nuts.

To grind nuts for Mexican Wedding Cookies (page 154) or for sprinkling between the filo sheets for Suddenly Last Summer (page 92), use a mortar and pestle or a small food processor. If you add a little of the sugar that will be mixed with the nuts to the food processor while grinding, it will help keep the nuts from turning into nut butter. Go easy with the pulse switch. You don't want to process the nuts to a paste.

SAMMYSNAPS

makes about 4 dozen 4-inch cookies

The photographer for this book, Frankie Frankeny, has been a good friend of mine as well as a regular customer for years. She used to come to the first Citizen Cake in the South of Market with her dachshund, Sammy, who inspired this memorable gingersnap. The Sammysnap, which was exactly the same color as Sammy, became one of our most popular cookies. These days we take the same ginger dough, cut it into small rounds, and use a crème fraîche filling to make ginger sandwich cookies. We miss Sammy, but Frankie's current dachshunds, Sunnie and Sydnie, still pay us visits, and we are always glad to see them.

You can use any cookie cutter you like to make these gingery, fragrant cookies. If you feel the need to own a dachshund cookie cutter (and who could blame you), check kitchenware stores or see Resources.

12 tablespoons (6 ounces) unsalted butter, softened but still cool

1 cup plus 1 tablespoon (about 7$1/2$ ounces) granulated sugar

$1/4$ cup (2$3/4$ ounces by weight) unsulfured dark molasses

1 (1$1/2$ ounces) large egg

2 cups plus 3 tablespoons (11 ounces) all-purpose flour

1 teaspoon baking soda

1 teaspoon ground cinnamon

1 teaspoon ground cloves

$1/4$ teaspoon kosher salt

1 tablespoon minced crystallized ginger

FOR PEOPLE, NOT FOR DOGS

In a large bowl, using a stand mixer fitted with the paddle attachment or a handheld mixer, cream the butter on medium speed for 1 to 2 minutes, or until creamy. Add the sugar and molasses and beat for 2 to 3 minutes, or until smooth, stopping if necessary to scrape any butter or molasses from the bottom or sides of the bowl. Add the egg and beat until smooth.

In a medium bowl, stir together the flour, baking soda, cinnamon, cloves, salt, and ginger. Add the flour mixture to the butter mixture and beat for about 1 minute, or just until combined. Transfer the dough to a sheet of plastic wrap and wrap tightly. Refrigerate for at least 30 minutes or up to overnight. If you chill it overnight, let it sit at room temperature for 10 to 15 minutes before you begin rolling it out.

Position racks in the upper third and lower third of the oven and preheat the oven to 350°F. Line 2 baking sheets with parchment paper.

Divide the dough in half. On a lightly floured work surface, roll out half of the dough into an 11-inch square about $1/4$ inch thick. You can use any cookie cutters you like to cut out shapes. Using a spatula, transfer the cookies to the prepared pans, spacing them about 1 inch apart. Push the scraps together, reroll them, and cut out additional cookies. Repeat with the remaining half of the dough while the first batch bakes.

Bake the cookies, rotating the pans after about 5 minutes, for 10 to 12 minutes, or just until crisp. Transfer to racks and let cool.

The cookies will keep in an airtight container at room temperature for up to 3 days.

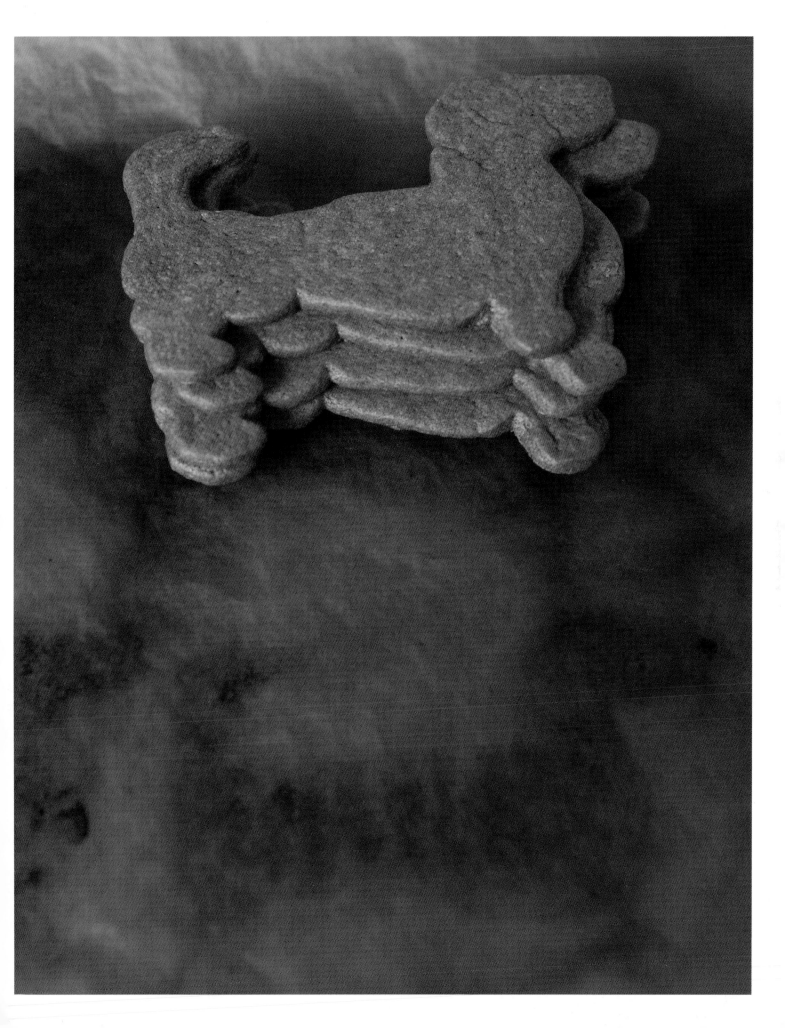

You can make some
components in advance:

UP TO 2 WEEKS BEFORE

➥ make the cookie
dough

UP TO 2 DAYS BEFORE

➥ bake the cookies

THE DAY BEFORE

➥ make the rose
custard

**A FEW HOURS
BEFORE SERVING**

➥ make the crisps

JUST BEFORE SERVING

➥ plate the dessert

MINIMALIST VERSION

Serve the custard with
the caramel crisps, and
don't bother making
the cookies. Garnish
the plate with organic
rose petals or seasonal
fruit if you like.

ROSEBUD

rose custard, caramel crisps, saffron pistachio cookies

serves 4

I created the first version of a rose custard in 1993 as a way to pay homage to the beautiful cuisine of chef Traci Des Jardins. I wanted to give her a bouquet of roses in edible form. Traci was the chef at Rubicon when I was the pastry chef, and she is now the chef-owner of Jardinière, Mijita, and Acme Chophouse, all in San Francisco. Rose Petal Crème Brûlée became one of my signature dishes.

Rosebud has the same rose custard as the original dessert, but we had fun taking the custard out of the ramekin and changing the focus to the part of the dessert that people like the best: the crisp sugar disk on top of the custard. Normally you would caramelize the sugar with a torch, but I figured out a way to bake the sugar disk separately, which means I can either stack the disks with custard and create a simple Napoleon or accent a custard with as many disks as I want.

The unusual thing about this recipe is that you let the custard break when it's cooking over simmering water. It looks like a complete disaster, and when new cooks are training at Citizen Cake, they always think they are ruining it. But a few minutes with an immersion blender whips the custard into beautiful shape.

When you are preparing the custard, use a tall pan (a stockpot is good) and fill it at least three-fourths full of water. Check the water level halfway through cooking to make sure there is still sufficient water in the pot.

You can also use the custard for a tart filling, which we do at the pâtisserie. Make the tart shells for A Chocolate Tart Named Desire (page 57) and bake as directed. Fill the baked tart shells with the chilled custard and add a caramel crisp to the top. Or, to make my original Rose Petal Crème Brûlée, spoon the custard into a ramekin, sprinkle sugar on top, torch it to caramelize, and garnish with a rose petal.

Saffron Pistachio Cookies

8 tablespoons (4 ounces) unsalted butter

1/4 teaspoon saffron threads

1 cup (5 ounces) all-purpose flour

1 teaspoon kosher salt

3/4 cup (3 ounces) powdered sugar, sifted

1 (1 1/2 ounces by weight) large egg, at room temperature

3/4 cup (about 3 ounces) shelled pistachio nuts

2 tablespoons (1 ounce) turbinado sugar

Rose Custard

2 cups heavy cream

1/2 cup (3 1/2 ounces) plus 1 tablespoon granulated sugar

1/2 vanilla bean

4 (2 ounces by weight) large egg yolks

2 teaspoons Grand Marnier

1/2 teaspoon rose water

To Make the SAFFRON PISTACHIO COOKIES

In a small saucepan, melt 4 tablespoons (2 ounces) of the butter over medium heat. When the butter has melted but is not yet brown, reduce the heat to medium-low, add the saffron threads, and stir once or twice. Remove the pan from the heat and set aside.

In a bowl, stir together the flour and salt. In a large bowl, using a stand mixer fitted with the paddle attachment or a handheld mixer, cream together the remaining 4 tablespoons butter and the powdered sugar on medium speed for 2 minutes, or until smooth. Add the egg and beat for about 30 seconds, or until well combined.

In a mortar with a pestle or in a small food processor, combine the pistachios and turbinado sugar and grind or pulse until finely ground. Add the pistachio-sugar mixture to the butter-sugar mixture and beat on low speed just until combined, stopping as needed to scrape the bottom and sides of the bowl. Add the flour mixture in two additions, stirring well after each addition. Pour in the saffron butter and stir to combine.

Divide the dough in half and roll each half into a log 1 inch in diameter. Wrap in plastic wrap and refrigerate for at least 1 hour or up to 2 weeks. This makes more dough than you need for this recipe. You can store 1 log in the freezer for up to 2 months. While the dough is chilling, you can begin making the rose custard.

Position the racks in the upper third and lower third of the oven and preheat the oven to 350°F. Line 2 baking sheets with parchment paper.

Using a sharp knife, cut the dough into 1/4- to 1/2-inch-thick slices. Arrange the slices on the prepared pans, spacing them 1/2 inch apart.

Bake the cookies, rotating the pans after about 6 minutes, for 12 to 15 minutes. These cookies are best when they are toasty (they taste almost savory to me), so don't take them out of the oven until they have a good amount of color. Let cool on the pans on racks. This recipe makes a big batch, but because they are so good with coffee or tea and will keep for a few days in an airtight container at room temperature, it is not a hardship to have extra. You should have about 5 dozen cookies if you bake all the dough.

To Make the ROSE CUSTARD

Fill a stockpot or other tall pot three-fourths full of water, set over medium heat, and bring to a gentle simmer. Reduce the heat to low or medium-low. Meanwhile, pour the cream into a saucepan and add the 1 tablespoon granulated sugar. Split the vanilla bean lengthwise and, with the tip of the knife, scrape the seeds into the saucepan, and then toss in the empty pod. Place the saucepan over medium-high heat and cook for 5 to 7 minutes, or until the cream comes to a rolling boil. Watch closely, as the mixture can bubble up quickly. Remove from the heat and set aside.

In a large heatproof bowl that will rest on the rim of the stockpot, whisk together the egg yolks and the $^{1}/_{2}$ cup sugar. Whisk a few tablespoons of the hot cream mixture into the egg mixture. Then, while whisking steadily, slowly add the rest of the hot cream mixture to the egg mixture.

Rest the bowl on the rim of the stockpot, making sure the bottom of the bowl does not touch the water. Cook the custard, whisking every 5 to 10 minutes, for about $1^{1}/_{2}$ hours, or until the mixture is so broken that it cannot be whisked back together. Yes, $1^{1}/_{2}$ hours is a long time, but think of this as like making chicken stock. You don't need to stand over the stove the whole time. Stir every 5 to 10 minutes while you work on something else nearby, such as slicing and baking the cookies and making the crisps. Check the water level halfway through cooking to make sure there is sufficient water in the pot.

After about $1^{1}/_{4}$ hours, set up an ice bath by half filling a large bowl with ice and water. When the custard is ready, remove the bowl from over the simmering water and nest it in the ice bath. Let cool for 15 minutes, then remove and discard the vanilla pod. Using an immersion blender, whip the custard until it is smooth again.

Stir the Grand Marnier and rose water into the custard. Cover and refrigerate for at least 2 hours or up to overnight. Or, spoon the custard into ramekins before refrigerating. (If you are using the custard as a tart filling, make sure to refrigerate it for 2 hours before spooning it into the pastry shell.) You should have about $1^{3}/_{4}$ cups.

To Make the CARAMEL CRISPS

Position racks in the upper third and lower third of the oven and preheat the oven to 350°F. Line 2 baking sheets with parchment paper.

In a small bowl, stir together the sugar, corn syrup, and butter until a paste forms. Pinch off marble-sized pieces of the paste and set them on the prepared pans, spacing them about 3 inches apart. You should have 8 crisps.

Bake the crisps for 10 to 12 minutes, or until they are completely flat, caramelized, and the color of dark brown sugar. Don't overbake, as they will continue to darken and caramelize as they cool. When removing the baking sheets from the oven, be sure to keep them level. The mixture is a very hot liquid at this point, and the crisps will run into one another if the pans are tilted. Place the pans on cooling racks. Allow the crisps to cool completely on the paper on the pans before you try to move them. This will take about 15 minutes.

To Plate the Dessert

Set a spoonful of custard in the center of each plate. To get the crest, just bring the spoon up very slowly and let the top droop over. Carefully stand 2 crisps in the custard. Set 2 cookies off to the side.

Caramel Crisps

3 tablespoons ($1^{1}/_{4}$ ounces) granulated sugar

1 tablespoon light corn syrup

1 teaspoon unsalted butter, softened but still cool

SHAGALICIOUS

serves 8 to 10

More exotic than a lemon cake, this dessert satisfies Lemaniacs but has a sexy twist: passion fruit filling. I have been a passion fruit evangelist from the moment I first tasted the fruit. The filling for this cake is so bright and creamy that it is even more unforgettable than the cake's stunning looks. The secret behind the filling is passion fruit puree.

When I was building the original cake, it didn't seem to need the shards and straws I like to put on my cakes. The simple adornment of shredded coconut made it look like a shag-covered ottoman. This was during the first Austin Powers movie ("yeah baby"), so we named the cake the Retro Tropical Shag and called it The Shag for short. The Shag has been so popular that it inspired a passion fruit and rum cocktail we serve in the restaurant, the Shagadelic (page 187)—and has led other bakeries to copy the cake.

You can make this recipe, a simplified version of the Retro Tropical Shag, in about half the time it takes to make the original. The great thing about this cake—aside from its amazing flavor and fabulous appearance—is how forgiving it is. If you are nervous about making a three-layer cake, this is an excellent place to start, because the exterior of whipped cream and coconut disguises any flaws.

This cake tastes best when you bake, layer, and frost it the day before serving, so the rum syrup has time to soak into it. None of the components should be made any further in advance.

Genoise

2 tablespoons (1 ounce) unsalted butter
3 (4¹/2 ounces by weight) large eggs
¹/2 cup (3¹/2 ounces) granulated sugar
³/4 cup (3³/4 ounces) all-purpose flour
Pinch of kosher salt

To Make the GENOISE

Position a rack in the center of the oven and preheat the oven to 350°F. Butter a quarter sheet pan (9¹/2 by 13 inches) or a 9 by 13 by 2-inch baking pan and line with parchment paper.

In a small saucepan, melt the butter over medium to medium-high heat and heat for 3 to 5 minutes, or until it browns. It will continue to darken after you pull it off the heat, so don't overdo it. Remove the pan from the heat and set aside.

Fill a large saucepan one-third full of water, place over medium-high heat, and bring to a simmer. Combine the eggs and sugar in a large heatproof bowl and whisk together until light in color. Place the bowl over (not touching) the simmering water and whisk for 2 to 4 minutes, or until the sugar has dissolved. Test it by rubbing the mixture between your finger and thumb. If it feels at all gritty, it is not ready. The mixture will be warm but not too hot.

Scrape out the contents of the bowl into the bowl of a stand mixer fitted with the whip attachment, or leave it in the bowl if using a handheld mixer. Whip on high speed for about 5 minutes, or until the batter is cool, thick, and doubled in volume. Fold a large spoonful of the batter into the cooled browned butter, and then fold the butter mixture back into the batter. Sift in the flour in two additions, folding gently after each addition, and then fold in the salt. Don't overwork the batter or you will deflate all the air bubbles you just created. The batter will have flecks from the brown butter. Scrape the batter into the prepared pan. Smooth the top gently, but don't overdo it.

Bake the cake for about 10 minutes, or until golden. (Go ahead and make the rum syrup while the cake bakes.) Let the cake cool completely in the pan on a cooling rack. Run a knife blade around the inside edge of the pan to loosen the cake, and then invert the pan onto a larger baking sheet or cutting board and lift off the pan. Peel off the parchment paper from the bottom of the cake.

To Make the RUM SYRUP

In a small saucepan, combine the sugar, water, and lime juice. Split the vanilla bean lengthwise and, with the tip of the knife, scrape the seeds into the saucepan, and then toss in the empty pod. Place the pan over medium-high heat and bring to a rolling boil. Reduce the heat to medium-low and simmer for 2 minutes. Remove the pan from the heat, add the rum, and set aside to cool. You should have about 3/4 cup.

This is a fabulous syrup for moistening a genoise. There is not a lot of fat in a genoise, so it is pretty dry without the syrup. In old-world countries, cooks pour on enough liquid to drench the cake, but I prefer a cake that is plumped up but not soaking wet.

To Make the PASSION FRUIT DIPLOMAT CREAM

In a small saucepan, combine the passion fruit puree (or the orange juice mixture) and 1/3 cup (2 1/4 ounces) of the sugar. Place over high heat and bring to a boil. Remove the pan from the heat.

In a small bowl, stir together the cornstarch and water to make a thin slurry. In a medium bowl, whisk together the egg yolks and the remaining 1/3 cup sugar until blended. Whisk in the cornstarch slurry.

Whisk a few tablespoons of the hot passion fruit puree into the yolk mixture. Then, while whisking steadily, slowly add the rest of the hot puree to the yolk mixture. Return the mixture to the saucepan and place over medium heat. Cook, whisking constantly, for about 5 minutes, or until thickened.

Remove the pan from the heat and add the butter 1 tablespoon at a time, stirring after each addition until the butter is melted and the mixture is smooth. Pour the mixture into a bowl and cover with plastic wrap, pressing the wrap directly onto the surface to prevent a skin from forming. Let

Rum Syrup

1/2 cup (3 1/2 ounces) granulated sugar

1/2 cup water

1 tablespoon fresh lime juice

1/2 vanilla bean

1 tablespoon white rum

Passion Fruit Diplomat Cream

1/2 cup passion fruit puree, or 1/4 cup fresh orange juice combined with 2 tablespoons fresh lemon juice and 2 tablespoons passion fruit brandy, such as Alizé Gold Passion brand

2/3 cup (4 1/2 ounces) granulated sugar

1 tablespoon cornstarch

1 tablespoon plus 1 1/2 teaspoons water

2 (1 ounce by weight) large egg yolks

2 tablespoons (1 ounce) unsalted butter

1 cup heavy cream

stand for 15 to 20 minutes, or until completely cooled. You want the passion fruit cream to be cool, but not ice-cold, when you fold the cream into it. You should have about 1¼ cups.

In a bowl, using a mixer on high speed or a whisk, whip the cream until it forms stiff peaks. The peaks must stiff so that the cream will hold its body when mixed with the passion fruit cream. Whisk a large spoonful of the whipped cream into the passion fruit cream to lighten it. Using a rubber spatula, gently fold the rest of the whipped cream into the passion fruit cream, using soft strokes to keep the air bubbles in the whipped cream from deflating. This is the filling for the cake layers. You should have about 3 cups.

To Assemble the Cake Layers

Trim the edges of the cake so they are even, and then cut the cake crosswise into thirds. Each third will be about 9 by 4 inches. Place one-third of the cake upside down on a serving tray. (I like to turn the sections upside down because the bottom soaks up the syrup better than the top does.) Using a pastry brush, brush the cake with about one-third of the rum syrup. Using either an offset or an icing spatula, smooth on about half of the filling (about 1½ cups). Lightly place a second third of the cake, upside down, on top of the filling. (Cookware stores sell special oversized cake spatulas that are handy for moving big sections of cake, but a clean piece of cardboard works, too.) Brush the cake with half of the remaining syrup and then smooth on the rest of the filling. Lightly place the final third of the cake upside down on the filling and brush with the remaining rum syrup.

Refrigerate the cake for 15 minutes while you whip the cream for the exterior. Chilling the cake makes the whipped cream go on a little more smoothly.

To Make the COCONUT SHAG FINISH

In a bowl, using a mixer on medium-high speed or a whisk, beat together the cream and powdered sugar for 1 minute. Just before soft peaks form, add the rum and vanilla and continue to whip until stiff peaks form.

Using an offset or icing spatula, spread about one-third of the whipped cream in a thick layer over the top of the cake. Frost the sides of the cake with the remaining cream.

Sprinkle the top of the cake with about one-third of the coconut. Gently press the rest of the coconut into the whipped cream on the sides of the cake. Sprinkle any remaining coconut over the top. The cake will be about 9 inches long, 4 inches wide, and 3 inches high. Cover the cake loosely with plastic wrap and refrigerate for at least 1 hour or preferably overnight, so the rum syrup really soaks into the genoise, before serving.

YEAH BABY

Coconut Shag Finish

½ cup heavy cream

2 tablespoons (½ ounce) powdered sugar, sifted

¾ teaspoon white rum

¼ teaspoon pure vanilla extract

1 to 1½ cups (2 to 3 ounces) unsweetened shredded dried coconut

CUPCAKES

the cupcake phenomenon began sweeping the country a few years ago, and it makes a lot of sense. Cupcakes are indulgent and restrained at the same time. The size is a perfect individual portion, especially to go. They also inspire nostalgia, making you feel like a kid again.

When I decided to open Citizen Cupcake, I knew I wanted to reexamine the form of this classic sweet. Just having cake and frosting can be wonderful (as long as it is not too sugary sweet), but the architecture of a cupcake invites many other possibilities. To me, the coolest thing about cupcakes is not adding glitter sprinkles or fluorescent frostings, but playing around with my favorite flavor combinations, filling them with a surprising injection of caramel or ganache, and then adding things like salted nuts, coconut, citrus zest, or more chocolate chunks to the frosting.

We offer an incredible selection of cupcakes that changes throughout the week and the seasons. We also make plain vanilla cupcakes, and chocolate ones, too, and both stand out because we use great ingredients. In this chapter, I am featuring a few of our favorite creations, including Lemania Cupcakes (page 173), which have an injection of lemon curd for that extra oomph, and our Rocky Road Cupcakes (page 175), with chocolate cake, chocolate frosting, marshmallows, walnuts, and a drizzle of chocolate. Not for the faint of heart!

Try experimenting with injections and flavor combos and explore new ways to frost and decorate. There are no restrictions on where you can take your own cupcakes.

cupcake tips

The cupcakes in this chapter are quite different from the standard cupcakes found in many bakeries. The tricks and equipment tips that follow will help you to make rock-star cupcakes with attitude.

Baking Cupcakes

Nonstick muffin pans outfitted with paper liners ensure that you will be able to save any cupcakes that rise up beyond the capacity of the muffin-pan cups. Let the cupcakes cool in the pan on a cooling rack for 10 minutes, gently loosen them from the pan, and then let cool in the pan completely.

Filling Cupcakes with a Squirt Bottle

I like to use a plastic squirt bottle to inject a filling into my cupcakes. Eight-ounce bottles work well, and you can find them in baking or cookware stores.

Check the opening on the bottle. Most likely the opening on the squirt bottle will be too small to handle thick fillings. Use a standard pair of scissors to snip off the tip so it is about 1/4 inch wide.

Whether you are filling a cupcake with caramel sauce, chocolate, or lemon curd, you can control the filling's consistency. Applying heat will make it more liquid. Have a shallow bowl of warm water sitting by. Make sure the bowl isn't so deep or wide that your squirt bottle will submerge and take on water. If your filling gets too hard or slow moving, stand the squirt bottle in the warm water for a few minutes until the filling softens. Have a towel nearby for wiping the bottle before you start filling your cupcakes.

You can make any of the fillings in this book ahead of time, refrigerate them, spoon them into the squirt bottle, and then let the filling warm up in warm water while the cupcakes bake. Be careful the water isn't too hot, or the fillings will squirt out too quickly.

Gently squeeze the warmed squirt bottle so the filling comes right to the tip. Insert the tip into the top center of the cupcake. Squeeze the squirt bottle and you can almost feel the cupcake take on weight. When you see the top of the cupcake rise just slightly, stop squeezing the bottle and slowly pull the tip out of the cupcake. You are going to cover the cupcake with frosting, so don't worry if a little of the filling runs out of the top.

Filling Cupcakes with a Pastry Bag

First check the consistency of the filling and rewarm if necessary. When the filling is warm enough to flow easily, spoon it into a pastry bag fitted with a plain 1/2-inch or 1/4-inch tip.

Squeeze the bag to test how quickly the filling comes out. Push the tip into the top of the cupcake and gently squeeze the bag to pipe in the filling. When you see the top of the cupcake rise just slightly, pull the pastry bag tip out of the cupcake. A little filling runoff is not a problem.

No Bottle? No Bag? No Problem

If you don't have a squirt bottle or pastry bag, you can still fill your cupcakes. Pry an opening into the top of the cupcake and use a baby offset spatula or a small knife or spoon to slip a little filling inside the cupcake. Or, peel the paper off of the cupcake and cut the cupcake in half. Using a spreading knife, add filling to the cut side of each half, gently push the cupcake back together, and then frost it.

You can make some components in advance:

UP TO 1 WEEK BEFORE

➥ make the lemon curd

A FEW HOURS BEFORE

➥ make the cupcakes

➥ warm the lemon curd and fill the cupcakes

JUST BEFORE SERVING

➥ make the frosting

➥ frost and garnish the cupcakes

LEMANIA CUPCAKES

buttermilk cupcakes, eggless lemon curd filling, vanilla meringue frosting, lemon zest

makes **12** cupcakes

Inge, the mother of my partner, Sabrina, is one of Citizen Cake's most die-hard Lemaniacs. She will drive across the Golden Gate Bridge to Citizen Cake to buy up every lemon tart in the store, which she takes home and freezes. I created this cupcake for Inge and for all the Lemaniacs who have made our lemon desserts so successful over the years.

The cupcake itself is actually a moist buttermilk, not lemon, cupcake, which means you can fill and frost it just about any way you like. For example, take this same cupcake, fill it with Pastry Cream (page 203), drizzle on Dark Chocolate Sauce (page 207), and you have Boston cream cupcakes.

To Make the BUTTERMILK CUPCAKES

Position a rack in the center of the oven and preheat the oven to 325°F. Line a 12-cup standard nonstick muffin pan (or two 6-cup pans) with paper liners.

In a medium bowl, sift together the flour, baking powder, and baking soda. Add the salt and set aside. In a small bowl, stir together the buttermilk and vanilla and set aside.

In a large bowl, using a stand mixer fitted with the paddle attachment or a handheld mixer, cream together the butter and sugar on medium speed for about 4 minutes, or until light and fluffy, stopping to scrape down the sides of the bowl as needed. Add the eggs one at a time, beating well after each addition until incorporated. On low speed, add the flour mixture in three additions and the buttermilk mixture in two additions, beginning and ending with the flour mixture and beating for about 30 seconds after each addition, or until combined. Divide the batter evenly among the prepared muffin-pan cups.

Bake the cupcakes, rotating the pan after about 12 minutes, for 23 to 25 minutes, or until they are lightly golden and a skewer inserted into the center comes out clean. Let cool in the pan on a cooling rack for 10 minutes, gently loosen the cupcakes from the pan, and then let them cool completely in the pan before removing them.

Buttermilk Cupcakes

2 cups (9 ounces) cake flour

2 teaspoons baking powder

1/4 teaspoon baking soda

1/2 teaspoon kosher salt

3/4 cup (6 1/4 ounces by weight) buttermilk, at room temperature

1/2 teaspoon pure vanilla extract

8 tablespoons (4 ounces) unsalted butter, softened but still cool

1 cup plus 2 tablespoons (8 ounces) granulated sugar

2 (3 ounces by weight) large eggs, at room temperature

To Fill the Cupcakes with LEMON CURD

Inject the lemon curd into the cooled cupcakes, following the directions on page 171.

Filling

1 cup Eggless Lemon Curd (page 204)

Vanilla Meringue Frosting

3/4 cup (5 1/4 ounces) granulated sugar

3 tablespoons water

1/4 teaspoon cream of tartar

2 (2 ounces by weight) large egg whites

1 teaspoon pure vanilla extract

2 lemons for grating

To Make the VANILLA MERINGUE FROSTING

In a medium saucepan, combine the sugar, water, and cream of tartar and stir just to moisten the sugar. Clip a candy thermometer onto the side of the pan and place over high heat. Bring to a boil and cook for about 3 minutes, or until the syrup registers 280°F on the thermometer. Remove from the heat.

In a medium bowl, using a handheld mixer on medium speed, whip the egg whites until soft peaks form. (The volume of egg whites is too small to use a stand mixer.) Turn the mixer to low speed and slowly drizzle the hot sugar syrup into the egg whites (try to keep the hot syrup from hitting the beaters). Turn the mixer to high speed and continue whipping the frosting for 5 to 8 minutes, or until it is at room temperature. Beat in the vanilla (or any other flavoring you like, but err on the side of caution and add no more than 1 teaspoon and then taste before you add more). You should have about 2 cups.

To Frost and Garnish the Cupcakes

You can finish the cupcakes in one of two ways: Frost them with an offset or icing spatula, creating dramatic spikes if you like, and then grate lemon zest directly on top. Or, frost them, fire up your torch, brown the frosting, and then grate lemon zest directly on top.

You can make some
components in advance:

UP TO 1 WEEK BEFORE

➡ make the
   marshmallows

A FEW HOURS BEFORE

➡ make the cupcakes

➡ make the frosting

➡ frost and garnish
   the cupcakes

ROCKY ROAD CUPCAKES

dark chocolate cupcakes, dark chocolate buttercream frosting, marshmallows,
walnuts

makes **12** cupcakes

The basic components of rocky road—chocolate, walnuts, marshmallows—work
across different dessert formats, including ice cream, brownies, and these
cupcakes. The cupcakes themselves are basic chocolate and, like the buttermilk
ones in Lemania Cupcakes (page 173), can be taken in lots of directions. They
have wonderfully pure flavors and are already over the top, so I don't think any
filling is necessary.

Dark Chocolate Cupcakes

1 cup (5 ounces) all-purpose flour

3/4 cup (2 ounces) unsweetened cocoa powder, preferably natural

2 teaspoons baking powder

1/4 teaspoon baking soda

1/2 teaspoon kosher salt

1/4 cup plus 3 tablespoons (about 4 ounces by weight) buttermilk

3 tablespoons water

1/2 teaspoon pure vanilla extract

8 tablespoons (4 ounces) unsalted butter, cut into 1/2-inch pieces

2 ounces bittersweet chocolate, preferably 70% cacao, coarsely chopped (about 1/2 cup)

3/4 cup plus 2 tablespoons (6 ounces) granulated sugar

1/4 cup plus 3 tablespoons (3 3/4 ounces) firmly packed dark brown sugar

2 (3 ounces by weight) large eggs, at room temperature

Dark Chocolate Buttercream Frosting

Buttercream Frosting (page 217)

4 ounces bittersweet chocolate, preferably 70% cacao, coarsely chopped (scant 1 cup)

2 ounces bittersweet chocolate, preferably 70% cacao, coarsely chopped (about 1/2 cup)

2 teaspoons canola oil

6 marshmallows, made with gelatin (page 212) or xanthan gum (page 213), each cut into eight 1/4-inch pieces, or 48 store-bought miniature marshmallows

1/2 to 3/4 cup (2 to 3 ounces) walnut halves or pieces

To Make the DARK CHOCOLATE CUPCAKES

Position a rack in the center of the oven and preheat the oven to 325°F. Line a 12-cup standard nonstick muffin pan (or two 6-cup pans) with paper liners.

In a medium bowl, sift together the flour, cocoa powder, baking powder, and baking soda. Add the salt and set aside. In a large bowl, stir together the buttermilk, water, and vanilla and set aside.

Bring a few inches of water to a gentle simmer in a saucepan. Combine the butter and chocolate in a heatproof bowl and place over (not touching) the simmering water (or use a double boiler). Heat slowly, stirring occasionally, until nearly melted, and then remove the bowl from the heat and whisk until smooth. Add the granulated and brown sugars and stir until blended. Add the eggs one at a time, beating after each addition until combined. Scrape the chocolate mixture into the buttermilk mixture and whisk until smooth.

Add the flour mixture to the chocolate-buttermilk mixture in three additions, beating after each addition just until combined. Divide the batter evenly among the prepared muffin-tin cups; each paper liner will be filled almost to the top.

Bake the cupcakes, rotating the pan after about 10 minutes, for 20 to 22 minutes, or until a skewer inserted into the center of a cupcake comes out clean. Let cool in the pan on a cooling rack for 10 minutes, gently loosen the cupcakes from the pan, and then let them cool completely in the pan before removing them.

To Make the DARK CHOCOLATE BUTTERCREAM FROSTING

Make the buttercream frosting as directed. Melt the chocolate as you did for the cupcake batter, and then whisk the chocolate into the frosting. You should have a generous 2 cups.

To Frost and Garnish the Cupcakes

Melt the chocolate as you did for the cupcake batter. Add the canola oil and whisk until smooth. You should have 1/4 cup.

Using an offset or icing spatula, frost the cupcakes and then garnish with the marshmallow pieces and walnuts. Finish each cupcake with a drizzle of chocolate.

*You can make some
components in advance:*

UP TO 1 WEEK BEFORE

- make the caramel
  sauce

A FEW HOURS BEFORE

- make the cupcakes

- warm the caramel
  and fill the cupcakes

- make the frosting

JUST BEFORE SERVING

- frost and garnish
  the cupcakes

CANDY BAR CUPCAKES

brown sugar cupcakes, caramel filling, peanut butter frosting, salted peanuts

makes **12** cupcakes

Over the years, I have done my own dessert versions of well-known candy bars, and the concept of a Snickers bar has shown up more than once. There are several generations of Americans who have never gotten over the magical combination of salty peanuts, caramel, and an aeration of nougat and chocolate. While my versions of these components aren't as sweet as those of the famous candy bar, people seem to be just as crazy for the combination.

To Make the BROWN SUGAR CUPCAKES

Position a rack in the center of the oven and preheat the oven to 325°F. Line a 12-cup standard nonstick muffin pan (or two 6-cup pans) with paper liners.

In a medium bowl, sift together the flour and baking powder. Add the salt and set aside. In a large bowl, using a stand mixer fitted with the paddle attachment or a handheld mixer, cream together the butter and brown and granulated sugars on medium speed for 3 to 4 minutes, or until light and fluffy, stopping to scrape down the sides of the bowl as needed. Add the eggs one at a time, beating well after each addition until incorporated. Beat in the vanilla.

On low speed, add the flour mixture in three additions and the milk in two additions, beginning and ending with the dry ingredients and beating after each addition for about 15 seconds, or until combined. Divide the batter evenly among the prepared muffin-pan cups.

Bake the cupcakes, rotating the pan after about 10 minutes, for 20 to 25 minutes, or until golden and a skewer inserted into the center of a cupcake comes out clean. Let cool in the pan on a cooling rack for 10 minutes, gently loosen the cupcakes from the pan, and then let them cool completely in the pan before removing them.

Brown Sugar Cupcakes

- 1 1/2 cups plus 2 tablespoons (8 ounces)
  all-purpose flour

- 1 teaspoon baking powder

- 1/2 teaspoon kosher salt

- 8 tablespoons (4 ounces) unsalted butter,
  softened but still cool

- 3/4 cup (6 1/4 ounces) firmly packed dark brown
  sugar

- 1/4 cup plus 1 tablespoon (2 1/4 ounces) granulated
  sugar

- 2 (3 ounces by weight) large eggs, at room
  temperature

- 1/2 teaspoon pure vanilla extract

- 3/4 cup whole milk

To Fill the Cupcakes with CARAMEL SAUCE

Inject the caramel sauce into the cooled cupcakes, following the directions on page 171.

Filling

3/4 cup Basic Caramel Sauce (page 210)

Peanut Butter Frosting

4 ounces milk chocolate, coarsely chopped (2/3 cup)

3 ounces bittersweet chocolate, preferably 70% cacao, coarsely chopped (about 2/3 cup)

1/2 cup heavy cream

3 to 3 1/2 tablespoons (about 2 ounces) peanut butter

1/2 cup (about 4 ounces) Buttercream Frosting (page 217)

1/2 to 3/4 cup (2 to 3 ounces) salted roasted peanuts

Fleur de sel for sprinkling

To Make the PEANUT BUTTER FROSTING

In a heatproof bowl, combine the milk chocolate and bittersweet chocolate and set aside. In a small saucepan, heat the cream over medium heat for 4 to 5 minutes, or just until it comes to a boil (small bubbles will appear around the edges of the pan). Remove the pan from the heat, pour the hot cream over the chocolate, and stir until the mixture is smooth. Stir in the peanut butter. Let the mixture cool for 10 to 20 minutes, then whisk in the butter frosting. You should have about 1 1/4 cups.

To Frost and Garnish the Cupcakes

Spread the frosting on the cupcakes with an offset or icing spatula, or pipe it on with a pastry bag fitted with a medium star tip. Garnish with the peanuts and sprinkle with a few grains of *fleur de sel*.

POKEMON'S CUPCAKE ...THAT'S WHAT I WOULD CALL IT.

OKAY, OKAY—I'LL MAKE UP ANOTHER POKEMON DESSERT.

You can make some components in advance:

UP TO 3 DAYS BEFORE

➡ make the toffee filling

➡ make the frosting

A FEW HOURS BEFORE

➡ make the cupcakes

➡ warm the filling and fill the cupcakes

JUST BEFORE SERVING

➡ frost and garnish the cupcakes

STICKY TOFFEE CUPCAKES

date cupcakes, toffee filling, coconut cream cheese frosting, flaked coconut

makes **12** cupcakes

This cupcake doesn't have a standard vanilla or chocolate base, but instead goes out on a limb, with dates making it fabulously moist and flavorful. It is inspired by sticky toffee pudding, a much-loved dessert in Britain and Australia that is basically brown sugar, butter, and cream—and who doesn't like that?

The toffee filling is incredibly sweet and buttery. I like sweet things, but they must have some salt tossed in, and this filling does. The frosting is also fantastic. If you want to make it without the coconut flavor, just substitute heavy cream for the coconut milk.

Use good dates for this recipe. Farmers' markets generally offer the best quality. If you are buying dates at a grocery store, look for whole ones that are plump, moist, and free of cracks. Don't choose pitted dates, because they lose a lot of their moisture after their pits are pulled.

To Make the TOFFEE FILLING

In a medium saucepan, melt the butter over medium-high heat. Clip a candy thermometer onto the side of the pan, add the brown sugar and cream, and stir just to moisten the sugar. Bring to a boil and cook for about 5 minutes, or until the mixture registers 225°F on the thermometer. Remove the pan from the heat, stir in the vanilla and salt, and set aside to cool. Cover and refrigerate until ready to use or for up to 3 days. You should have ¾ cup.

Toffee Filling

2 tablespoons (1 ounce) unsalted butter

½ cup (4¼ ounces) firmly packed dark brown sugar

½ cup heavy cream

¼ teaspoon pure vanilla extract

Small pinch of kosher salt

To Make the DATE CUPCAKES

Position a rack in the center of the oven and preheat the oven to 350°F. Line a 12-cup standard nonstick muffin pan (or two 6-cup pans) with paper liners.

In a small saucepan, bring the water to a boil and add the baking soda. Place the dates in a small heatproof bowl, pour in the hot liquid, and stir briefly to separate the pieces. Set aside.

In a medium bowl, sift together the flour and baking powder. Add the salt and set aside. In a large bowl, using a stand mixer fitted with the paddle attachment or a handheld mixer, cream together the butter and sugar on medium speed for 3 to 4 minutes, or until light and fluffy, stopping to scrape down the sides of the bowl as needed. Add the eggs one at a time, beating well after each addition until incorporated. Beat in the vanilla.

Date Cupcakes

1 cup water

1 teaspoon baking soda

11 ounces dates, preferably Medjool, pitted and chopped into ¼-inch pieces (about 6 ounces after pitting)

1½ cups (7½ ounces) all-purpose flour

2 teaspoons baking powder

Pinch of kosher salt

4 tablespoons (2 ounces) unsalted butter, softened but still cool

¾ cup (6¼ ounces) firmly packed dark brown sugar

2 (3 ounces by weight) large eggs, at room temperature

½ teaspoon pure vanilla extract

On low speed, add the flour mixture in three additions, beating after each addition for about 15 seconds, or until combined. Using a rubber spatula, fold in the date mixture, including any water that has not been absorbed by the dates. Divide the batter evenly among the prepared muffin-pan cups.

Bake the cupcakes, rotating the pan after about 9 minutes, for 18 to 20 minutes, or until golden and a skewer inserted into the center comes out clean. Let cool in the pan on a cooling rack for 10 minutes, gently loosen the cupcakes from the pan, and then let them cool completely in the pan before removing them.

To Fill the Cupcakes with TOFFEE FILLING

Inject the toffee filling into the cooled cupcakes, following the directions on page 171.

To Make the COCONUT CREAM CHEESE FROSTING

Coconut Cream Cheese Frosting

6 tablespoons (3 ounces) unsalted butter, softened but still cool

3 ounces (about 1/3 cup) cream cheese, softened but still cool

3 cups (12 ounces) powdered sugar

4 tablespoons (2 1/4 ounces by weight) coconut milk

In a bowl, using a stand mixer fitted with the paddle attachment or a hand-held mixer, cream together the butter and cream cheese on medium speed for 2 to 3 minutes, or until light and fluffy. Sift 1 1/2 cups (6 ounces) of the powdered sugar into the bowl and stir until smooth. Pour in 2 tablespoons of the coconut milk and again stir until smooth. Repeat with the remaining powdered sugar, followed by the remaining coconut milk. Use immediately, or cover and refrigerate for up to 3 days and let come to room temperature before using. You should have about 2 cups.

To Frost and Garnish the Cupcakes

1 to 1 1/2 cups (2 to 3 ounces) unsweetened large dried coconut flakes (see Resources)

Spread the frosting on the cupcakes with an offset or icing spatula, or pipe it on with a pastry bag fitted with a medium star tip. Top with the coconut.

s Willy Wonka says in my favorite movie, "Candy is dandy but liquor is quicker." Drinks have been such a hit at Citizen Cake that I decided to include a few of my favorite libations and liquid desserts here. We began by offering classic cocktails like martinis, margaritas, and gimlets, all made with premium ingredients, but soon found that drinks were another arena that invited playing around with flavors. In addition to the classics, we now have an ever-changing specialty drinks menu with about fifteen options that are as seasonal, varied, and sometimes off-the-wall as our desserts. All of the drinks in this chapter are easy to make, with the possible exception of the marshmallows that go into the Indian Rose Milk (page 196), but you can choose to leave out the marshmallows and still serve a terrific drink.

I love to invent new drinks, but at the restaurant it is very much a collective effort. Our general manager, Angie Heeney, who started at Citizen Cake working behind the bar, has contributed such drinks as The Winter Cup, a wintry whiskey lemonade, and a Coconut Collins. Matt Conway, who is a bartender and server at Citizen Cake, makes a killer blood orange sorbet–Negroni cocktail that he calls Blood on the Sun. And John Mark, wine director for both Citizen Cake and Orson, is the creative mind behind the Violet Beauregard (page 191) and many of our other popular drinks.

John and I go way back to my early cooking days at Café Claude, where he worked as a waiter while studying French. I have always been serious in the kitchen—friendly, but serious. John made work more fun. He seemed to love everything I made, wanted to know more about each dish, and always managed to make me laugh. John is the kind of server who knows about everything on the menu but is never pretentious about it, greets regular customers by name, and always seems to be having a blast doing all of it. But there is also his starch standard. John believes in shined shoes, pressed clothing, and the general importance of starch in a well-run restaurant: starched aprons for the waitstaff, starched white tablecloths. John tells our waiters there are two keys to success: starch and presetting a table with the appropriate silverware for the next course. It goes without saying that when John makes a drink, there is never a speared olive, cherry, or lemon twist out of place.

CANDY IS DANDY
but liquor is quicker.

SHAGADELIC

serves 2

Passion fruit is one of my favorite fruits. When our Shag cake became a big hit (see the home version on page 164), it was only a matter of time before we came up with a matching cocktail. When this taxi-yellow drink in a martini glass rimmed with coconut comes your way, it almost seems to be showing off, trying to compete with the cake for your attention. The cake is hard to beat, but this cocktail has its own fan club.

You can use corn syrup, agave nectar, or simple syrup to hold the lacy coconut garter belt around the lip of the glass.

In a spice grinder or coffee grinder, finely grind the coconut. Pile the coconut on a saucer.

Dip your finger into the corn syrup and run it around the rims of 2 glasses. (Don't cheat and use a lime or lemon half, because the coconut won't stay on the glass.) Dip the rim of each glass into the coconut, making sure the entire rim is coated.

In a cocktail shaker, combine the passion fruit juice, Cointreau, white and coconut rums, and lime juice. Fill the shaker with ice, cover, and shake.

Strain into the coconut-rimmed glasses and add a cherry to each glass. Serve immediately, taking care not to slosh the coconut off the rims.

2 tablespoons unsweetened shredded dried coconut

1 teaspoon corn syrup, Simple Syrup (page 215), or agave nectar (see Resources)

1/2 cup (4 ounces) bottled passion fruit juice, such as Looza brand

1 tablespoon (1/2 ounce) Cointreau

1/4 cup (2 ounces) white rum, such as 10 Cane brand

2 tablespoons (1 ounce) coconut rum, such as Malibu brand

Juice of 1/2 lime

Ice cubes

2 maraschino cherries

WATERMELON MARGARITA

serves **2** to **4**

I am a margarita purist and generally drink a simple on-the-rocks blend of tequila, Cointreau, and lime juice in a glass with a salted rim. But I do love adding fresh watermelon juice, which makes the classic margarita both gorgeous and delicious. Chile is the twist here, resulting in a fabulous mix of sweet, tart, and spicy.

You can use either red or yellow watermelon for this summertime drink, and making juice from a whole watermelon is easy. Just cut big chunks of melon away from the rind, slide the chunks into your blender, puree, and then strain through a medium-mesh strainer. (Don't strain through a fine-mesh strainer; you want enough fruit in the drink to give it color.) If you can't find a seedless melon, blend for just a few seconds with the seeds before straining. Don't grind too much or the seeds will add a peppery note to the cocktail.

A small seedless watermelon weighing about 6 pounds will give you about 5 cups of juice. You only need a little of that juice for this drink. Pour the extra into ice-cube trays and freeze to make melon cubes, which will keep the margaritas cool without diluting them. This melon-ice idea came from our tester, Amy Vogler, but I have to admit that I am almost never able to wait long enough for the ice to set up.

I like to sprinkle yellow chile powder on a red margarita and dark red chile powder on a yellow margarita, but the flavor and aroma, rather than the color, are what are important. As long as it is fresh, any chile powder will work for the garnish.

1 tablespoon kosher salt or margarita salt

1 juicy lime

1 teaspoon corn syrup (optional)

1 cup (8 ounces) fresh watermelon juice (see headnote)

1 cup (8 ounces) tequila

1/4 cup (2 ounces) Cointreau

Ice cubes

2 to 4 pinches of chile powder (optional)

Spread the salt on a saucer. Cut the lime in half, and set aside half of the lime to use later. Cut the other half into 2 wedges, or 4 wedges if making 4 drinks. Run 1 wedge around the rim of each glass, then dip each rim in the salt, making sure you coat the entire rim. Or, instead of lime juice, dip your finger in a little corn syrup and run it around the rim. The salt adheres better than when you use lime juice, and you get a nice sweet-and-salt flavor.

Pour the watermelon juice, tequila, and Cointreau into a cocktail shaker and squeeze in the juice from the reserved lime half. Fill the shaker with ice, cover, and shake.

Fill the salt-rimmed glasses with ice and strain the watermelon mixture into the glasses. Top each margarita with a pinch of cayenne.

VIOLET BEAUREGARD

serves 2

Infusing vodka with fresh blueberries is easy, but you have to start two weeks before you plan to serve your Violet Beauregards. John Mark came up with this luscious drink when a friend brought him a batch of fresh blueberries from Maine. John was so taken with the berries that he used them to make his own blueberry vodka. Unless you are feeling ambitious, you can just infuse a high-quality vodka such as Hangar One with fresh blueberries, which is what gives this drink its beautiful color of violet bordering on fuchsia.

John named this drink after one of the bad children in *Charlie and the Chocolate Factory*, one of the most inspiring books and movies ever. We will sometimes break off in the middle of a normal conversation to recite lines from the movie to each other. For us, dialogue like "Violet, you're turning violet" or "I've got a blueberry for a daughter" never gets old.

To Infuse the VODKA

Start with a full bottle of your favorite vodka. Pour out 1 cup and use it for something else. Wash the blueberries and dry them on a clean kitchen towel. Drop them, one by one, into the vodka bottle, cap the bottle, and set it in a cool, dark place for at least 2 weeks or up to 1 year. Leave the blueberries in the bottle and the vodka will just get better.

Blueberry-Infused Vodka

1 bottle (750 milliliters) premium vodka

1 cup (about 5 ounces) blueberries

To Make the Cocktails

Chill 2 glasses in the freezer for at least 30 minutes.

In a cocktail shaker, combine the vodka, Cointreau, and lemon juice. Fill the shaker with ice, cover, and shake.

Strain into the chilled glasses. Drop 2 or 3 blueberries into the bottom of each glass and serve immediately.

3/4 cup (6 ounces) blueberry-infused vodka

1/4 cup plus 2 tablespoons (3 ounces) Cointreau

1 tablespoon (1/2 ounce) fresh lemon juice

Ice cubes

6 blueberries

LOVE LETTER

serves 2

This is a divine combination of rum and raspberries with a hint of rose. When I first came up with this cocktail, I wanted to call it The Secret Admirer because the name has such sex appeal, but then I decided it was a more meaningful cocktail and not just a quick flirtation, so I named it the Love Letter. It's an homage to Pierre Hermé, one of the greatest pastry chefs of our time, who loves the combination of raspberry, rose, and lychee.

You don't need fresh raspberries for this drink. Start with either bottled raspberry juice or a raspberry-strawberry blend, like the kind found in the nonrefrigerated juice section of Whole Foods or other good grocery stores. Or, use frozen raspberry juice concentrate and dilute according to the directions on the can.

¼ cup (2 ounces) raspberry juice

1 tablespoon (½ ounce) Cointreau

¼ cup (2 ounces) white rum, such as
    10 Cane brand

    Juice of ½ lime

½ teaspoon rose water (see Resources)

    Ice cubes

2 to 4 organic rose petals, preferably red

Chill 2 glasses in the freezer for at least 30 minutes.

In a cocktail shaker, combine the raspberry juice, Cointreau, rum, lime juice, and rose water. Fill the shaker with ice, cover, and shake.

Half fill the chilled glasses with ice and strain the cocktail into the glasses. Float 1 or 2 rose petals on top of each drink and serve immediately.

I HOPE HE LIKES THIS.

STRONG HOT CHOCOLATE

serves 4

I developed this drink for chocoholics, which wasn't hard because I am one. A cross between hot chocolate and chocolate sauce, it stands up to a shot of brandy or whiskey if you want your hot chocolate X-rated. It is also a good stand-in for the shot of coffee that is traditionally poured over ice cream for *affogato* (see the variation below).

In a 1-quart saucepan, combine the milk and cream. Split the vanilla bean lengthwise and, with the tip of the knife, scrape the seeds into the saucepan, and then toss in the pod. Whisk in the cocoa powder and brown sugar, place over medium heat, and whisk the mixture for 5 to 7 minutes, or until it is frothy and simmering.

Place the chocolate in a heatproof bowl. Remove and discard the vanilla pod from the hot milk mixture and pour the mixture over the chocolate. Add the salt (but not more than 3 grains) and whisk until the hot chocolate is smooth.

Divide the hot chocolate among cups, top each cup with 2 marshmallows or a dollop of whipped cream, and serve. Or, allow the chocolate to cool completely, then cover tightly and store in the refrigerator for up to 3 days. Reheat gently just before serving.

1 1/2 cups (12 ounces) whole milk

1/2 cup (4 ounces) heavy cream

1/2 vanilla bean

2 tablespoons (about 1/4 ounce) unsweetened cocoa powder, preferably natural

2 tablespoons (1 ounce) firmly packed dark brown sugar

2 ounces bittersweet chocolate, preferably 70% cacao, coarsely chopped (about 1/2 cup)

A few grains of *fleur de sel*

8 marshmallows, made with gelatin (page 212) or xanthan gum (page 213), or whipped cream

variation

HOT CHOCOLATE AFFOGATO

Place 3 mini scoops of vanilla gelato, homemade (page 205) or store-bought, in each tall glass. Put 2 to 4 tablespoons (1 to 2 ounces) of Strong Hot Chocolate in each shot glass. Serve each person a glass of gelato and a shot glass of chocolate, and let them pour the chocolate over the ice cream.

INDIAN ROSE MILK

serves 4

I made this warming combination of cardamom, rose water, milk, and honey for a *Bon Appétit* Chef Ski event in Beaver Creek, Colorado, and it was a huge hit with both the guests and my fellow chefs, especially après-ski. Adding a saffron marshmallow pays tribute to a classic Indian flavor composition, but if you don't have time to whip up homemade marshmallows, a pinch of saffron and a splash of rose water are a good stand-in. Because there is no caffeine in this drink, it works any time, night or day.

3 to 4 whole cardamom pods

1/4 teaspoon black peppercorns

4 cups (1 quart) whole milk

1/2 cup (5 ounces by weight) honey

1 tablespoon (1/2 ounce) rose water (see Resources)

8 saffron rose marshmallows (page 213) or 4 small pinches of saffron threads and a little rose water

In a mortar, crush together the cardamom pods, papery husks and all, and peppercorns with a pestle. If you don't have a mortar and pestle, crush the cardamom lightly with a rolling pin. (If you can't find whole cardamom pods, you can use ground cardamom, but your drink won't be as fragrant or flavorful. Start by adding 1 teaspoon ground cardamom to the milk mixture, taste, and see if you would like to add more.)

In a saucepan, combine the milk, honey, and crushed cardamom and peppercorns. You will strain this after heating, so don't worry about the husks in the milk. Place the pan over medium heat and heat, stirring to dissolve the honey, for 3 to 5 minutes, or until the milk comes to a simmer. Remove the pan from the heat and allow the milk to steep for 15 to 20 minutes, or until it absorbs the flavor of the cardamom. The longer the milk sits, the stronger it will taste, but don't allow it to steep for more than 25 minutes or it will be bitter.

Strain the milk through a fine-mesh strainer into a clean saucepan and place the pan over medium heat. Bring the milk to a simmer, remove the pan from the heat, and add the rose water.

Divide the milk among glasses or cups and top each serving with 2 marshmallows, or with a pinch of saffron and a splash of rose water.

8

CORE RECIPES

When I create or remodel a dessert idea, there are certain materials that I use to build a structure for the concept. These core recipes—divided in this chapter into foundations, supports, and accents—will give you the tools you need to create many of the desserts in this book, and hopefully inspire you to create your own crossover dessert concepts.

199

FOUNDATIONS

CHOUX PASTE (AKA PÂTE À CHOUX)

The dough used to make the churros in Spanish Quincition (page 130) can be converted into a classic *pâte à choux* to make the pastry puffs for cream puffs, profiteroles, or a *croquembouche.* Simply omit the cheese and pepper, double the remaining dough ingredients, and prepare and mix the dough as directed. You will have enough dough to make about 18 pastry puffs.

To make the pastry puffs, position a rack in the center of the oven and preheat the oven to 400°F. Butter a baking sheet and then line with parchment paper. (The butter will keep the paper in place.)

Spoon the dough into a pastry bag fitted with a 1/2-inch plain tip, or have a spoon ready. Pipe the pastry into mounds about 1 inch in diameter onto the prepared baking sheet, spacing them about 2 inches apart. Or, gently scoop up a spoonful of the pastry to form each mound. Make each mound about the size of a large marble, but don't get too hung up on size. Dot each mound with a drop of water and press your thumb or finger lightly on top to flatten any thread of paste that may have formed when you piped out the pastry.

Bake the puffs for 15 to 20 minutes, or until golden. Lower the oven temperature to 350°F and continue to bake for 20 to 25 minutes longer, or until the puffs are light brown. Turn off the oven and leave the puffs inside for another 10 to 15 minutes, but keep an eye on them and remove the pan from the oven before they become too dark.

Remove the puffs from the oven and let cool completely on the pan on a wire rack before filling them. Use the puffs the same day you bake them.

USES

➤ *For the puffs*
Make cream puffs: Spoon 1 1/4 cups Pastry Cream (page 203), mousseline (see Uses, page 203), or whipped cream into a pastry bag fitted with a 1/4-inch plain tip, pierce the bottom of a puff with the tip, and pipe in the filling.

➤ *For the puffs*
Make profiteroles: Slice each pastry puff in half horizontally, spoon ice cream (any flavor) onto the bottom half, and replace the top. Serve drizzled with Dark Chocolate Sauce (page 207).

➤ *For the puffs*
Make a *croquembouche*: Stack cream puffs or profiteroles in a pyramid and coat with spun sugar; the sugar will harden into a glossy, crunchy finish.

➤ *For the dough*
Make *gougères*: After adding the eggs to the dough, gently stir in 1 cup grated Gruyère, Parmesan, or Gouda. Add a little salt and white pepper, a pinch of cayenne pepper or nutmeg, and 1/2 teaspoon minced fresh thyme or chives. Form and bake the puffs as directed and serve warm as an appetizer.

TART DOUGH

The tart dough I use in A Chocolate Tart Named Desire (page 57) is great because it is easy to make, strong enough to hold all kinds of fillings, and delicious. I usually double the dough recipe, divide it into four portions, and then wrap three portions and put them in the freezer, where they will keep for up to 2 months. That way, I already have pastry on hand when I want to bake tarts. Just remember to transfer a wrapped dough portion from the freezer to the refrigerator at least 24 hours before you plan to use it.

USES

➤ Bake the dough in a tart ring or tart pan, let cool, and layer the bottom of the tart shell with Pastry Cream (page 203). Top with sliced fruit and glaze the fruit with apricot marmalade.

➤ Bake the dough in tartlet pans, let cool, and fill the tart shells with the rose custard used for Rosebud (page 161).

PUFF PASTRY

The puff pastry used for Apple Galettes (page 100) is wonderfully light and flaky. It's so easy to prepare, it is often called blitz puff pastry. You can use it to make a rustic fruit galette, as described here.

USES

- Make a rustic fruit galette: Toss 2 cups sliced fruit with sugar (to taste), a little flour, and a dash of cinnamon or nutmeg. Roll out the dough into a large round and place it on a baking sheet. Arrange the fruit in the center of the dough, leaving a 2-inch border. Fold the border up and over the fruit, forming loose pleats. Bake until the pastry is a deep golden brown.

- For an elegant appetizer, cut the dough into rounds, bake, and top with crème fraîche (page 221) and caviar.

- Top chicken pot pies.

SHORTCAKE BISCUIT DOUGH

The same biscuit dough used for Citizen Shortcake (page 97) can also be used to make scones.

USES

- To make scones, add any single flavoring or combination of flavorings to the dough: 1/2 cup dried cherries or chopped dried apricots, 1/2 cup nuts, 2 ounces coarsely chopped bittersweet chocolate, 2 tablespoons crushed cacao nibs, 2 teaspoons ground cinnamon or cardamom, 1 1/2 teaspoons freshly grated nutmeg. Shape and bake the scones as described for the biscuits.

CRÈME ANGLAISE

makes about 2 cups

This silky custard sauce, flecked with vanilla, is the foundation for many classic recipes. It is cooked, strained, and then cooled quickly in an ice bath.

Set up an ice bath by half filling a large bowl with ice and water. Have ready a heatproof storage container or bowl (large enough to hold about 3 cups liquid) that fits in the ice bath and a fine-mesh strainer or chinois.

In a medium saucepan, combine the milk and cream. Split the vanilla bean lengthwise and, with the tip of the knife, scrape the seeds into the saucepan, and then toss in the empty pod. Place the pan over medium heat. In a medium bowl, whisk together the egg yolks and sugar until smooth.

After about 5 minutes, when the milk mixture just begins to boil (small bubbles will appear around the edges of the pan), remove the pan from the heat. Whisk a few tablespoons of the hot milk mixture into the egg mixture. Then, while whisking steadily, slowly add the rest of the hot liquid to the egg mixture. Return the mixture to the saucepan and place over medium-low heat. Cook, stirring constantly but gently with a wooden spoon or heatproof spatula, for about 3 minutes, or until the custard begins to thicken. The custard is done when the trace of foam on the surface is gone, and you can run your finger across the back of the custard-coated spoon and the line holds.

Immediately remove the pan from the heat and strain the custard, pouring it into the heatproof bowl. I like to set a metal ladle into the custard, to help draw off some of the heat. Let the custard cool in its ice bath for at least 15 to 20 minutes, and then cover and refrigerate for at least 2 hours. It will keep, tightly covered, for up to 2 days.

1 cup whole milk

1 cup heavy cream

1/2 vanilla bean

6 (3 ounces by weight) large egg yolks

1/2 cup (3 1/2 ounces) granulated sugar

USES

- Pour around warm Chocolate Crottin Cakes (page 74).

- Spoon around spicy Chipotle Gingerbread (page 118).

- Pour over Peaches Sautéed in Wine and Honey (page 94).

- Refrigerate for 2 hours, then add any flavoring you like and freeze in an ice cream maker according to the manufacturer's directions.

IN THIS BOOK

Battleship Potemkin (page 143)

NorCal (An Homage to Laura Chenel) (page 147)

CUSTARDS

PASTRY CREAM

makes about 1¹/₄ cups

This core recipe begins with the same ingredients as Crème Anglaise (opposite), except that butter is used instead of cream and cornstarch is added. The cornstarch makes this cream thick enough to be the filling in a cream puff, or the first step of *chibouste*, pastry cream lightened with meringue.

In a medium bowl, whisk together the egg yolks, 2 tablespoons (1 ounce) of the sugar, and the cornstarch. Set aside.

In a medium saucepan, combine the milk and the remaining 3 tablespoons (1¹/₄ ounces) sugar and place over medium heat. Heat for about 2 minutes, or just until the mixture comes to a boil (small bubbles will appear around the edges of the pan). Remove the pan from the heat. Whisk a few tablespoons of the hot milk mixture into the egg yolk mixture. While whisking steadily, slowly add the rest of the hot milk mixture. Return the mixture to the saucepan and place over medium heat. Cook, stirring constantly but gently with a wooden spoon or heatproof spatula, for 1 to 2 minutes, or until the custard begins to thicken. (If you are anxious about overcooking your pastry cream, cook it over medium-low heat for 5 to 6 minutes.)

Once the pastry cream starts to thicken, it will do so almost instantaneously. Whisk continuously, making sure to get in the corners and across every inch of the pan bottom. Remove the pan from the heat as soon as the pastry cream is the consistency of an éclair filling. If you are not sure about the consistency, pull the pan off the heat and check the custard. You can always put it back on the heat if it needs to thicken a bit more.

Pour the mixture into a heatproof bowl and immediately whisk in the butter. To store the pastry cream, cover with plastic wrap, pressing the wrap directly onto the surface to prevent a skin from forming. Let cool to room temperature. (If you would like to cool it more quickly, set up an ice bath.) Refrigerate for at least 1 hour or up to overnight.

3 (1¹/₂ ounces by weight) large egg yolks

¹/₄ cup plus 1 tablespoon (2¹/₄ ounces) granulated sugar

3 tablespoons (³/₄ ounce) cornstarch

1 cup whole milk

2 tablespoons (1 ounce) unsalted butter

USES

- Mix with unsalted butter (use the same amount by weight of butter and pastry cream) to form a mousseline, my filling of choice for cream puffs. Use a stand mixer fitted with the whip attachment or a hand-held mixer to beat together the butter and pastry cream.

- Whisk into whipped cream to make diplomat cream for use as a filling between cake layers, as in Shagalicious (page 164).

- Use as a filling for any of the cupcakes on pages 173 to 181. To make Boston cream cupcakes, fill buttermilk cupcakes (page 173) with pastry cream and top with Dark Chocolate Ganache (page 206).

IN THIS BOOK

Black on Black (page 64)

EGGLESS LEMON CURD

makes about 2¼ cups

This method of mashing together citrus zest and sugar extracts the maximum amount of flavor from the zest, and you can store the mixture in your freezer for months. Use any peak-of-season citrus fruit—bergamot oranges, mandarin oranges, tangerines, Key limes, grapefruits, Meyer lemons—as long as the peel is brightly colored and shiny. Here is the key to making other citrus curds with this recipe: use fresh lemon juice for ¼ cup of the juice and the juice from the featured citrus fruit for the other ½ cup juice. The lemon juice won't hide the flavor of the other citrus but will actually make it taste brighter.

For more about agar agar, see Secret Agent (page 140). And two more things about this superb gelling medium: First, it can handle heat, so you can serve this curd cold, warm, slightly warm, or reheated and completely melted. Also, keep in mind that the gelling power of various forms of agar agar can vary. If the curd comes out too thick, you can heat it to thin it out, or you can remake it using less agar agar. Anywhere from 1 to 2 tablespoons—either powder or flakes—will work for this recipe. We used 2 tablespoons Eden brand agar agar, available from Whole Foods stores or health food stores (see Resources).

Place the lemon zest on a cutting board and mound 1 teaspoon of the sugar on top. Cut the zest and sugar together with a knife, alternately chopping and rubbing the mixture with the flat side of the knife. Gradually, the mixture will transform into a smooth paste.

In a 2-quart or larger saucepan, combine the zest paste, remaining sugar, lemon juice, butter, and agar agar. Bring to a boil over medium heat, whisking continuously and taking care to get into the edges of the pan bottom with your whisk. After 4 to 5 minutes, reduce the heat to medium-low and simmer for 2 to 3 minutes, or until you are sure the agar agar is dissolved. Pour the mixture into a heatproof bowl, whisk in the sweetened condensed milk, and let cool at room temperature for 10 to 15 minutes. Cover and refrigerate for at least 2 hours, but preferably overnight. This curd is a little darker than usual lemon curd—closer to the color of honey than a bright lemon yellow. It will keep in the refrigerator for up to 1 week.

EGGLESS KEY LIME CURD

Substitute 2 teaspoons Key lime zest (from about 4 limes) for the lemon zest, and substitute ¼ cup plus 2 tablespoons fresh Key lime juice (from about 10 limes) for an equal amount of the lemon juice. Proceed as directed for Eggless Lemon Curd.

---

2 teaspoons lemon zest strips, about ⅛ inch wide (from about 1 lemon)

¾ cup (5¼ ounces) granulated sugar

¾ cup fresh lemon juice (from 4 to 5 lemons)

8 tablespoons (4 ounces) unsalted butter, cut into 1-inch chunks

2 tablespoons agar agar flakes or powder

½ cup (6 ounces by weight) sweetened condensed milk

USES

- Serve any citrus curd with Graham Crackers (page 214) or Streusel (page 218) and a small spoonful of whipped cream.

- Plate any citrus curd with the coconut *panna cotta* from Cocoshok (page 55).

- Use grapefruit zest and juice instead of lime zest and juice in eggless key lime curd and serve with avocado slices, cilantro-mint oil (page 220), sea salt, and a sprinkle of muscovado sugar for a great palate-cleansing course.

IN THIS BOOK

Lemon Meringue Pie = Lemon Drop (page 71)

Lemania Cupcakes (page 173)

VANILLA GELATO

makes about 3 1/2 cups

This is my favorite recipe for gelato because it calls for more milk than cream, which makes it lighter than a standard gelato and very smooth. It has just the right amount of vanilla flavor.

Set up an ice bath by half filling a large bowl with ice and water. Have ready a heatproof storage container or bowl that fits in the ice bath and a fine-mesh strainer or chinois.

In a bowl, whisk together the egg yolks and cornstarch to make a slurry. Set aside.

In a saucepan, combine the milk, sugar, and corn syrup. Split the vanilla bean lengthwise and, with the tip of the knife, scrape the seeds into the saucepan, and then toss in the empty pod. Place over medium heat and heat, stirring occasionally, for 7 to 9 minutes, or just until the mixture comes to a boil (small bubbles will appear around the edges of the pan). Remove the pan from the heat and remove and discard the vanilla pod.

Whisk a few tablespoons of the hot milk mixture into the egg mixture. Then, while whisking steadily, slowly add the rest of the hot milk mixture. Return the mixture to the saucepan and place over medium heat. Cook, whisking gently, for about 2 minutes, or until the mixture has thickened slightly.

Pour the custard through the strainer into the heatproof container. Stir in the cream and 1/4 teaspoon salt. I like a pronounced salt flavor in this gelato, so taste the custard and add up to 1/4 teaspoon more salt if you like. Nest the container in the ice bath. When the custard is completely cool, cover and refrigerate for at least 1 hour or up to overnight.

Pour the custard into an ice cream maker and freeze according to the manufacturer's directions. Store in a covered container in the freezer for 1 to 2 hours before serving. It will keep for 1 week but will taste best if served within 3 days.

2 (1 ounce by weight) large egg yolks

2 teaspoons cornstarch

2 cups plus 1 teaspoon whole milk

1/4 cup (1 3/4 ounces) granulated sugar

1/4 cup (about 2 3/4 ounces by weight) light corn syrup

1/2 vanilla bean

1 cup heavy cream, well chilled

1/4 to 1/2 teaspoon kosher salt

USES

- Make a tin roof sundae with Dark Chocolate Sauce (page 207) and salted Spanish peanuts.

- Plate with sautéed blackberries (page 98) and Streusel (page 218).

- Top with Pecan Caramel Sauce (page 110).

IN THIS BOOK

Untitled II: Chocolate with Raspberry and Fennel Tones (page 79)

Upside-Down Pineapple Parfait (page 80)

Hot Chocolate Affogato (page 195)

SUPPORTS

DARK CHOCOLATE GANACHE

makes about 1 cup

This ganache has only three ingredients, so you need to make them count by using very good dark chocolate.

Bring a few inches of water to a gentle simmer in a saucepan. Put the chocolate in a heatproof bowl and place over (not touching) the simmering water (or use a double boiler). Heat slowly for 3 to 5 minutes, or until about half of the chocolate is melted, and then remove the bowl from the heat and set aside.

In a small saucepan, combine the cream and honey over medium heat. Heat for 2 to 3 minutes, or just until the mixture comes to a boil (small bubbles will appear around the edges of the pan). Remove the pan from the heat, pour the hot cream mixture over the chocolate, and whisk together until the chocolate has melted and the mixture is smooth.

Cover the bowl with parchment paper or plastic wrap, pressing it directly onto the surface of the ganache. Let the ganache cool at room temperature for about 2 hours. Don't try to speed this up by putting the warm ganache in the refrigerator, or its structure will change. Once the ganache is at room temperature, you can refrigerate it for a day or two.

4 ounces bittersweet chocolate, preferably 70% cacao, coarsely chopped (scant 1 cup)

1/2 cup plus 2 tablespoons heavy cream

1 tablespoon honey

USES

- Use instead of icing to cement together any architectural elements, like the steps in Battleship Potemkin (page 143).

- Whip the ganache and use it to fill layer cakes or roulades.

- Make truffles, following the instructions on page 145. One cup of ganache will make about 18 truffles. For classic truffles, dip them in melted bittersweet chocolate before immediately rolling in the cocoa powder. You will need 6 ounces (about 1 1/4 cups) bittersweet chocolate and 1/4 cup (about 1/2 ounce) cocoa powder for dipping and rolling.

IN THIS BOOK
Battleship Potemkin (page 143)

DARK CHOCOLATE SAUCE

makes about 1¹/₄ cups

This sauce is dark, satiny, and completely addictive. I use Scharffen Berger or Valrhona bittersweet chocolate, both 70% cacao, but any good chocolate will do. I have also used El Rey, Guittard, Ghirardelli, and Cocoa Barry for this recipe, and they have all been subtly different but fantastic.

Place the chocolate in a medium heatproof bowl. In a small saucepan, combine the cream and corn syrup over low heat and cook for about 5 minutes, or just until the mixture begins to boil (small bubbles will appear around the edges of the pan). Remove from the heat.

Pour the hot cream mixture over the chocolate, let stand for 1 minute, and then whisk until smooth.

In another small saucepan, combine the cocoa powder and water and place over medium heat. Whisk for 2 to 3 minutes, or until thickened, and remove from the heat. Pour the cocoa mixture into the chocolate mixture and whisk to combine. Add the butter and salt and whisk until the butter melts and the sauce is smooth.

I prefer to use this sauce immediately, but you can store it, tightly covered, in the refrigerator for up 1 week.

The sauce hardens when refrigerated. To reheat it, either set the bowl in a warm water bath or heat half of the sauce in the microwave in 10-second blasts, stirring between blasts so it doesn't burn. If using the microwave method, stir the melted portion into the rest of the sauce. If the reheated sauce appears broken or grainy, add 1 to 2 teaspoons of cold heavy cream or water and stir until smooth.

MILK CHOCOLATE SAUCE

Follow the directions for Dark Chocolate Sauce, but substitute 4 ounces of good-quality milk chocolate for the bittersweet chocolate. I generally use El Rey, but you can use any premium brand. Store it and reheat it the same way.

4 ounces bittersweet chocolate, preferably 70% cacao, chopped into ¹/₂-inch pieces (scant 1 cup)

¹/₂ cup heavy cream

2 tablespoons (1¹/₂ ounces by weight) light corn syrup or honey

3 tablespoons (¹/₂ ounce) unsweetened cocoa powder, preferably natural

¹/₄ cup water

2 tablespoons (1 ounce) unsalted butter, at room temperature

¹/₈ teaspoon kosher salt

USES

- Use as a filling for any of the cupcakes on pages 173 to 181.
- Serve a ramekin of the warm sauce with homemade graham crackers (page 214) and marshmallows (page 212), or store-bought if you are pressed for time.
- Drizzle it over anything: cakes, cupcakes, gelato, sundaes, ice cream sandwiches, bare skin.

IN THIS BOOK

Chocolate Chip Mania (page 35)

The Real McCoy Ice Cream Sandwich (page 49)

CocoShok (page 53)

A Chocolate Tart Named Desire (page 57)

S'More A Palooza (page 61)

WHITE CHOCOLATE SAUCE

makes 1 cup

You can use any premium chocolate for this sauce. El Rey, which is made with unbleached cocoa butter, retains the aroma and flavor of chocolate. White chocolate from Valrhona is also a good choice; it is particularly smooth because they conch it for so long.

Place the chocolate in a medium heatproof bowl. In a small saucepan, heat the cream over low heat for about 5 minutes, or just until it begins to boil (small bubbles will appear around the edges of the pan). Remove from the heat.

Pour the hot cream over the chocolate, let stand for 1 minute, and then stir until the chocolate melts completely. Add the butter and salt and stir until the butter melts and the sauce is smooth.

You can use the sauce immediately or store it, tightly covered, in the refrigerator for up 1 week.

The sauce hardens when refrigerated. To reheat it, either set the bowl in a warm water bath, or heat half of the sauce in the microwave in 10-second blasts, stirring between blasts so it doesn't burn. If using the microwave method, stir the melted portion into the rest of the sauce. If the reheated sauce appears broken or grainy, add 1 to 2 teaspoons of cold heavy cream or water and stir until smooth.

6 ounces white chocolate, chopped into 1/4-inch pieces (about 1 1/4 cups)

1/2 cup heavy cream

2 tablespoons (1 ounce) unsalted butter, at room temperature

1/8 teaspoon kosher salt

USES

- Serve with Chocolate Chibouste (page 66), *fleur de sel*, and curry powder.
- Serve with any kind of citrus curd (page 204) and Streusel (page 218).
- Substitute for one of the components in Bananas Foster Cane Split (page 133).
- Make a pool of sauce around fresh blueberries and sprinkle grated lemon zest on top.

IN THIS BOOK
Chocolate Chip Mania (page 35)

FRUIT SAUCE

makes about 1 cup

A fruit sauce is a way to intensify the flavor of perfectly ripe fruit. I often use this sauce as a finishing touch when I want to emphasize the flavor of the same fruit that I am using in the dessert. Many different types of fruit will work in this recipe, including blackberries, raspberries, blueberries, apricots, peaches, pears, strawberries, plums, Concord grapes, fresh currants, and even tomatoes.

Guar gum or xanthan gum is the magic ingredient, allowing you to whip up a fruit sauce in minutes (see Secret Agent, page 140). You can make the fruit sauce without a gum, but it won't have the same viscosity.

The sauce won't taste exactly the same each time you make it. Fruits change from season to season and from farm to farm, so the flavor of the sauce will too. Plus, even fruits in the same season from the same farmer can vary in water and sugar content.

This is a "taste as you go" recipe. The measurements for sugar, water, and lemon juice are guidelines. For tart fruits such as currants, you will want to add a few more tablespoons of sugar. For very ripe, juicy fruits, such as peaches, start with 3 tablespoons of water and see if you need more. Lemon juice acts as a seasoning for fruit, brightening its flavor. With all three ingredients, add a little and then taste to see if it needs more.

1 cup (about 5 ounces) ripe berries or chopped fruit

1/4 cup (1 3/4 ounces) granulated sugar or (3 ounces by weight) honey, plus more if needed

3 to 4 tablespoons water, plus more if needed

1/2 teaspoon guar gum, or 1/4 teaspoon xanthan gum (optional)

1/4 teaspoon fresh lemon juice, plus more if needed

USES

- Make a plum dipping sauce for plain churros (use the churros recipe on page 130, omitting the Manchego and pepper) and sprinkle with cinnamon or five spice.
- Stir the sauce into 2 cups Crème Anglaise (page 202) and freeze in an ice cream maker for a fruit-flavored ice cream.
- Pool chilled tomato fruit sauce around strawberry halves and basil ice cream (infuse Crème Anglaise, page 202, with basil leaves) and sprinkle with *fleur de sel*.

In a small saucepan, combine the fruit, sugar, and 3 tablespoons water and place over medium heat. Heat for about 3 minutes, or just until the mixture comes to a boil (small bubbles will appear around the edges of the pan). Remove from the heat and let stand for 10 to 20 minutes, or until slightly cooled. Taste the mixture and if it is not sweet enough for you, add a little more sugar, bring it back to a boil, let it cool slightly, and then retaste.

Stir in the gum, scrape the mixture into a stand blender, and process until smooth. Or, puree the mixture in the pan with an immersion blender until smooth. (If you use an immersion blender, be sure the mixture has cooled before turning on the blender, to avoid splattering hot fruit.)

Add the 1/4 teaspoon lemon juice, stir or blend for just a few seconds to combine, and then strain the sauce through a medium-mesh strainer into a clean bowl. You can also serve it without straining it or strain the sauce then add a few berry seeds back to the sauce. Taste and add a few more drops of lemon juice if you like. If the sauce is too thick, stir in another tablespoon or so of water until it is the desired consistency.

You can use the sauce immediately, or you can store it, tightly covered, in the refrigerator for up 4 days.

WINE-SOAKED CHERRIES

makes about 1 cup

These dark, decadent cherries will keep for up to 2 months. I make batches of them at the end of summer when the last of the cherries are in the market.

In a saucepan, combine the wine and sugar and place over medium-high heat. Heat, stirring to dissolve the sugar, for about 2 minutes, or until the mixture comes to a boil. Lower the heat to medium-low and simmer for 4 to 5 minutes, or until the liquid is reduced by half, forming a syrup. Pour the syrup into a heatproof bowl and let cool for 2 minutes.

Stir the cherries and pepper into the syrup and let stand at room temperature for 15 minutes. Serve the cherries right away, or cover tightly and refrigerate for up to 2 months.

1/2 cup Cabernet Sauvignon or Zinfandel

3 tablespoons (about 1 1/4 ounces) granulated sugar

1 cup (about 4 ounces) halved and pitted Bing cherries

Small pinch of freshly ground black pepper

USES

➥ Spoon over Vanilla Mochi Cake (page 82) and top with whipped cream and pistachios.

➥ Serve with Cheesecake Custard (page 116) and cacao nibs.

IN THIS BOOK

Black on Black (page 64)
Cherries of the Corn (page 127)

BASIC CARAMEL SAUCE

makes about 1 1/2 cups

Who doesn't love caramel sauce? To prepare it, start with a very clean pan, preferably one of heavy aluminum lined with stainless steel so the sugar doesn't crystallize on the sides. Also, use a 2-quart or larger pan with high sides, as caramel can bubble up. And if you don't need this much caramel sauce, the recipe is easily cut in half. I have given instructions for using a candy thermometer, but you really don't need one.

In a medium saucepan, mix together the water, cream of tartar, and sugar. Add the corn syrup and stir just until combined. Place the pan over high heat and cover. Cook for 2 to 3 minutes, or until the mixture comes to a full rolling boil. Remove the lid, clip a candy thermometer onto the side of the pan, and cook the syrup until it registers 350°F on the thermometer, or until it is dark amber, 7 to 10 minutes.

Remove the pan from the heat and add the butter. Carefully add the cream, standing back because it will sizzle and pop. The caramel may seize up (form clumps), but that's fine. The lumps will melt when the caramel is put back over the heat.

Place the pan over medium-low heat and stir gently with a wooden spoon, a heatproof spatula, or a whisk. Bring the mixture back to a boil and, as soon as you see bubbles around the edges of the pan, remove it from the heat and strain the mixture through a strainer into a heatproof container. Stir in the salt and vanilla and set aside to cool. Use immediately, or cover tightly and refrigerate for up to 2 weeks.

BRANDY CARAMEL SAUCE

Follow the directions for Basic Caramel Sauce, adding 1 to 2 tablespoons of brandy with the vanilla. Makes about 1 1/2 cups.

PASSION FRUIT CARAMEL SAUCE

Follow the directions for Basic Caramel Sauce, substituting 1/2 cup of passion fruit juice (such as Looza brand) for the 1 cup cream. This sauce doesn't have the same creamy texture as basic caramel sauce, but it is thick and rich and has a lighter, fresher taste that I like. Makes about 3/4 cup.

SPICED CARAMEL SAUCE

I use cinnamon, cardamom, and rosemary for this sauce, but you can use just one of them or you can try other spices that you like. Substitute the following for the cream in Basic Caramel Sauce: In a small saucepan, combine the cream, 1 cinnamon stick, 4 crushed cardamom pods, and 1 fresh rosemary sprig (optional) over medium heat and heat for about 5 minutes, or just until the cream comes to a boil (small bubbles will appear around the edges of the pan). Remove from the heat and let the mixture steep for 20 minutes, then strain the cream through a strainer. Unlike the basic sauce, which will keep in the refrigerator for about 2 weeks, this sauce loses its spiciness after about 4 days. Makes about 1 1/2 cups.

1/4 cup water

1/8 teaspoon cream of tartar or fresh lemon juice

1 cup (7 ounces) granulated sugar

2 tablespoons (1 1/2 ounces by weight) light corn syrup

1 tablespoon (1/2 ounce) unsalted butter

1 cup heavy cream

1/2 teaspoon kosher salt

1/2 teaspoon pure vanilla extract

USES

- Pour a few spoonfuls of caramel sauce into hot cider or caffe latte.

- Drizzle caramel sauce over Grilled Figs (page 138) dotted with Gorgonzola and topped with walnuts or Walnut-Thyme Streusel (page 94).

- Add 1/2 cup of caramel sauce to Crème Anglaise (page 202) and freeze in an ice cream maker for caramel ice cream.

- Create your own caramel ripple ice cream by packing down scoops of ice cream as you remove it from your ice cream maker and spooning on caramel between layers.

- Use as a filling for any of the cupcakes on pages 173 to 181.

CHOCOLATE CARAMEL SAUCE

This variation is easy. Chop about 4 ounces of bittersweet chocolate (scant 1 cup), add it to the warm Basic Caramel Sauce after mixing in the salt and vanilla, and stir until smooth. Makes about 2 cups.

NUTTY, SALTY CARAMEL SAUCE

Adding salt to the buttery sweetness of caramel is a passion of mine. For this recipe, follow the directions for Basic Caramel Sauce, adding 1/2 cup (2 ounces) salted skinless roasted peanuts after you add the butter. If you are using unsalted peanuts, increase the salt to 1 teaspoon. The nuts will get soggy, so use this sauce within a day of making it. Makes about 2 cups.

PECAN CARAMEL SAUCE

See A Veil of Vanilla (page 108) for this sauce, which calls for a slightly different method than Basic Caramel Sauce.

MARSHMALLOWS 1.0
(Gelatin Version)

makes thirty-two 2 by 1 by 1-inch marshmallows

Add a gelling agent to a meringue and you have marshmallows. We first made marshmallows for our hot cocoa in Citizen Cake's original South of Market location and were soon infatuated with them. They began to sneak into our ice creams, cookies, and even our chocolate bunnies during Easter. Once I encountered gums (see Secret Agent, page 140), I became even more excited about the different ways to make marshmallows. The freshness and texture are reason enough to make your own, and once you start flavoring them, you will be infatuated, too.

Here are two ways to make marshmallows, one with gelatin and one with xanthan gum. You can pour warm marshmallow into any size pan, as long as you line it with parchment paper and sprinkle generously with cornstarch.

Line a baking sheet or an 8-inch square pan with parchment paper and sprinkle generously with cornstarch.

In a small bowl, sprinkle the gelatin over the 2 tablespoons water and set aside to soften while you make the sugar syrup.

In a 2-quart or larger saucepan, combine the remaining 1/4 cup water, the cream of tartar, sugar, corn syrup, and vanilla bean and stir just to moisten evenly. Place over high heat and bring to boil. Lower the heat to medium, clip a candy thermometer onto the side of the pan, and cook the syrup until it registers 248°F on the thermometer. Don't wait until the syrup gets that hot before you begin whipping the egg whites, however. I usually start whipping them when the thermometer reads 175°F.

In a bowl, using a stand mixer fitted with the whip attachment or a handheld mixer, whip the egg whites on low to medium speed, stopping the mixer when they look frothy and still a little soft. This will take about 2 minutes. They won't become glossy until you add the syrup.

When the syrup has reached 248°F, take the pan off the heat, add the gelatin mixture, and stir with a whisk or heatproof spatula for 30 seconds to 1 minute, or until the gelatin dissolves. Carefully remove the vanilla bean and discard it.

If you are using a handheld mixer, you need to be extremely careful: working with syrup this hot is like working with hot lava. With the mixer on low speed, very slowly drizzle the syrup into the egg whites, aiming for a spot midway between the beater and the side of the bowl. If you drip syrup onto the beater, it will be flung against the sides of the bowl and never be fully incorporated into the beaten egg whites. Instead, these splatters will appear as tiny hardened lumps of syrup in the marshmallows. Don't worry about this too much, as it isn't a big deal. Just try to aim as carefully as possible to avoid the beater.

Once all the syrup has been incorporated into the egg whites, turn the mixer to high speed and beat for 2 to 3 minutes, or until the meringue begins to pull away from the sides of the bowl and gather around the beater. The marshmallow mixture will have cooled quite a bit, but the bottom and lower sides of the bowl will still be very warm to the touch.

Cornstarch for dusting the pan and covering the marshmallows

Canola oil cooking spray

1 tablespoon plus 1 teaspoon powdered gelatin

1/4 cup plus 2 tablespoons water

Pinch of cream of tartar

1 1/4 cups plus 1 tablespoon (9 ounces) granulated sugar

3/4 cup (9 ounces by weight) light corn syrup

1/2 vanilla bean

3 (3 ounces by weight) large egg whites

IN THIS BOOK

S'More A Palooza (page 61)

S'More Brownies (page 153)

Rocky Road Cupcakes (page 175)

Strong Hot Chocolate (page 195)

Hot Chocolate Affogato (page 195)

Indian Rose Milk (page 196)

Spray a silicone spatula with cooking oil and use it to scrape the mixture out of the bowl onto the prepared pan, and then spread it out. Work quickly, before the mixture begins to set, and don't worry if it is not spread perfectly in the pan. Top the mixture with a generous amount of cornstarch, cover the pan with plastic wrap, and refrigerate for about 4 hours, or until set.

Uncover the pan and, using scissors, cut the sheet of marshmallows into pieces 2 inches long by 1 inch wide by 1 inch thick, or into any size or shape desired, dipping the scissors into cornstarch before each cut. Pat off any excess cornstarch before serving. These marshmallows are softer and a bit stickier than store-bought marshmallows, so once they are cut, store them in a single layer, not touching, in an airtight container at room temperature. They will keep for up to 1 week.

MARSHMALLOWS 2.0 (Xanthan Gum Version)

Prepare the pan as directed for Marshmallows 1.0. Omit the gelatin step and proceed as directed. As soon as you have added all of the hot syrup to the egg whites, add 1¹/₂ teaspoons xanthan gum (see Resources) while continuing to whip. Then continue as directed to complete the recipe.

flavorings for marshmallows

ou can add almost any flavoring to marshmallows, usually mixing in between ¹/₄ teaspoon and 1 teaspoon when the mixture is just about ready to be poured onto the pan.

Single Flavorings

Ground cloves: ¹/₈ teaspoon for a mild flavor, ¹/₄ teaspoon for an intense flavor

Ground cardamom, cinnamon, coriander, or most other ground spices: ¹/₄ to ¹/₂ teaspoon

Grated citrus zest: ¹/₄ to ¹/₂ teaspoon

Saffron threads: ¹/₂ to 1 teaspoon

Peppermint oil: 1 teaspoon

Flavor Combinations

Saffron rose: Add ¹/₄ teaspoon saffron threads mixed with ¹/₂ teaspoon rose water. Try it with Indian Rose Milk (page 196).

Orange cacao nibs: Add ¹/₂ teaspoon grated orange zest and about ¹/₄ cup (1 ounce) cacao nibs.

GRAHAM CRACKERS

makes twenty-four 3-inch square crackers

I like a wheaty flavor and texture that you don't find in most commercial graham crackers. So I began making my own grahams shortly after opening the first Citizen Cake.

In a medium bowl or large liquid measuring cup, stir together the whole wheat and all-purpose flours and salt and set aside. In a small cup or bowl, stir together the baking soda and water until the soda dissolves and set aside.

In a stand mixer fitted with the paddle attachment (or by hand in a bowl with a wooden spoon), cream together the butter and sugar on medium speed for 1 to 2 minutes, or until thoroughly combined and slightly paler. Add the honey and molasses and continue to mix for 30 seconds to 1 minute, or until combined. Add the egg and mix for 15 to 20 seconds, or until incorporated. Add the baking soda mixture and mix for about 30 seconds, or until combined. Add half of the flour mixture and mix for 15 to 30 seconds, or until incorporated. Then add the remaining flour mixture and mix for 15 to 30 seconds longer, or until combined.

Lay 2 large pieces of plastic wrap on a work surface. Divide the dough in half and place half on each sheet. Shape each half into a block or flatten it into a disk, and wrap in the plastic wrap. Refrigerate the dough for at least 4 hours or preferably overnight. You can also freeze half or all of the dough for up to 1 month.

Position racks in the upper third and lower third of the oven and preheat the oven to 325°F. Line 2 baking sheets with parchment paper.

Check to see that your dough is firm enough to work with. It should be a little sticky but still hold together. Lightly dust the work surface with flour. Unwrap half of the dough and knead it a few times on the floured surface. Dust a rolling pin with flour and then roll out the dough into a rectangle about 12 by 9 inches and 1/4 inch thick, adding more flour to the work surface as needed to prevent the dough from sticking.

I like to bake the rectangle as a single piece and then break it into randomly sized shards after it has cooled. You can also cut the dough into a dozen 3-inch squares or into any other shape or size you like. Either way— in one piece or many pieces—transfer the dough to one of the prepared baking sheets. Repeat with the second half of the dough, transferring it to the second baking sheet.

Bake the cookies for 20 to 25 minutes, or until the color of graham crackers. The cookies will puff during baking but will flatten as they cool. Let the grahams cool completely on the pans on cooling racks before removing them. They keep for 1 week in an airtight container at room temperature, or they can be frozen for up to 1 month.

1 1/2 cups plus 2 tablespoons (8 ounces) whole wheat flour

3/4 cup plus 1 tablespoon (4 ounces) all-purpose flour

1/2 teaspoon kosher salt

1/2 teaspoon baking soda

1 tablespoon cold water

4 tablespoons (2 ounces) unsalted butter, softened but still cool

1/2 cup (3 1/2 ounces) granulated sugar

1/4 cup plus 2 tablespoons (4 3/4 ounces by weight) honey

2 tablespoons (1 1/2 ounces by weight) unsulfured dark molasses

1 (1 1/2 ounces by weight) large egg

USES

➤ Make classic s'mores with homemade marshmallows (page 212) and really good dark chocolate.

➤ Serve with a citrus curd (page 204) and a spoonful of whipped cream.

IN THIS BOOK

S'More A Palooza (page 61)

Waking Up in a City That Never Sleeps (page 115)

S'More Brownies (page 153)

ACCENTS

SIMPLE SYRUP

makes about 2 cups

Simple syrup is a combination of sugar and water, boiled for just a few minutes until it forms a syrup. I keep this in my refrigerator for making lemonade, mixing cocktails (and for rimming the glass with salt for margaritas), and making sorbets.

In a small saucepan, combine the sugar and water and place over high heat, stirring occasionally. When the water begins to show small bubbles, lower the heat to medium-low and simmer for 5 minutes. At this point, the sugar should be dissolved. Pour into a storage container, let cool to room temperature, and then cover and refrigerate. The syrup keeps almost indefinitely.

2 cups (14 ounces) granulated sugar

1 cup water

IN THIS BOOK

Waking Up in a City That Never Sleeps (page 115)

Shagadelic (page 187)

INFUSED SIMPLE SYRUP

makes about 1 1/2 cups

I first made infused simple syrups for plated desserts when I was at Rubicon, and I like the fact that one of these unassuming syrups can bring a secret flavor component to a dessert or a cocktail. You can flavor the syrup with fresh ginger, cloves, lemon zest, kaffir lime leaves, or dozens of other options. This is definitely a good place to experiment with flavor combinations, such as chai spices or basil and tomato.

Steeping time will vary depending on whether you are using a fruit, herb, or spice. Ten minutes is a good place to start, but taste as you go and decide if you want the infusion to be stronger.

In a small saucepan, combine the sugar, water, and corn syrup and place over medium to medium-high heat, stirring occasionally. Heat for about 5 minutes, or until the mixture just comes to a boil. Then reduce the heat to low and simmer for 1 minute. Remove the pan from the heat, add one or two of the flavorings, and let steep for about 10 minutes.

Pour the syrup through a fine-mesh strainer into a clean container. Add 2 drops of lemon juice, and then taste and adjust with more lemon juice if needed. Let cool to room temperature, and then cover and refrigerate. The syrup will keep for at least 1 week.

1 cup (7 ounces) granulated sugar

1 cup water

1/2 cup (5 3/4 ounces by weight) light corn syrup

Choice of flavoring: 6 quarter-sized disks peeled fresh ginger, 8 kaffir lime leaves, zest of 1 lemon (with pith removed), 12 whole cloves, or 1 cup (about 1 ounce) fresh mint leaves

2 or 3 drops fresh lemon juice, or more if using lemon zest

USES

- Experiment with flavors for cocktails, such as vodka mixed with ginger-infused syrup and ginger ale.

- Drizzle a syrup infused with lemon and black pepper over fruit, especially berries.

- Drizzle on a plate next to shortcake, meringues, or *panna cotta*.

- Add flavor to gelato or ice cream bases or to Crème Anglaise (page 202).

- Make a clove-infused syrup and use it to poach pears.

IN THIS BOOK

Citizen Shortcake (page 97)

Shagalicious (page 164)

ROYAL ICING

makes about 1/2 cup

This icing hardens well and dries to a nice matte finish, so it is just right for icing cookies, cementing the walls of a gingerbread house, or making the shards for Gingerbread Bauhaus (page 117).

In a medium bowl, combine the egg white and cream of tartar. Using a whisk or a handheld mixer on high speed, whip the egg white until foamy. Add the sugar 1/4 cup at a time and beat for 3 to 5 minutes by hand or for 2 to 3 minutes on medium speed, or until a thick, smooth icing forms.

Use the icing immediately, or store in an airtight container in the refrigerator for up to 1 week.

1 (1 ounce by weight) large egg white

Pinch of cream of tartar (less than 1/8 teaspoon) or a few drops of fresh lemon juice

1 1/4 cups (5 ounces) powdered sugar, sifted

USES
- Cement together the walls of a gingerbread house.
- Decorate cookies or gingerbread people.
- Use for piping out words on cakes or cookies.

IN THIS BOOK
Gingerbread Bauhaus (page 117)

SEVEN-MINUTE ICING AND FILLING

makes about 2 3/4 cups

This classic frosting is the filling for our signature Citizen Cake cupcakes, which are chocolate cupcakes (the same ones we use in Rocky Road Cupcakes on page 175) topped with Dark Chocolate Ganache (page 206). We finish each cupcake by spelling out Citizen on top in Royal Icing (above).

Bring a few inches of water to a gentle simmer in a saucepan. Put the egg whites, salt, sugar, and corn syrup in a heatproof bowl and place it over (not touching) the simmering water (or use a double boiler). Using a handheld mixer on medium speed, beat for 7 minutes, or until the mixture has an easily spreadable consistency. Add the vanilla when you have just about finished beating.

Remove from the heat and let the frosting cool slightly, but don't wait too long. The frosting stays fluffy and keeps its sheen if you use it while it is still warm to the touch.

3 (3 ounces by weight) large egg whites

Pinch of kosher salt

3/4 cup (5 1/4 ounces) granulated sugar

2 tablespoons (1 1/2 ounces by weight) light corn syrup

1/2 teaspoon pure vanilla extract

USES
- Use to fill or frost any of the cupcakes on pages 173 to 181.
- Use to frost any layer cake.

BUTTERCREAM FROSTING

makes about 2 cups

You can use this old-fashioned thick, smooth frosting for cakes and cup-cakes, and as the filling for sandwich cookies. The small amount of lemon juice is just enough to brighten the flavor of the frosting without giving it a lemon taste.

In a large bowl, using a stand mixer fitted with the paddle attachment or a handheld mixer, cream the butter on medium speed for 30 seconds to 1 minute, or until light and creamy. Gradually add the sugar while continuing to beat, stopping to scrape down the sides of the bowl as necessary. When all of the sugar has been incorporated, add the salt, milk, vanilla, and lemon juice, beating well after each addition. Then continue to beat on high speed for 5 to 6 minutes, or until the frosting is fluffy.

I prefer to use this frosting the same day it is made, but it will keep, tightly covered, in the refrigerator for 2 to 3 days.

8 tablespoons (4 ounces) unsalted butter, softened but still cool

2 1/2 cups (10 ounces) powdered sugar, sifted

1/2 teaspoon kosher salt

1 tablespoon plus 1 teaspoon whole milk

1 teaspoon pure vanilla extract

1 teaspoon fresh lemon juice

USES

- Roll out the ginger dough for Sammy-snaps (page 158), cut into rounds, and bake as directed. Use this frosting as a filling to make sandwich cookies.

- Use to frost any of the cupcakes on pages 173 to 181.

- Use to frost any layer cake.

IN THIS BOOK

Rocky Road Cupcakes (page 175)

Candy Bar Cupcakes (page 179)

CLARIFIED BUTTER

makes about 5 tablespoons

Clarified butter is butter that has been cooked over low heat until it separates and the milk solids sink to the bottom of the pan. You can cook with it at high temperatures without fear of it burning.

Place the butter in a small pan over low heat. Without stirring, allow the butter to melt completely. As soon as the butter has separated and the milk solids have collected on the bottom of the pan, remove the pan from the heat. Skim off any froth from the surface and then carefully pour the clear, golden liquid into a spouted heatproof measuring cup, leaving the solids behind in the pan. Discard the solids. Allow the clarified butter to cool to room temperature. Transfer to an airtight container and refrigerate for up to 1 month.

8 tablespoons (4 ounces) unsalted butter

USES

- Ideal for whenever you need to sauté in butter over relatively high heat.

- Brush on filo dough to prevent cracking.

IN THIS BOOK

The M Word (page 137)

STREUSEL

makes 1³/₄ cups

Streusel is more than a sweet cinnamon topping for coffeecake. It can be savory, cheesy, spicy, or nutty, and it can work with many flavors. I like the crunchiness and the melt-in-your-mouth character of streusel that has been cooked separately on a baking sheet instead of baked on a cake, crisp, or tart. We use a lot of different streusel-type components at Citizen Cake and call them by different names, such as Point Reyes Blue Cheese Crumbles (page 110) or Cheddar Crumbles (page 106), just because streusel falls short in description—although I do like the word *streusel* in Cacao Nib Streusel (below). Both the Cheddar and the blue cheese versions are good to eat out of hand with a glass of wine.

Position a rack in the center of the oven and preheat the oven to 350°F. Line a baking sheet with parchment paper.

In a medium bowl, stir together the sugar, flour, and salt. Split the vanilla bean lengthwise and, with the tip of the knife, scrape the seeds into the bowl. Stir until the seeds are distributed evenly. Using your fingers, a pastry blender, or two knives, work in the butter until the mixture resembles gravel. (I prefer to use my hands, but you can use any of the methods.)

Dump the mixture onto the prepared baking sheet dump, shake the pan to spread the mixture a little, and bake for 10 minutes. Remove from the oven and rake through the streusel with a fork, like you would rake granola, moving it out from the center to the edges, where it cooks fastest. Bake for another 8 to 10 minutes, and then rake again, moving any dark pieces along the edges to the center and any underdone center bits to the edge. Then continue to bake for 5 to 7 minutes longer, or until the streusel is a nice and even deep gold.

Remove from the oven and let cool completely. Use immediately, or store in an airtight container in the refrigerator for up to 2 weeks.

CACAO NIB STREUSEL

Cacao nibs have the dark, earthy flavor of chocolate without any sweetness. That's because the nibs are cacao beans that have been roasted but not yet made into chocolate. Nibs add a wonderful nutlike crunch to streusel or to whatever you are baking (see Resources).

Proceed as directed for Streusel, reducing the amount of flour to ¹/₂ cup (2¹/₂ ounces) and adding ¹/₃ cup (³/₄ ounce) unsweetened cocoa powder to the dry ingredients. After incorporating the butter into the mixture, scatter ¹/₄ cup (1 ounce) cacao nibs over the top and toss together to mix thoroughly. Bake, cool, and store as directed.

¹/₂ cup (3¹/₂ ounces) granulated sugar

1 cup (5 ounces) all-purpose flour

¹/₂ teaspoon kosher salt

1 vanilla bean, split

4 tablespoons (2 ounces) cold unsalted butter, cut into ¹/₂-inch pieces

USES

- Place a mound of streusel next to baked apples and vanilla ice cream.
- Set streusel on a plate next to fruit (apples, pears, any stone fruit) that has been sautéed in a little butter and muscat.
- Serve with yogurt and fresh fruit.
- Make a small nest of streusel for fruit, ice cream, or sorbet.
- Place small bowls of streusel around the room during cocktail parties. Refill often.

IN THIS BOOK

Suddenly Last Summer (page 92)

Apple of My Eye (page 105)

A Veil of Vanilla (page 108)

Bananas Foster Cane Split (page 133)

Battleship Potemkin (page 143)

VANILLA GEL

makes about 1/2 cup

When I visited Japan, I discovered the wonderful gels that bakers make for confections. As soon as I returned home, I began experimenting with gelatin and various flavors, and I discovered that gels are surprisingly easy to make. I am giving you two versions, one made with milk and vanilla and one made with pomegranate juice. You can change the flavors by infusing the milk with spices or trying any kind of juice you like, fresh or bottled. Some juices, such as kiwifruit and pineapple, won't work because they contain enzymes that prevent the gel from setting.

There are two methods for molding the gel. You can line a loaf pan or a 5-inch square baking dish or plastic storage container with plastic wrap, allowing it to overhang the sides and smoothing out any wrinkles. Or, you can use a baking dish without lining it. The plastic wrap simply makes it a bit easier to get the gel out of the mold.

In a cup or small bowl, sprinkle the gelatin over the water and set it aside to soften while you heat the milk.

In a small saucepan, combine the milk, sugar, and vanilla over medium heat. Heat, stirring, for 2 to 3 minutes, or until the sugar dissolves and the milk is hot, then remove from the heat. Or, combine the milk, sugar, and vanilla in a microwave-safe container and heat in the microwave for about 1 minute, or until the sugar dissolves and the milk is hot.

Add the gelatin mixture to the hot milk mixture and stir for 30 seconds to 1 minute, or until the gelatin has dissolved. Strain the liquid through a fine-mesh strainer into a heatproof container and let cool for 5 to 10 minutes. Then pour the strained liquid into the readied container, lined or not, and let cool to room temperature.

Cover the container with plastic wrap, being careful that the wrap doesn't touch the cooled gel, and refrigerate for about 2 hours, or until the gel is set, before using. The gel will keep for 1 week.

When ready to serve, if you have lined the container, grasp the overhanging plastic wrap and lift out the gel, place it on a work surface, and cut into cubes, squares, circles, or whatever shape appeals to you. If you have used an unlined mold, cut the shapes right in the container.

POMEGRANATE GEL

Proceed as directed for Vanilla Gel, increasing the amount of water used in softening the gelatin to 1 tablespoon, substituting 1/2 cup bottled pomegranate juice for the milk, and omitting the vanilla.

1 teaspoon powdered gelatin

2 teaspoons water

1/2 cup whole milk

1 tablespoon granulated sugar

1/2 teaspoon pure vanilla extract or 1/2 vanilla bean

USES

- Make healthy gel shots for kids in small cups using any fruit juice they like.
- Use gels in place of gelato or ice cream.

IN THIS BOOK

A Veil of Vanilla (page 108)

Gingerbread Bauhaus (page 117)

Bananas Foster Cane Split (page 133)

HERB OIL

makes about 1/4 cup

Not just for savory dishes, herb oils crank up the volume in a dessert. A few drops of a vibrant herb oil add visual flair and another flavor accent to a dish. You can make this oil from any herb you like, or from a combination of herbs. Use the equivalent of 20 large leaves (such as mint, basil, or shiso) or 20 sprigs from small-leafed herbs (such as cilantro, thyme, or parsley).

Bring a small saucepan of water to a boil. While the water is heating, set up an ice bath by half filling a small bowl with ice and water.

Add the basil leaves or cilantro sprigs and the mint leaves to the boiling water and blanch for 15 seconds. Using a slotted spoon or tongs, immediately plunge the leaves or sprigs into the ice bath. The herbs should be bright green at this point. Remove the herbs from the ice bath and set them on paper towels to drain for a few minutes.

Finely chop the herbs and place them in a blender. Add the oil, salt, and lemon juice and blend on high speed for 2 minutes. Strain the oil through a fine-mesh strainer into a container. There will be small flecks of green in the oil; if you want an oil with no flecks, line the sieve with cheesecloth. Cover and store at room temperature. The color fades quickly, so use within a few hours.

10 fresh basil leaves or leafy sprigs of cilantro

10 fresh mint leaves

1/4 cup (1 3/4 ounces by weight) canola oil

Pinch of kosher salt

1 teaspoon fresh lemon juice

USES

- Top basil ice cream (infuse Crème Anglaise, page 202, with basil leaves) and tomato fruit sauce (page 208) with basil oil.

- Plate Carrot Caketons (page 86) with Coconut Cream (page 82) and top with cilantro oil.

- Top Vanilla Mochi Cake (page 82) with sesame ice cream (add 2 teaspoons sesame oil to Crème Anglaise, page 202) and shiso oil.

IN THIS BOOK

The Real McCoy Ice Cream Sandwich (page 49)

Lemon Meringue Pie = Lemon Drop (page 71)

Bananas Foster Cane Split (page 133)

CAREMI, TRAINED IN MARTIAL ARTS, TAKES A SHOT AT THE ANNOYING DISTRACTION...

CRÈME FRAÎCHE

makes 4 cups

Tart, creamy crème fraîche tastes more interesting than plain whipped cream and can be used to top sweet or savory dishes.

Combine the cream and buttermilk in a bowl or other container. Let the mixture thicken at room temperature for at least 8 hours or up to overnight, then cover and refrigerate. It will keep for 1 week.

4 cups heavy cream
2 tablespoons buttermilk

USES

- Whip together equal amounts of heavy cream and crème fraîche and dollop on hot chocolate, shortcakes, fruit cobblers, tarts, or cakes.
- Whisk together equal amounts of crème fraîche and vanilla frosting (page 174) and use as a filling for ginger sandwich cookies made from Sammysnaps dough (page 158).
- Spoon onto blinis, toast points, or Puff Pastry (page 201) and top with caviar.

IN THIS BOOK

Lovelova (page 89)

Citizen Shortcake (page 97)

Apple Galettes (page 99)

A Veil of Vanilla (page 108)

Cherries of the Corn (page 127)

CAREMI, I LOVE YOUR INTENSITY AND DEDICATION TO YOUR ART.
XO ELIZABETH

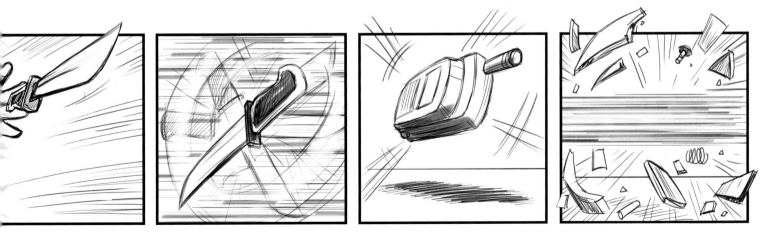

RESOURCES

Agar Agar

Eden Foods
www.edenfoods.com

Whole Foods stores
www.wholefoods.com

Agave Nectar

Whole Foods stores
www.wholefoods.com

Almond Meal

Bob's Red Mill
www.bobsredmill.com

Trader Joe's stores
www.traderjoes.com

Whole Foods stores
www.wholefoods.com

Altoids, Liquorice Flavor

Altoids
www.altoids.com and click on shoppe

Trader Joe's stores
www.traderjoes.com

Brandied Cherries

Trader Joe's stores
www.traderjoes.com

Whole Foods stores
www.wholefoods.com

Williams-Sonoma stores
www.williams-sonoma.com

Cacao Nibs

Scharffen Berger
www.scharffenberger.com

Whole Foods stores
www.wholefoods.com

Chocolate, Dark

El Rey
www.elreychocolate.com

Ghirardelli
www.ghirardelli.com

Guittard
www.guittard.com

Scharffen Berger
www.scharffenberger.com

Valrhona
www.valrhona.com

Chocolate, White

El Rey
www.elreychocolate.com

Ghirardelli
www.ghirardelli.com

Guittard
www.guittard.com

Valrhona
www.valrhona.com

Cocoa Powder, Natural

Scharffen Berger
www.scharffenberger.com

Coconut, Unsweetened Large Flakes

Let's Do . . . Organic brand, distributed by Edward & Sons Trading Co.
www.edwardandsons.com

Whole Foods stores
www.wholefoods.com

Dachshund Cookie Cutters

The Cookie Cutter Shop
www.thecookiecuttershop.com

Dachshund Gifts
www.dachshundgifts.com

Dark Chocolate.
See Chocolate, Dark.

Fennel Pollen

Dean & Deluca stores
www.deananddeluca.com

Sugar Ranch
www.fennelpollen.com

Filo Dough

Athens and Apollo brands are in the freezer section of most grocery stores. Fillo Factory organic filo is available in most Whole Foods stores.

Athens
www.athens.com

The Fillo Factory
www.fillofactory.com

Whole Foods stores
www.wholefoods.com

Goat Cheese

Laura Chenel's chèvre
www.cowgirlcreamery.com

Grits (Polenta)

Anson Mills Grits
www.ansonmills.com

Bob's Red Mill
www.bobsredmill.com

Whole Foods stores
www.wholefoods.com

Guar Gum

Bob's Red Mill
www.bobsredmill.com

Hazelnut Oil

Safeway stores
www.safeway.com

Sur La Table stores
www.surlatable.com

Whole Foods stores
www.wholefoods.com

Williams-Sonoma stores
www.williams-sonoma.com

Hazelnut Paste

Sur La Table stores
www.surlatable.com

Whole Foods stores
www.wholefoods.com

Williams-Sonoma stores
www.williams-sonoma.com

Honey

Marshall's Farm Honey
www.marshallsfarmhoney.com

Maraschino Cherries

Williams-Sonoma stores
www.williams-sonoma.com

Mastic Gum

Dayna's Market
www.daynasmarket.com

Gum Mastic
www.gummastic.gr (at time of writing, website is in Greek only)

Mastiha Shop
www.mastihashop.com

Mochiko. *See* Rice Flour.

Nut Oils. *See* Hazelnut Oil and Pistachio Oil.

Orange Flower Water

Dean & Deluca stores
www.deananddeluca.com

Mymouné
www.mymoune.com

Also try Turkish, Lebanese, and Middle Eastern shops.

Pimentón, Mild and Hot

Dean & Deluca stores
www.deananddeluca.com

Pink Peppercorns

Dean & Deluca stores
www.deananddeluca.com

Morton and Bassett
www.worldpantry.com

Pistachio Oil

L'Epicerie
www.lepicerie.com

Market Hall Foods
www.markethallfoods.com

Polenta. *See* Grits.

Rice Flour, Glutinous (Sweet)

Most Asian markets and well-stocked supermarkets carry this rice flour.

Koda Farms
www.kodafarms.com

Safeway stores
www.safeway.com

Rose Water

Dean & Deluca stores
www.deananddeluca.com

Mymouné
www.mymoune.com

Also try Turkish, Lebanese, and Middle Eastern shops.

Spices

Dayna's Market
www.daynasmarket.com

Dean & Deluca stores
www.deananddeluca.com

L'Epicerie
www.lepicerie.com

Sugar, Artisanal

Billington's
www.wholesomesweeteners.com

India Tree
www.indiatree.com

Sugar India
www.sugarindia.com

Thai Tapioca

ImportFood.com
www.importfood.com/nrtp1405.html

White Chocolate. *See* Chocolate, White.

Xanthan Gum

Bob's Red Mill
www.bobsredmill.com

INDEX

CONVERSION CHARTS

VOLUME

Formulas:

1 teaspoon = 4.93 milliliter
1 tablespoon = 14.79 milliliter/3 teaspoons
1 cup = 236.59 milliliter/16 tablespoons
1 liter = 202.88 teaspoons/67.63 tablespoons/4.23 cups

U.S.	Imperial	Metric
1 tablespoon	1/2 fl oz	15 ml
2 tablespoons	1 fl oz	30 ml
1/4 cup	2 fl oz	60 ml
1/3 cup	3 fl oz	90 ml
1/2 cup	4 fl oz	120 ml
2/3 cup	5 fl oz (1/4 pint)	150 ml
3/4 cup	6 fl oz	180 ml
1 cup	8 fl oz (1/3 pint)	240 ml
1 1/4 cups	10 fl oz (1/2 pint)	300 ml
2 cups (1 pint)	16 fl oz (2/3 pint)	480 ml
2 1/2 cups	20 fl oz (1 pint)	600 ml
1 quart	32 fl oz (1 2/3 pint)	1 l

WEIGHT

Formulas:

1 ounce = 28.35 grams
1 pound = 453.59 grams/16 ounces
1 kilogram = 2.2 pounds

U.S./Imperial	Metric
1/2 oz	15 g
1 oz	30 g
2 oz	60 g
1/4 lb	125 g
1/3 lb	150 g
1/2 lb	225 g
3/4 lb	350 g
1 lb	450 g

LENGTH

Formulas:

1 inch = 2.54 cm
1 foot = .3 m/12 inches
1 cm = .39 inch
1 m = 3.28 feet/39.37 inches

Inch	Metric
1/4 inch	6 mm
1/2 inch	1.25 cm
3/4 inch	2 cm
1 inch	2.5 cm
6 inches (1/2 foot)	15 cm
12 inches (1 foot)	30 cm

TEMPERATURE

Formulas:

$9/5 \text{ C} + 32 = \text{F}$
$(\text{F} - 32) \times 5/9 = \text{C}$

Fahrenheit	Celsius/Gas Mark
250°F	120°C/gas mark 1/2
275°F	135°C/gas mark 1
300°F	150°C/gas mark 2
325°F	160°C/gas mark 3
350°F	180 or 175°C/gas mark 4
375°F	190°C/gas mark 5
400°F	200°C/gas mark 6
425°F	220°C/gas mark 7
450°F	230°C/gas mark 8
475°F	245°C/gas mark 9
500°F	260°C